**Defence expenditure,
industrial conversion
and local employment**

Defence expenditure, industrial conversion and local employment

Edited by Liba Paukert
and Peter Richards

International Labour Office   Geneva

Paukert, L., Richards, P. (eds.)
Defence expenditure, industrial conversion and local employment
Geneva, International Labour Office, 1991
/Disarmament/, /Employment/, /Defence/, /Public expenditure/, /Defence industry/, /Industrial restructuring/, /Comparative analysis/, /China/, /Germany, Federal Republic of/, /Italy/, /UK/, /USA/, /USSR/. 01.02.4
ISBN 92-2-107287-8 (paperback)
ISBN 92-2-107288-6 (hardback)

ILO Cataloguing in Publication Data

Printed in Switzerland

IRL

Preface

This manuscript was substantially completed in the days before détente and the revival in Eastern Europe of the search for liberal democracy. By the second half of 1990 it had become clear that writing about the consequences of disarmament, at least for the industrialised countries, was neither the recital of fairy tales nor propaganda. On the contrary, disarmament was beginning to change significantly the way in which many economic and social issues were viewed. It was therefore the more propitious that the ILO had begun a disarmament and employment research programme in 1984.

The initial stimulus for this was given by the resolution adopted by the International Labour Conference in 1981 (resolution concerning the economic and social consequences of disarmament). This resolution deplored "the considerable waste of resources resulting from the armaments race, particularly the nuclear arms race" and expressed a conviction that the ILO "should continue to contribute, within its own specific field of competence, to the process of détente and disarmament". To that end the ILO was to undertake studies and research, to be aided by information to be provided by member States. The ILO, i.e. the Office, was thus asked by its Conference of member States to encourage the process of disarmament by writing and commissioning studies which would analyse information within its field of competence.

Since the ILO's field of competence clearly relates to issues of labour policy and employment, the information that was asked for and the studies written dealt with the characteristics of the workforce associated with defence spending, and to a lesser extent with certain characteristics of the enterprises they worked in. To limit the extent of the inquiry, emphasis was placed on civilian workers in the secondary sector, i.e. excluding issues relating to the demobilisation of the armed forces or to clerical and Ministry of Defence manpower, and to the extent possible on civilians producing an output that was uniquely demanded by the military. Initial attempts to collect quantitative data on such employment from governments had limited success – because rarely are statistics organised that way. The chapter in this volume by Dunne demonstrates the use that can be made of available statistics given they way they are collected.

The focus of the ILO's effort was on conversion. The concept of conversion is not precise. In the context of general and complete disarmament, conversion is a measure to raise confidence and reduce international mistrust. Weapons-producing facilities are adapted to produce alternative products in a manner that would make it very expensive for them to be returned to their earlier function. But all capital stock has a limited life and conversion costs can easily exceed the present value of discounted future profit streams. Furthermore, enterprises "convert" by reducing dependence on defence sales, frequently by taking over civilian industries. Scrapping may be a common and, for disarmament purposes, desirable means of conversion.

For the ILO, and for the defence workforce, conversion means something else. Labour skills should not go to waste or remain unused for more than a brief, "frictional", period. Enterprises may behave in one way or another, machinery may or may not have an alternative use – given prevailing prices and interest rates – but conditions have to be such that involuntary unemployment is minimised, or eliminated, and further employment is remunerative. Thus a whole range of issues is opened, ranging from retraining – which, how chosen, by whom, how financed – to unemployment insurance, to displacement of new jobseekers, and to slowing the pace of change and persuading the State to break normal rules of market intervention. Furthermore, this labour conversion can take place against a host of different institutional backgrounds in terms, on the one side, of state ownership of the means of production and, on the other, of state intervention in labour markets, up to and including the guarantee of employment.

One more, macro-economic, element has to be added. If conversion follows substantial disarmament there will be corresponding effects on fiscal policy. A conversion scenario should take these into account, but, by definition it cannot do so in advance, since fiscal policy is determined by other factors and considerations. It is a mark of the greater realism of the disarmament debate in 1990 that the United Nations is not attempting to specify a fiscal policy target. In the debate on the relationship of disarmament to development, to which the ILO contributed, it was axiomatic that defence cuts were a corollary of increased aid flows, which gave assumptions on which global models could be constructed.

The current volume is largely the outcome of an expert meeting which the ILO organised in May 1989. It deals mainly, but not exclusively, with local, i.e. metropolitan or regional, labour markets. It also looks at the manpower effects of changes in missile procurement following the Intermediate-Range Nuclear Forces (INF) Treaty while the concluding chapter draws on a wider range of ILO research. The present time is one of great hope for arms reduction so that consideration of the manpower issues involved is overdue.

Contents

Chapter 1

Introduction

In most countries defence expenditure is a very important component of government expenditure. It shares with a large part of other government expenditure the property that its output is difficult, if not impossible, to measure. Reasonable levels of expenditure on arms and on military personnel provide security, which may be considered as vital to society, but which cannot be quantified or assessed in economic terms. The level of defence expenditure is decided by governments, on political, historical, ideological, ethical and other grounds. Government decisions on defence expenditure have to take into account economic constraints, and many important technical questions of an economic nature are involved in the process of decision-making. But economic arguments do not prevail in the determination of increases or decreases in defence spending.

On the other hand, the amount and pattern of defence expenditure have tangible effects on the economy, both in the short run and in the long run. While obvious benefits can be derived from defence spending, there are also costs which nations have to bear and which may be higher than is commonly assumed. An increase in defence expenditure can add to aggregate demand and can accelerate technical change. On the other hand, defence cuts which are not compensated by other forms of public or private expenditure will be associated with job loss and declining short-term growth.

Military spending, however, has a number of negative consequences which may not be immediately evident. The level and structure of investment, the orientation of R & D and productivity growth can be negatively affected. Other effects are ambivalent, e.g. the impact on the foreign trade structure and the balance of payments, or on regional resource allocation and regional development. A distinction can be made between defence spending's short-term and the long-term effects. The short-term effects are demand-type effects: other things being equal, a rise in military spending increases aggregate demand and leads to job creation, while a cut in military spending leads to job suppression and to short-term adjustment problems. But the long-term effects of defence expenditure are of a structural nature and most authors agree that, security considerations apart, their final impact on the economy is negative. It has been increasingly argued that defence expenditure has no particular economic benefits that could not be achieved by other forms of public or private spending, even in those developing countries where the creation of military industry has been associated with faster economic growth. Furthermore, it is recognised as a factor reducing flexibility in enterprise behaviour, and given the frequent use of cost-plus contracts, leading to resource hoarding, overskilling and the generation of inflation. Its expansion can thus easily have effects which run counter to the generally desired objectives of greater enterprise and labour market efficiency.

That defence expenditure has a negative impact on investment is supported by a considerable amount of evidence.[1] That war materials can rarely be used for productive investment is clear and has been discussed at various levels for a long time. Classical economists, such as Adam Smith and David Ricardo, saw certain basic levels of military expenditure as a requirement of national sovereignty, but viewed military expenditure as a drain on capital accumulation, slowing down investment and economic growth. They were not against military expenditure, but were implicitly concerned about an excessive level of it. They held that state expenditures on war and war preparation were financed out of profits and came at the expense of investment into new productive capacity and additional productive employment, being "withdrawn from the productive capital of the nation".[2]

Much has been added to the analysis of this issue since classical times. Today, however, there is ample empirical evidence that high levels of defence spending are associated with low levels of investment. For example, a regression of the share of gross investment and of military expenditure in GDP in 18 industrialised market economy countries, for which the data are readily available, shows that there is a significant negative relationship between the two variables. The regression results illustrated in figure 1.1 refer to 1986, but the outcome is broadly similar also for other recent years. Of course, the graph in figure 1.1 needs some qualifications. It is shown here mainly as a heuristic device illustrating the existence of a negative relationship having a close impact on some of the central issues examined in this volume. But, the inverse correlation between defence expenditure and investment illustrated in figure 1.1 cannot be interpreted as a short-term effect. It is rather a long-term structural relationship (any cross-country relationship being, in a sense, a long-term relationship by nature, whereas an examination of time-series data tends to look for short-run dynamic effects). Beyond this simple illustrative exercise, however, there is considerable econometric evidence of a significant negative relationship between military expenditure and investment.[3] The causal relationship between the share

---

[1] The discussion partly draws on A. Adams and D. Gold: *Does a defence dollar make a difference?* (Washington, DC, Center on Budget and Policy Priorities, 1987); and on Michael D. Oden: *A military dollar really is different: The economic impacts of military spending reconsidered* (Lansing, Michigan, Employment Research Associates, 1988).

[2] David Ricardo: *The principles of political economy and taxation* (London, J. M. Dent & Sons, 1973; original edition 1817).

[3] Wassily Leontief and Faye Duchin: *Military spending facts and figures — Worldwide implications and future outlook* (New York, Oxford University Press, 1983); R. P. Smith: "Military expenditure and capitalism", in *Cambridge Journal of Economics* (Cambridge, UK, 1977, No. 1); idem: "Military expenditure and capitalism: A reply", in *Cambridge Journal of Economics*, 1978, No. 2; idem: "Military expenditure and investment in OECD countries 1954-1972", in *Journal of Comparative Economics* (New York, 1980, No. 4); M. Anderson, J. Brugmann and G. Erickcek: *The price of the Pentagon* (Lansing, Michigan, Employment Research Associates, 1982).

Figure 1.1. Regression between the share of investment and military expenditure in GDP in 18 industrialised market economy countries in 1986

log (Investment % of GDP)

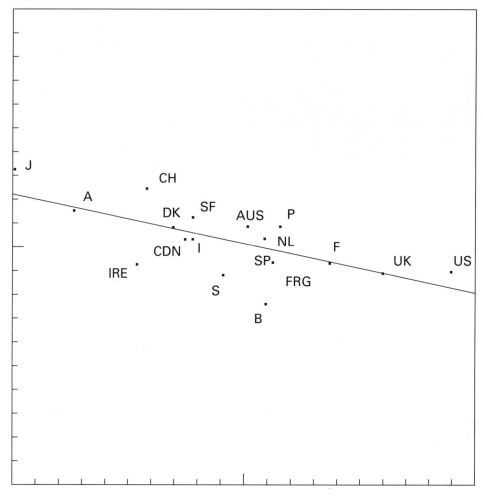

log (Military expenditure % of GDP)

log I = 3.2375 - 0.2169 log MILEX   (R-square = 0.4920)
I = Gross domestic investment as % of GDP
MILEX = Military expenditure as % of GDP

Sources. World Bank: *World Development Report, 1988* (Oxford University Press); Stockholm International Peace Research Institute: *World Armaments and Disarmament: SIPRI Yearbook, 1988* (Oxford, Oxford University Press).

of investment and military expenditure in GDP remains a matter of debate. Is it that military expenditure crowds out other investment-encouraging forms of government expenditure? Is it that some, more militarised countries, have low savings, and hence low investment rates? Although a number of case studies have tried to establish the linkages between military expenditure and growth, the results are inconclusive and considerable research remains to be done.

Long-term observations, from the beginning of this century, show that in leading industrialised countries the share of defence expenditure in GDP increased considerably until the mid-1950s and then fluctuated, while the share of investment has not declined. Instead, the share of private consumption went down, in accordance with the well-known Engel effect.[4] This secular trend makes the analysis of the trade-off between defence expenditure and the level of investment more difficult.

Defence expenditure is not only associated with the level of investment but it also affects its structure. Military outlays have specific effects on different industries and this breakdown has implications for aggregate economic performance. Much defence expenditure is directed at present to high technology production in the engineering and chemical sectors of industry (explosives, propellants, etc.), which devote a substantial share of their output to armaments. Industries which do not benefit from contracts of this kind may find it harder to finance the investment needed to achieve cost-minimising productivity gains. If productivity-generating investment is held back, this is bound to have negative effects for overall economic performance.

A related issue concerns the economic effects of defence spending on research and development. The large amounts spent on military R & D in the main industrialised countries have yielded some spectacular results and a part of modern advanced technology consists of the more or less direct spin-offs of military discoveries. Military funding has allowed some R & D activities to be pursued consistently and in depth. But a high level of military R & D takes away resources (human and capital) from civilian research which probably reduces the rate of productivity growth in the bulk of industry and, at the least, makes products less competitive abroad. If enterprises were prepared, or were encouraged, to invest comparable – or simply higher – amounts directly into civilian R & D, the question is what the results would be. Would the ensuing pool of technology be of a more general application?

In fact, there are several questions related to the spin-off problem: the first is what amount of R & D outlays would have actually gone into civilian technological innovation in the absence of government-financed military R & D, without comparable government funding. The second is what percentage of military R & D can have civilian spin-offs and with what time-lag. The third concerns the mutual influence of military and civilian R & D, i.e. it asks whether part of civilian R & D is geared to applying the results of military

---

[4] Kenneth Boulding: "The impact of the defense industry on the American economy", in *The consequences of reduced military spending* (Lexington, Mass., Lexington Books, 1973). Engel's law is that food expenditure declines relatively as income rises.

research, or is the link very weak, particularly because of the secrecy surrounding military R & D.

A number of studies have demonstrated the existence of a negative cross-country relationship between the level of military R & D activities and productivity growth in industry.[5] While this is linked to the investment issue, defence R & D absorbs large financial means and much of the best qualified scientific and technical personnel, which the defence industry tends to "hoard". A more equal distribution of resources and of high level skills would in principle allow productivity problems to be solved more widely across the board in industry. Clearly, spin-offs from military R & D are not the most efficient way of advancing civilian technology or raising productivity.

A slow growth of productivity may lead to imbalances in foreign trade as non-military industries find it difficult to compete on foreign markets. This, however, is only one aspect of the possible impact of a military build-up on the balance of payments. Imports of high-technology parts, necessary for military production in all but the most advanced industrialised countries, can be considerable. On the other hand, with the expansion of the market for armaments in non-producing countries observed in recent decades arms exports became profitable, and this may well have considerably improved the balance of payments of some arms suppliers. However, a "defence-dependent" export structure has drawbacks, because of the instability of the world armaments market and because it further draws resources away from other types of industry. But these longer-term considerations easily give way to immediate earning prospects.[6] And, as has been often remarked, most policy-makers tend to ignore long-term risks. Another argument against a "defence-dependent" export structure is that the international armaments market is extremely competitive and, as domestic demand for armaments falls, will probably become more so. Armaments exported are probably largely sold at close to their marginal cost, most of the fixed and development costs being covered by the home government's orders. But to the extent that with a different structure of government expenditure, other sectors could follow the same pricing policy in foreign markets, arms exports confer no particular advantage to the balance of payments.

While the apparently negative effect of defence expenditure on investment, on civilian R & D and on productivity can be expected to have serious repercussions on economic growth, empirical evidence does not support this. Existing literature shows both positive and negative relationships between defence expenditure and growth.[7] The reason seems to be that, while defence

---

[5] M. Oden, op. cit., 1988, bibliography.

[6] The contrast between the short term and the long term was stressed by A. K. Sen, comment on "Defence spending as a priority", by A. Brody in C. Schmidt (ed.) *Peace, defence and economic analysis* (Basingstoke, Hants., Macmillan, 1987).

[7] See, for example, A. Szymanski: "Military spending and economic stagnation", in *American Journal of Sociology* (Chicago), 1973, Vol. 79, No. 1, pp. 1-14; and A. Cappelen, P. Gleditich and O. Berkholt: "Military spending and economic growth in the OECD countries", in *Journal of Peace Research* (Clemson, South Carolina), 1984, Vol. 21, No. 4. Studies which have

expenditure is certainly not without effect on economic growth, the effects are multiple and partly offset each other. A regression between the average share of defence expenditure in GDP and the average growth rate of GDP in the years 1980-86, in the IMECs, indicates the absence of any significant relationship between the two variables. (The regression sign is, however, negative.) In any event, the causes of economic growth are not themselves well understood and different factors of production contribute different weights to overall growth according to the country and period considered. Defence expenditure would thus be unlikely to have a uniform effect on the causes of growth irrespective of country or period.

It can be argued that such exercises implicitly assume that some resources will be devoted to military expenditure. It is impossible to study the hypothetical case where no resources at all would be needed. But in such circumstances resources would be allocated more in line with priorities set either by the market or by more human and social considerations. Both scenarios might well be expected to raise levels of output or of welfare, or both.

The impact of defence expenditure on economic growth is broadly paralleled by its impact on employment. Defence expenditure may create considerable employment in some circumstances. Its effect on mopping up mass unemployment in the 1930s crisis is still widely remembered. Defence spending like any other form of spending clearly creates jobs, directly and indirectly. However, as reviewed in Chapter 2, alternative forms of public and private spending may create more employment, even in the short run and particularly in the long run. Simulation studies carried out by researchers have established that a given amount of expenditure is likely to create more employment when invested in the civilian sector than in the defence sector.[8]

The debate is complicated by the composition of military expenditure – for military and civilian personnel, for construction and maintenance, for armaments of various types, and for civilian goods and services – and by the different direct and indirect employment effects of the various types of military spending. The same amount creates more employment if spent on wages or personnel costs than if spent on armaments. But, even with weapons procurement, the employment effect depends on the structure of the defence

suggested positive relationships between military spending and GNP growth include: David Cuputo: "New perspectives on the public policy implications of defense spending and welfare expenditures in four modern democracies", in *Policy Science* (Norwell, Mass.), 1975, Vol. 6, pp. 436-437; and Miroslav Nincic and Thomas Cusak: "The political economy of US military spending", in *Journal of Peace Research*, 1979, Vol. 16, No. 2, p. 106. C. Nardinelli and G. B. Ackerman: "Defense expenditures and American capitalism", in *Armed Forces and Society* (Cabin John, Maryland), Nov. 1976, Vol. 3, No. 1.

[8] D. Gold: *Misguided expenditure: An analysis of the proposed MX missile system* (New York, Council on Economic Priorities, 1981), especially table 5, Bezdek, supra no. 11; Chase Econometric Associates: *Economic impact of the B-1 Program on the US economy* (Bala Cynwyd, Pennsylvania, Chase Econometrics, 1975); Carolyn Kay Brancato and Linda LeGrande: "Impact on employment of defense versus non-defense government spending", Congressional Research Service Issue Brief MB82246 (Washington, DC, Library of Congress, 1984). Congressional Budget Office: *Defense spending and the economy* (Washington, DC, US Government Printing Office, 1983).

industry and on the type of equipment procured. In general, a large part of procurement outlays go to the high-technology, capital-intensive industrial branches and this is one of the reasons for the relatively low job-creating effect of defence industry expenditure.

Summing up, there is considerable evidence that the opportunity cost of defence spending is high, also in terms of employment creation, particularly in a longer-run perspective.

However, the immediate effect of defence cuts – if they are at all important – would probably be unemployment, at least in most countries. What the size and duration of the unemployment would be and what would be its effect on the labour force is an important issue to be examined. In general, the size and duration of unemployment would depend, first of all, on the size and the composition of the defence cuts; secondly, it would depend on the general economic situation – prosperity or recession – the general policy framework adopted and on the labour market conditions and structure; and finally, it would be affected by the capacity and willingness of defence industry enterprises to convert to civilian production.

The problems created by defence cuts and by the resulting redundancies are inevitably particularly serious at the local level because individuals and households cannot be perfectly mobile while the defence industry tends to be geographically concentrated for strategic, historical, industrial and other reasons. The uneven distribution of military outlays among regions in all the countries for which information is available has an impact on the structure of the regional economy, on regional growth and on the local labour markets, which acquire special characteristics with the presence of defence enterprises. But, despite certain different characteristics, basically the problem of defence cuts would be one of industrial restructuring, similar to other industrial restructuring problems which many IMECs have had to face in recent years, when, for example, heavy industries such as steel or shipbuilding were affected by a sharp fall in demand, rising foreign competition, and other external and internal factors. In the USSR most defence conversion tasks might not exceed in magnitude the current problems of economic restructuring or "perestroika" although in one sense they would be additional to it. In another sense dethroning military industry should help the process of economic reform. Some experience in the industrial, managerial, labour relocation and retraining and other fields is available – at the national as well as international level – which could be drawn on to reduce hardship to the existing workforce. However, a wide range of issues needs to be considered, as is discussed in many of the chapters of this study, which concentrates on the impact of defence expenditure on the regional labour markets and on local employment.

Much that has been written about the conversion of the defence industry has been in the context of relatively small changes in the amount and content of defence spending in a given political setting. Conversion problems in a market economy thus can be contrasted with those in a centrally planned economy. In fact, however, the topicality of conversion has only arisen because of inter-related political changes. The USSR's need to raise general consumption levels has led both to a change in its economic strategy and to political changes in the rest of Eastern Europe. In turn this will very probably lead to a replacement of the command economy management system by a virtual market system. What other foreign policy and security changes will come about is a matter for speculation. Changes are being made in the areas of price liberalisation, wage setting and foreign trade; however, full-fledged reform and the achievement of enterprise autonomy and well-functioning capital markets will take longer.

But while détente may be general in the industrialised countries, it is by no means global. Developing countries' appetite for arms imports depends partly on the depth of their pockets and many cannot afford expensive weaponry. Others, however, can, so that sales abroad are a real alternative for many traditional producers. Defence cuts at home may simply generate greater competition abroad and the encouragement of an arms build-up by Japan, for example, although détente may be accompanied by a sharpened reluctance to export military equipment to human rights offenders. In addition, it is unlikely that the appetite of arms producers in developing countries to expand their own foreign sales will be in any way lessened by events in industrialised countries.

To the extent that changes in the industrialised countries are genuinely towards peace, are non-trivial and lead to different patterns of international relations and alliances, their impact on arms manufacture could be very wide-reaching. Military establishments may be significantly reduced and arms become less sophisticated, which would in some respects resemble a return to the 1920s and early 1930s. Other observers stress the impossibility of putting a genie back into the bottle, and fear that weapons will become more research-intensive as military establishments fall and indeed as conventional arms are cut. As a result, the "worst case" scenario could be that there would be no financial savings from government defence cuts, but a fall in defence-related output in manufacturing and a greater claim by the military on scientific manpower. Clearly the defence industry, especially in the larger industrialised countries, could evolve in very different ways over the next 10-20 years.

In addition, the Soviet Union's current Warsaw Treaty Organisation (WTO) allies are a special case. On the one hand they are eager to move towards the establishment of a market economy, yet even the nature of the ownership of their industrial assets is unclear. Furthermore, their future security needs are almost impossible to predict, as are the markets for their defence products. Presumably there will be a decline in the output of their defence industries which, however, supply only a limited range of products, and efforts will be made to convert a (large) part of the defence plant and workforce to production of other goods. None the less the process will probably be less subject to control than in the Soviet Union. There will probably be far less development of new and more technologically developed weapons systems than is likely in the Soviet Union, although Czechoslovakia, for example, may develop certain specialised lines and, indeed, could find Western markets.

To the extent that defence industries in Eastern Europe are integrated into the defence production and procurement system of the Soviet Union, it is likely that they will face problems of over-capacity. Conversely, however, it is difficult to see precisely how much, if any, of the defence industry can be expected to survive in relatively small States, especially where government revenues are anyway under considerable strain and where most of the weaponry used has been produced by the USSR. Will some kind of co-operation in defence production emerge between these WTO members, might they choose some sort of specialised co-operation with neutral States of Western Europe, or might their defence production appear to operate at such high unit costs that they will mainly rely on imports, very possibly continuing their reliance on the Soviet Union – a solution which might solve more than one problem since they could export their manufactured goods in exchange? In any event these countries are unfortunately convinced that unemployment will increase in the near future and that many low-skilled workers will be made redundant. On top of that, defence production and employment are likely to fall. If defence production generally operated at higher than average levels of efficiency, then the labour shake-out should help in finding a rational use for scarce skills. But, as in all adjustment episodes, long-run benefits will entail short-run costs and if the latter are too high the adjustment process may be stopped half-way. Furthermore, if defence production continues as a branch of industry under public ownership, efficiency targets may not be reached.

The present study starts by assessing the magnitude of the problem of defence employment conversion at the national level, using a macro-economic approach. It examines, in Chapter 2, the possible size of the defence industry workforce in some of the major industrialised countries and reviews various studies of the theoretical impacts of changes in defence expenditure on the level of economic activity and employment. It critically appraises quantitative, mostly econometric, studies made earlier in Canada, France, the Federal Republic of Germany, Norway, Sweden, the United Kingdom and the United States.

Four regional case studies follow, focusing on the regional and occupational dependence on defence contracting in areas with a high share of defence production, namely the Greater London area (Chapter 3), the Greater Munich area (Chapter 4), Rome province (Chapter 5), and the State of Michigan (Chapter 6). The first three of these chapters follow a broadly similar outline. They first try to determine the degree of dependence on defence contracting in the region as a whole. They identify the leading companies in the defence sector and provide an estimate of the number of workers each of them employed, and of the number employed in the regions. They then produce a skill and occupational profile for the leading defence industry facilities and where possible a skill and occupational profile for the region as a whole, in order to determine the differences that exist in terms of skill and occupational characteristics between the defence industry and the civil industry. Unemployment and job vacancies are examined. The aim of these chapters is to assess the regional economy's capacity to absorb labour released from the military-industrial sector. They also study the effect of reductions in defence procurement at the enterprise level. Employers' and trade unions' attitudes to conversion are analysed and their respective policies and strategies on defence conversion are surveyed. In particular, the Michigan study offers a description of the unemployment and other social benefits which would accrue to laid-off defence industry workers.

While Chapters 3 to 6 treat defence cuts as a somewhat theoretical possibility, the next four chapters describe actual experience of defence conversion. The signing of the Intermediate-range Nuclear Forces (INF) Treaty between the United States and the USSR, in 1987, created a situation where the conversion of military production became an immediate practical concern. Chapter 7 analyses the industrial, economic and employment impact of the INF Treaty on defence production and employment in the United States. Chapter 8 deals with conversion problems in the Soviet defence industry, in the light of the INF Treaty, with particular reference to the regional dimension, and Chapter 9 provides a description of the economic and employment impact of the INF Treaty on the Votkinsk plant in the Soviet Union. Chapter 10 reveals some little-known facts on defence cutbacks in China and on their employment implications.

Finally, Chapter 11 makes a comparative assessment of the consequences of defence industry conversion for employment and unemployment, based on the different country and regional experiences, and draws lessons for coping with defence industry conversion in the future.

To sum up, the point of departure of the study is that military spending and the existence of a large defence industry workforce have a number of negative impacts, especially in the long term. These negative impacts, particularly on investment, on the development of civilian technology and on the level and structure of employment, have to be taken into account when evaluating the total cost of defence expenditure. While in the short run defence cuts might result in unemployment – the scope of which would depend on the amount and structure of alternative government spending – in the long run a switch to civilian activities would have an employment-creating effect.

Chapter 2

Quantifying the relation of defence expenditure to employment

J. P. DUNNE

I. Introduction

The concern of this chapter is to evaluate and attempt to draw some comparative assessment from studies that have analysed one of the most easily measured and important economic effects of military expenditure, namely the employment consequences. This requires estimation of both the direct and the indirect employment effects, the latter generally requiring the use of some form of input-output model. Employment consequences need not simply mean the number of jobs created; the composition of the change in employment is also of importance. The sex mix of the jobs, the number of full-time and part-time, the number of skilled and unskilled, the geographical distribution, even the duration, will all have differing economic implications. While a few of the studies reviewed are a few years old, it is not believed that any significant new advance is omitted.

In the studies considered in this chapter a number of approaches have been adopted. If one is simply concerned with the number of persons directly employed on defence contracts, the simplest approach is to survey contractors and to ask them how many people they employ on defence contracts. Just such an approach was used in the United Kingdom up to 1973 but was abandoned because of alleged unreliability of the results. It has also been used in Sweden. It certainly does have its disadvantages, as it might be open to misrepresentation by contractors, and it is often difficult to distinguish between those workers involved on defence and those on civilian contracts when both groups are employed in the same enterprise, in which many tasks may in fact be shared. Of course, this approach is of little use for estimating the indirect employment effects of defence expenditure, that is, the employment embodied in the production of intermediate commodities used in the production of defence goods, and any income multiplier effects.

To estimate the indirect employment effect of military expenditure, it is necessary to use some form of input-output model. These models allow estimates of both direct and indirect industrial demand and employment to be made. In the studies under consideration here such models take three forms. First, the open comparative static model which uses standard input-output tables augmented by average labour coefficients for the industries to estimate the employment effects of military expenditure. Second, the closed static model which allows for the multiplier effects of employment related to military expenditure through its effect on private consumption. Finally, the dynamic model, where the basic input-output model is augmented with econometric equations to determine final demands and factor demands. Trends may also be introduced into the input-output structure to allow for changes in technology over time.

Comparing the results of these different forms of model across countries is made difficult by the fact that they will each provide different estimates of the employment effects of military expenditure. Clearly, a closed static model will give a higher value than an open static one, while the static and dynamic models will produce different estimates. This results in part from the dynamic models allowing for feedbacks and multiplier effects and from the fact that static models use average labour requirements to supplement the input-output coefficients, while the dynamic models use the marginal requirements. These will clearly differ as the average requirement simply reflects the overall labour input to produce the absolute level of output, while the marginal requirement reflects only the additional labour required to produce an increase in output. The former will produce figures for the employment creation of present military expenditure, while the latter will provide the relevant figures for the employment effects of an increase or decrease in military expenditure. In addition, the econometric estimates of the marginal employment-output elasticity will be influenced by the extent to which defence contractors have attempted to maintain their workforces, especially design teams and other skilled workers, in the face of fluctuating demand over the estimating period. If they have done so, then high average labour requirements could lead to low marginal labour requirements because of the existence of underutilised labour.

A further problem with this form of model relates to how defence-related employment is computed. The simplest method is to multiply the estimate of the output generated by military expenditure by the employment-output ratio for the industry which received the contract. This method abstracts from any differences which may exist between the production processes and the relative labour requirements of the military and non-military goods, yet they clearly can differ markedly. Defence contracts are often of a cost-plus nature with continuous involvement of the funding body and possibly numerous changes in specification, which contrasts markedly with the environment implied by production for a civilian consumer market with the pressures of heavy competition. So there can be large divergences within the same industrial category and even the same firm. Thus the use of industrial results based on averages can thus be misleading when gauging the employment effects of military expenditure. In addition, difficulties in making comparisons can result from differences in the definition and presentation of industrial groupings. These will differ between countries and in fact can differ within studies in the level of detail provided.

Apart from these more technical questions, difficulties in making comparisons will be caused by the fact that studies vary in the way they present their analysis, the questions they ask and the scenarios they each envisage as being relevant. Estimating the level of employment associated with military expenditure is more straightforward than the more policy-oriented questions such as determining the effects of changes in the level of military expenditure. In such an analysis, it is necessary to bear in mind, if not to take directly into account, a number of considerations. It is important to ask whether the model can in fact answer the question posed. A large change might represent a change of regime from that which generated the historical data and hence there is little the model, based on this historical data, can say, and the effects of such a change are often felt in other countries as well. As noted in Chapter 1, this may be the current situation. Average labour requirement coefficients would not be relevant and some marginal estimates would be needed. It is also necessary within a dynamic model to have some way of updating input-output coefficients to allow for technological change; usually, this is simply done by the introduction of trends. It is also necessary to consider the policies that are likely to be undertaken in addition to the change in military expenditure, as part of a package with wider economic goals or attempts to compensate for the effects of military expenditure. This could be demand-side policies such as reallocation of defence expenditure to other government programmes rather than simply cutting total expenditure; supply-side policies such as aid to industry to convert military to civilian production, to retrain and to reorganise labour; and regional policies reflecting combinations of demand and supply-side policies within a regional or community perspective.

The macro-economic analysis of disarmament at the national level does tend to assume a highly mobile labour force and ignore economic, social and political costs in local communities. These and other employment aspects such as age, sex, occupation and educational composition of the labour force and the relative composition of the military/non-military sectors will affect the implications of model results, especially where they involve reallocations of expenditure.

Even within the general framework of input-output models, it must be remembered that models are simplifications of real processes. Types of models are constructed in various ways, designed to answer different types of questions, with contrasting underlying assumptions of economic behaviour, and different empirical and temporal bases. This point needs to be borne in mind when comparing the results of a number of models.

It is clear from this section that any analysis of the economic, or more specifically, the employment consequences of military expenditure will require the researchers to make numerous decisions. They will have to decide the model to use, the framework of analysis, the problem they are concerned with and practicalities such as availability of information and methods of overcoming data deficiencies. As a result, no two studies will be alike in all aspects of their analysis. Added to this are the problems we have outlined in making comparisons *per se*, and one can see that a comparative assessment of studies from different countries is both difficult and, of necessity, imprecise. There is, in general, enough common ground for some general comparative statements to be made but further detail is potentially at the cost of imprecision.

II. The studies reviewed

The *Canadian study*, CSDRM (1983), was the product of a Department of National Defence directive which gave the Centre for Studies in Defence Resources Management (CSDRM) three years to provide an assessment of the economic impact of defence expenditures and to develop a capability to provide such assessments on a continuing basis. It is by far the most comprehensive of the studies considered here including, as it does, a lengthy discussion of the issues involved in measuring the economic consequences of military expenditure and using three different types of models to provide estimates of aspects of these consequences.

The study rightly recognises that measuring the impact of military expenditure requires the use of a simplified model and that different models will be best suited to answer different questions, being based upon different assumptions about economic behaviour. For this reason, it presents the results of three models – a standard comparative static input-output model, a dynamic input-output model and a comparative static "neoclassical" model.

The difference between the standard input-output and the neoclassical models arises from their underlying assumptions. Unlike the former, the latter assumes fixed supplies of labour and capital, full employment of resources and profit maximisation, though both are inter-industry comparative static models. The dynamic model CANDIDE lies somewhere between the two in terms of assumptions but has a dynamic inter-industry structure. As mentioned, each model is considered best suited to answer particular types of questions. The standard input-output model is used to analyse the economic implications of defence expenditure; the effects of marginal increases in defence expenditure and its elimination are explored in the neoclassical model and the impact of alternative rates of growth of the defence budget over ten years are explored in the dynamic model.

To estimate the industrial employment generated by defence expenditure, the study used a standard input-output model. In fact, they used two forms of the model – an open model and a closed model, the latter allowing for multiplier effects of defence expenditure through its effect on income and consumption. Details are given for 191 industries, but there is in fact a high concentration of production with the top ten industries accounting for about 60 per cent of the employment generated in the private sector. Using the open input-output model, total indirect industrial employment was 46,121 work-years in 1980-81.

In looking at defence-related employment, the study applied job/output ratios to total defence output; in fact, they were based on earlier estimates adjusted for inflation. This implies the assumption that the average ratio for the industry is the same as that for defence-related production, a common though questionable assumption.

It would appear that the defence sector is not particularly important to the Canadian economy, accounting for only 1.4 per cent of GDP. It is, however, of significance to individual industries, for example, 15 per cent of the employment of aircraft and parts. In the same vein the regional model shows differing levels of dependence between the provinces. Defence spending and production are most significant to the maritime (Pacific) and least significant to the Western provinces (Winnipeg, Manitoba, etc.).

The dynamic CANDIDE model was used to compare the effects of a 6 per cent real growth rate in defence expenditure between 1980 and 1990 – scenario A – over a base run which assumed a 3 per cent real growth rate over that period. In addition, scenario B, where there was a compensated elimination of defence spending, maintaining defence at a bare minimum and reallocating the expenditure to other government programmes, was also compared to the base. For the increase in the growth of defence expenditure the method of financing was assumed to be a combination of increased taxation on the private sector, a transfer of funds, and printing money. The 3 per cent real growth assumption represented an estimate of the Canadian Government's five-year plan which was in action at the time. The capital component of the budget was assumed to increase by 12 per cent for five years with the other categories sharing the remainder, all portions of the budget increasing by 3 per cent for the rest of the decade. Under both scenarios employment increased, i.e. even with the compensated elimination of defence spending.

The *study available for France* (Ministère de la Défense, 1984) provides a survey of three previous Defence Ministry reports examining the economic consequences of defence expenditure. The first two of these studies used the AVATAR input-output model developed by INSEE while the third study used PROPAGE, a more complicated dynamic input-output model, also developed by INSEE.

AVATAR estimates implied that 66.5 billion francs of defence expenditure on goods and services in 1981 created 341,000 jobs. Aben and Smith (1986) provide more details on the 1981 figures for France comparing them with those for the United Kingdom.

The previous figures deal with the average effects of defence expenditure. The use of PROPAGE allows the measurement of the impact of defence expenditure through its dynamic structure. In the study, the specific form of the analysis is to examine the effects of increasing defence expenditure by 1 billion francs in 1982 prices. The results of this for 1982 were an increase in jobs of around 6,000 cumulated over five years. The simulations for later years show smaller effects.

In terms of the industrial effects, the employment effect was particularly concentrated in shipbuilding, aerospace and arms as one would expect, with these *industries militaires* accounting for 20 per cent of the employment creation. It is interesting to note that most of the employment effects in the armament industries are created in about a year with the further increases over the five-year horizon occurring in the other industries.

Military expenditure is certainly more important in France than in Canada though it still only supports about 5 per cent of the labour force, even when conscripts and gendarmerie are included. It shares with most countries the concentration of employment related to military expenditure within specific industries and areas, while at the aggregate level the simulation results illustrate that changes in military expenditure have rather small employment effects. A continued increase of a billion francs, in 1982 prices, has a cumulative effect after five years, equivalent to only 2.5 per cent of the labour force.

The *study conducted for Norway*, Bjerkholt et al. (1980), was the product of the UN research programme on disarmament and development. Its main aim was to examine how resources could be diverted from the arms race to increased development transfers to the Third World.

In analysing the effects of military expenditure on the Norwegian economy, the study used the 1978 version of MODIS IV, an inter-industry model with a high level of disaggregation. Although it has no regional breakdown, 200 commodities, 150 industries, 50 consumption categories, detailed government expenditure and several types of capital are distinguished. The model's basic input-output structure is embedded in a set of econometric equations. It is, however, a comparative static rather than a dynamic model.

The first use of the model was to update some previous work analysing the impact of reduced defence expenditure on the Norwegian economy. This exercise entailed reducing defence expenditure in 1978 by 1,000 million kronor, that is by 15 per cent, without any countermeasures. The estimated reduction in employment caused by this cut was 11,800 work-years with two-thirds of this effect being in directly created employment and the remaining third in indirectly generated employment.

The main part of the analysis involved estimating the effects of reductions in defence expenditure on the economy when combined with policies to channel the released resources as aid to developing countries. This was undertaken using a number of alternative policy options for aid transfer, as well as considering countermeasures to minimise the negative employment effects of the policies.

The scenarios considered in the study provide a base and three alternatives. The base is the "not disarm scenario" which corresponds to the NATO Council of Ministers' decision in 1978 to increase real military expenditure by 3 per cent per annum; this implies an assumption of a fixed share of national product for defence. The alternatives are the moderate one, a cut of 15 per cent in the 1978 level as suggested by the UN Expert Group; a radical alternative which would reduce defence expenditure to the average level for two neutral countries, Austria and Finland; and finally complete disarmament.

The total effect on GDP of the different disarmament options was found to be reasonably small and the loss of employment is only just over 4 percentage points or about 3 per cent of the labour force even for complete disarmament.

The *Swedish study*, Thorsson (1984), is an extremely comprehensive analysis of the possibilities and potential problems of conversion from military to civil production in Sweden. It differs from the other studies considered here in having much broader terms of reference and a rather different form of analysis in determining the employment consequences of military expenditure. In fact, the study does not use any form of input-output model and hence can only compute the direct employment consequences in the same manner as the other studies, the indirect estimates coming from a survey of the defence producers. As mentioned previously, this approach can have a number of problems such as double counting, the difficulty of distinguishing between military and civil work where both are carried out in the same plant, misrepresentation and the allocation of research and development. Although having the data at the level of the individual firm can be extremely useful in understanding the effects of defence expenditure on industry, it does cause problems in making comparisons as most studies use some form of industrial categorisation which is not necessarily directly related to the individual, often multi-product, firms.

Thorsson estimated that in 1984-85 defence expenditure of 25 billion Swedish kronor (US$3,000 million) supported 88,000 jobs and, if conscripts in training were included, to have had a total employment effect of 138,000 persons in 1980. The defence industry accounted for 18,000 and subcontracting for 4,000. This information is based on survey data and approximately 6,000 workers employed on defence-related production for export are not included.

Given the problems with using this survey approach and the somewhat arbitrary nature of some of the computations, one would not have much faith in the detail of these figures. Nevertheless, they probably provide a reasonable estimate of the total employment effect, with underestimates such as the lack of induced employment balancing out possible overestimates such as double counting for subcontractors.

The report looked at the geographical distribution of employment, with indirect employment allocated to regions according to their share of total employment. Defence agency direct employment was found to be relatively evenly distributed, except for a concentration in Stockholm. Industry employment, on the other hand, did tend to be concentrated in a smaller number of regions. While overall this implied a low level of dependence on defence-related employment at the subregional (county) level, dependence was in fact found to be very high for a number of local communities.

The report's disarmament scenario was a reduction of 50 per cent in Sweden's wartime organisation over a 25-year period, 1990-2015. Given these assumptions, an analysis of the employment effects of such a reduction in military expenditure was undertaken. Military personnel would be cut by half, a reduction of about 9,000 or 350 jobs per annum, civilian personnel would be reduced by more than 11,000, an average annual reduction of 400. Recognising the problems of such an evaluation, the study also provides an estimate of job reductions in the defence industries of 14,000, a loss of 560 per annum. It is considered likely that the reduction in orders would lead to a concentration of production within defence-related industries. Mergers, for example, would be likely in the electronics industry to allow domestic development and productive capacity to be maintained, a trend which could have marked regional and subregional consequences.

Overall, the estimate for job reductions is a total of 34,000. This, by the report's reasoning, implies 1,430 per year which is only 1 per cent of Sweden's labour force. This allows the authors to conclude that disarmament would present little serious problem from a macro-economic point of view. Problems would lie within the individual subregions and industries and much thought needs to be given to such problems of conversion.

The *West German study*, Filip-Kohn et al. (1980), is another produced in connection with the UN Group of Government Experts on the relationship between disarmament and development. It examines the extent to which sectoral production and employment in the Federal Republic of Germany depend both directly and indirectly on defence expenditures and on exports to developing countries. More specifically, it attempts to quantify the effects of a world-wide disarmament policy and a world-wide increase in development aid on West German sectoral output and employment.

The study uses the 1972 and 1976 input-output accounts with 34 production sectors, six final demand vectors and three primary input vectors to calculate the gross sectoral production required to achieve a particular final demand structure. The sectoral average job/output ratios are then used to calculate defence-related employment levels. The study has little discussion of the context of the analysis and recognises the deficiencies of the simplicity of its analysis. It does, however, provide a relatively high degree of industrial detail.

In 1972, according to the study, 848,000 jobs were generated directly and 136,000 indirectly, a total of 984,000 or 3.2 per cent of the total employment in the economy. By 1976, the total number of jobs supported by military expenditure was estimated to be 959,000, 3.3 per cent of total employment; 837,000 were directly and 121,000 indirectly generated. As would be expected, the industrial employment generation is concentrated in a small number of industries with the majority of the employment creation in the public sector (685,000 of the directly generated jobs). Manufacturing accounted for 85,000 direct and 64,000 indirect employment opportunities.

An attempt was made to estimate the effects of a 5 per cent and a 10 per cent cut in defence expenditure in 1972 and 1976. Overall, they found that a 5 per cent cut would reduce the number of employees by 50,000 through effects on domestic and export demand, and by 100,000 for a 10 per cent cut. The linearity of this result is quite striking and not surprising given the nature and simplicity of the model used; it holds even at the sectoral level.

The relative industrial effects are very much as one would expect, with vehicle building, electrical equipment, precision optics, metal products, wholesale trade and other services being the most affected industrial categories.

The study presents a detailed and careful analysis of the employment effects of military expenditure and one would expect reasonably precise estimates of the total employment generated. The model is of limited use for forecasting the effects of changes in military expenditure, however, being static, ignoring induced employment and using average rather than marginal labour/output coefficients.

For *the United Kingdom*, the results of an official Ministry of Defence study, Pite (1980), of the direct and indirect employment consequences of defence expenditure are available together with two recent independent studies, Bellany (1985) and Dunne and Smith (1984), which have investigated the employment effects of changes in the level of defence expenditure. The official figures show that in 1981 a defence budget of £12.5 billion was split between £5.3 billion in wages and salaries, which supported 534,000 jobs, and other current expenditures of £7.2 billion which generated direct and indirect employment of 600,000 jobs (330,000 direct and 274,000 indirect). The methods by which these figures are arrived at is described in Pite (1980). Until 1973, surveys were carried out but the data derived from them was considered unreliable and collection discontinued. Since then, some form of input-output analysis with various "in-house" adjustments has been used.

Dunne and Smith (1984) present a comprehensive analysis of the economic consequences of reducing British military expenditure, analysing the effects of a reduction from the present 5 to 3.5 per cent of GDP. This study used the Institute for Employment Research's version of the Cambridge Growth Project Model of Warwick University. In the first simulation, defence expenditure was reduced by £1 billion in 1970 prices and this was reallocated to other public expenditures proportionately to their share of total expenditure. In simulation B, no such compensating reallocation was made.

The model used is an input-output structure embedded in a set of econometric equations. It is dynamic and disaggregated into 40 industries, 49 consumption categories, five categories of government current expenditure, four categories of capital expenditure and so on. The simulation was undertaken from the years 1983 to 1990.

The results for the macro-economic indicators show quite small changes for simulation A, with an increase in total employment of about 1 per cent, 200,000, rising to over 250,000 by the fifth year. Even without compensation, the macro-economic effects are not large with employment falling by 149,000 in the first year and by 191,000 in the fifth year.

The main reduction in employment is as expected in government defence-related employment, a loss of 70,000 jobs, but this is more than offset in simulation A by the rise in other public employment of 124,000 to give the overall increase observed. Private sector employment is 77,000 higher in the first year and 130,000 by the fifth year. Construction is seen to be the main beneficiary and engineering the main casualty. In simulation B total employment in the first year is reduced by only 150,000 though this rises to almost 200,000 by the fifth. The study considers that most of the effects are probably the result of general deflation rather than specific to defence, and even by the fifth year the reduction is still under 0.8 per cent of the labour force.

Allowing for the adjustments, scenario A suggests that a cut in defence would cost about 250,000 jobs of which more than 150,000 would be in the public sector, while reallocation of the expenditure would create 350,000 jobs, 190,000 in the public sector; a net effect of an increase of 100,000 or 0.4 per cent of the labour force.

The official estimate for the employment supported by military expenditure in the United Kingdom is probably exaggerated, but at just over

1 million jobs it still only represents slightly over 4 per cent of the labour force. As with the other countries, defence-related employment is concentrated in certain industries and subregions, but the studies suggest that substantial reductions in defence spending could increase employment and be economically beneficial.

It is not surprising that *the United States* has shown the most concern in modelling the impact of defence expenditure and has the most advanced and detailed modelling framework. The pioneering work on the modelling of the economic effects of defence expenditure using input-output models was undertaken in the United States by Leontief et al. (1961, 1965). Since then, there have been numerous studies by academics, private consultants and the Government. In fact, the models used in such analyses by the Government are generally those provided by private consultants such as Data Resources Inc. (DRI).

The Department of Defense provides projections of defence purchases of products of any industry on request. They use the "Defense Economic Impact Modelling System" (DEIMS), a 400-industry dynamic input-output model embedded in an econometric model. The main intentions of the model were to give private industry useful forecasts of the impact of the budget on sales in the long and the short run, to act as a link between the planning and budgeting system and private sector suppliers, and thus to prepare private industry for its role in meeting the Department of Defense requirements. In fact, the projections have been made more widely available and submodels allow the forecasting of the occupational distribution of labour and of the demand for strategic materials, while a regional model allows state-level projections for each of the 50 states and the District of Columbia.

The structure of the input-output model developed by DRI has been improved by the use of a "defence translator" which adjusts the input-output links between the budget outlays and associated purchases to allow for the different compositions of weapons systems compared to other products. This is clearly an improvement over the other studies we have considered and was apparently developed because of the unreasonable results given by trial versions of the model which did not take into account the compositional differences between defence and non-defence production. There is certainly a mass of disaggregate data available for the United States economy which allows refinements of the modelling procedure. The question then becomes, however, whether we believe the numbers.

The results for the top 150 supplying sectors were provided with information for different expenditure categories though, as is usual, the defence output is concentrated in relatively few industries with 61 per cent of direct defence purchases accounted for by ten industrial groupings.

The Bureau of Labor Statistics produced a study of the employment consequences of defence expenditure in the United States. Although the study does in fact focus on the labour and material requirements of foreign defence sales, it also includes comparisons with the economy in general and the major industrial sectors. It is these results we shall consider here.

The study uses an inter-industry input-output model to provide the employment estimates, assuming directly proportional relationships between industrial sales and the output and employment required. The study provides results for the years 1972 to 1979, with productivity updates allowed for each year for each of the 158 sectors. The industry/occupational figures used in the model are those for 1978, though they consider this justifiable as the coefficients have generally been very stable.

The results of this analysis show total labour requirements including Department of Defense personnel to have declined constantly from 5.8 million in 1972 to 4.8 million in 1978 with a very slight increase in 1979 because of an increase in the private sector. Between 1972 and 1979, the armed forces strength fell from 2.6 million to 1.8 million, while defence-supported federal civil employment fell from 926,000 to 864,000 jobs. The study estimates that the defence creation of private sector jobs was 2.3 million in 1972 dropping to 1.8 million by 1979. Manufacturing accounted for 1,235,000 in 1972 and 986,000 in 1979. Effects are concentrated in a few industries, especially in engineering, electronics and transport, and are extremely important to those industries. The effect in business services does, however, seem to be rather large.

The United States clearly has the largest defence sector of all the countries considered and the highest proportion of GDP devoted to defence. The employment supported by defence expenditure, however, is still only just over 4 per cent of the labour force, with the United States having the lowest proportion of military expenditure spent on personnel. The United States does, of course, share with the other countries the problem of high dependence on defence employment within specific industries and subregions.

III. Comparison of methods and results

All the studies considered here, except that for Sweden, used some form of input-output model and all those, except the West German one, provided results from a dynamic input-output model, where the coefficients were embedded in a set of econometric relationships.

Some industrial detail for the employment effects of military expenditure was reported by all of the studies, though at different levels of aggregation and in different groupings. Sweden based its industrial analysis on survey results only, thus reporting information at the level of the firm rather than at an aggregate industry level. Such information is, of course, extremely useful but it does mean that the results are not directly comparable to the other studies and it also means that there are no estimates of indirect employment in that study.

As mentioned, all the studies, except that for the Federal Republic of Germany, provided results for macro-economic indicators beside aggregate output and employment. In fact, this study was the only one to focus solely on the industrial implications of military expenditure without regard to the other direct employment effects, in the armed forces and public administration. In addition, it was the only one not to give any consideration to the regional context of the analysis.

In the analysis of the employment effects of military expenditure, further important information can be gained by distinguishing types of workers. Clearly, differences in the structure of labour used by the defence industry, and in skill, occupation and sex mixes will have varying implications for the economic effects of military expenditure and for the effects of changes in it. In fact only the United States has, as part of the DEIMS system, an occupational model, though some of the other studies do discuss the issues involved with regard to their policy implications. There was no attempt to disaggregate by age or sex in the studies.

We have stressed that the technical aspects of the studies are important, but are in some ways conditional on the framework provided. The starting-point of the study, the scenarios, the defining of policies and policy options will all influence any particular study. There was in fact a wide variety of approaches in the studies. The studies in the Federal Republic of Germany, Norway and Sweden were the result of the UN disarmament and development initiative and explicitly introduced the use of savings on military expenditure as aid to developing countries into their modelling processes. The Norwegian study gives the most detailed analysis of this nature, giving results for the effects of reducing military expenditure for different aid-transfer policies. France and the United Kingdom simply shift the expenditure from military to other aggregate categories.

Table 2.1 summarises some information from the studies on the employment associated with military expenditure. These are average figures, that is the reported estimates of the number of jobs that military expenditure supports overall. The results are taken from the static input-output model estimates combined with official values for direct employment, where necessary, such as for military personnel. For Canada, the closed static model results are used; for France, they are the AVATAR 1981 results as reported in Aben and Smith (1986); for Norway, only the figures for direct employment could be extracted from the study as its main focus was on the effect of changing military expenditure; for Sweden, the figures are not based upon an input-output model; for the Federal Republic of Germany, details on the split between the categories of direct employment are not available; the reported results are based upon the static input-output model; for the United Kingdom, the figures are those supplied by the Ministry of Defence, which are in fact criticised in Dunne and Smith (1984); finally, the United States results are those from the Bureau of Labor Statistics study and only the total industrial employment can be obtained from this source.

The third line from bottom in table 2.1 gives the number of jobs supported by 1 million expenditure in constant (1980) US dollars. These results seem reasonable, though they do, of course, blur any distinction between expenditure on personnel and on capital. Sweden gives the lowest estimate but this may be discounted because of the lack of a formal model in the study, which probably led to an underestimate of indirect employment. Apart from Sweden,

Table 2.1. *Comparison of the effects of military expenditure in seven industrialised countries*

	Canada	France	Fed. Rep. of Germany	Norway	Sweden	United Kingdom	United States
Conscripts (thousand)	–	–	–	21.7	50.0	–	–
Service personnel (thousand)	–	573.0	–	13.5	20.0	331.0	2 102.0
Civilians (thousand)	–	80.0	–	10.7	32.0	203.0	864.0
Industrial employment (thousand)							
Direct	105.8[1]	–	837.0[2]	–	18.0	330.0	–
Indirect	120.5	–	121.0	–	18.0	270.0	–
Total employment (thousand)	226.3	451.0	959.0	–	–	–	1 844.2[3]
Total (thousand)	–	1 105.0[4]	–	–	138.0	1 134.0	4 810.3
Cost of personnel	–	10.5	–	14.1	20.3	17.9	9.9
Jobs per $1 million	48.8	63.1	52.2	–	23.3	49.7	36.0
Jobs as percentage of labour force	1.9	4.6	3.5	–	3.4	4.3	4.5
Military expenditure as percentage of GDP IISS (1985) figures	1.8	4.0	3.3	2.9	3.3	5.0	5.6
Year of study	1981	1981	1976	1978	1980	1981	1979

[1] Total direct employment. [2] Total direct employment composed of 152,000 direct industrial and 685,000 public sector employment. [3] Private sector employment. [4] Total including conscripts and gendarmerie (896,000 if they are excluded).
Sources. See text.

the United States is the lowest at 36 jobs, with the rest around or over 50, France providing the largest number at 63. There is clearly a wide dispersion of estimates for the employment consequences of military expenditure in these studies, but given the problems discussed earlier, it is difficult to say whether this is caused by inherent differences between the employment-supporting propensities of military expenditure in different countries or simply by differences between the countries. It is always possible that the number of jobs per million dollars might be more of a reflection of the success of the study in measuring indirect employment than anything to do with the job-supporting propensities of military expenditure.

    The final two rows present the employment supported by military expenditure as a proportion of the labour force and total military expenditure as a proportion of GDP, a statistic often used to represent the burden of such expenditure on an economy. Military employment does not appear to constitute a particularly high proportion of the labour force, although its effects are generally concentrated within particular industries and regions. It appears that the higher the burden of military expenditure, the higher the proportion of the labour force dependent on it for employment, as one would expect, but the countries with the highest burden also have lower employment shares than their expenditure share. This might be considered to reflect changes in the nature of military expenditure as it increases, from the lower technology labour-intensive basic defence to the higher technology, less labour-intensive luxury weapons.

    For most of the studies, some form of simulation was undertaken which examined the employment effects of a certain change in military expenditure. These results are summarised in table 2.2. Unfortunately, comparable results are not available for Sweden and it must be borne in mind that those for the Federal Republic of Germany come from a static model, while the rest used some form of dynamic model. The column headings give the country name and the year of the study; the first row the direction of the change (increase or decrease) assumed for military expenditure. Results were rebased to 1980 constant price US dollars. The second row gives the number of jobs per US$1 million expenditure in constant price US dollars that are implied by the results of the studies. Assuming symmetry between the effects of increases and decreases of military expenditure, a not uncontroversial assumption, allows a comparison of its job-creating abilities in the different countries. This shows the United Kingdom and the Federal Republic of Germany to have the highest number of jobs per US$ million, closely followed by Norway, all producing over 50 jobs, then comes France at 36, followed by the United States at 31 and finally Canada at 29. The West German result is close to that for the average effect because the study uses a static model; the differences are more marked for the other models, as would be expected, though the United States and United Kingdom are surprisingly close.

    Again it is not clear whether the dispersion reflects differences in the studies or in the propensity of military expenditure to create employment in these countries. Given the problems involved in attempting to make comparisons at this level of aggregation and generality, it does not seem worth

Table 2.2.   Comparison of the effects of a change in military expenditure in six industrialised countries

	Canada	France	Fed. Rep. of Germany	Norway	United Kingdom	United States
Year	1981	1982	1976	1978	1981	1984
Direction	inc.	inc.	dec.	dec.	dec.	inc.
Employment change (persons) per $1 million constant	28.8	36.1	54.1	52.1	54.8	31.4

Source. As table 2.1.

while attempting to compare more disaggregated results from the studies. Most of the industrial results show the effects of military expenditure concentrated in the industries one would expect, for example, engineering, aerospace and electronics, though industrial definitions and groupings differ across studies. The reports do imply that attempts to reduce military expenditure, which allowed for compensatory policies and planned conversion of resources, especially at the industrial and regional levels, would present few economic problems. Certainly, the employment effects of a policy of disarmament would be small relative to the effects of the restructuring that has taken place during the recession of the early 1980s and indeed the resources released could be used to enhance economic growth.

Unfortunately, the general conclusion of this chapter must be that the available analyses of the direct and indirect employment consequences of military expenditure do not invite comparisons across countries. The existence of differences between the questions asked, the types of models used and the frameworks of analysis, mean that it is not possible to isolate the differences in estimates that result from specific country effects. Given the general problems inherent in analysing the economic consequences of military expenditure within a country, it is not surprising that inter-country comparisons are difficult. In fact, attempting to draw any firm quantitative conclusions of a comparative nature could be misleading and produce figures imbued with spurious accuracy. Any such statements should be both general and well qualified.

Appendix

The studies considered in this chapter are the following:

Canada

Centre for Studies in Defence Resources Management, CSDRM. 1983. *The economic impact of Canadian defence expenditure*. Kingston, The Royal Military College of Canada; Summer.

Galigan, C. G. 1984. *The economic impact of Canadian defence expenditure: FY 1982-83 update*. Kingston, Centre for Studies in Defence Resources Management, The Royal Military College of Canada; Summer.

France

Aben, J. 1981. "Désarmement, activité et emploi", in *Défense Nationale* (Paris, Comité d'Etudes de Défense Nationale), May.

Aben, J.; Smith, R. P. 1986. "Defence and employment in the UK and France: A comprehensive study of the existing results", in C. Schmidt (ed.): *Peace, defence and economic analysis* (Basingstoke, Hants., Macmillan). 1987.

Ministère de la Défense. 1984. *Analyse économique des dépenses militaires*. Paris; Nov.

The Federal Republic of Germany

Filip-Kohn, R., et al. 1980. *Macro-economic effects of disarmament policies on sectoral production and employment in the Federal Republic of Germany with special emphasis on development policy issues*. Berlin (West), German Institute for Economic Research, Report; May. (This study has been updated by C. Wellman, *Abrüstung und Beschäftigung — ein Zielkonflikt*, Campus Verlag, Frankfurt, 1989.)

Norway

Bjerkholt, O., et al. 1980. *Disarmament and development: A study of conversion in Norway*. Oslo, International Peace Research Institute; S-7/80, May.

Sweden

Thorsson, I. 1984. *In pursuit of disarmament: Conversion from military to civil production in Sweden*, Vol. 1A. Stockholm, Liber.

The United Kingdom

Dunne, J. P.; Smith, R. P. 1984. "The economic consequences of reduced UK military expenditure", in *Cambridge Journal of Economics*, Sep., Vol. 8, No. 3.

Pite, C. 1980. "Employment and defence", in *Statistical News* (London, HMSO, Central Statistical Office), Vol. 4, No. 1.

The United States

Bureau of Labor Statistics. 1982. *Foreign defense sales and grants, fiscal years 1972-79: Labor and material requirements*. Washington, DC, Department of Labor; Jan.

Department of Defense: Defense Economic Impact Modelling System (DEIMS), print-outs of industrial detail forecast from, and various booklets on different aspects of, DEIMS.

Chapter 3

Defence employment and the local labour market of Greater London

SUE WILLETT

I. Introduction

Early research has shown that defence production tends to be geographically concentrated although there is little adequate understanding of the consequences of this for the localities involved. While research in this field in the United Kingdom has been constrained by an acute absence of adequate data on defence production and employment, some local economies have been highly dependent on Ministry of Defence (MoD) contracts which have considerably influenced their economic structure. In Greater London the defence industry generates a significant proportion of local employment and the main concern of this chapter is to identify those categories of workers most vulnerable to the labour force reductions associated with a decline in military spending.

II. The London labour market for manufacturing and defence employment

Most defence production takes place in what is loosely defined as the engineering industry; a broad spectrum from mechanical and electronic components to land vehicles, ships and aircraft. Engineering skills vary from mechanical engineers, fitters and toolmakers to draughtsmen and women, aerospace, electronics and software engineers. Different sectors of the engineering industry in the United Kingdom are in various stages of expansion or decline; mechanical engineering is in decline while instrument engineering has been expanding. These factors affect labour market conditions and, therefore, the demand for certain types of skill, both nationally and regionally.

In addition, new technology is having a profound effect on the restructuring of industry and its location. The Greater London economy has been profoundly affected in this way with significant implications for the possible absorption of labour displaced from the defence sector.

Greater London was earlier one of the principal manufacturing centres of the United Kingdom; in 1951 more than 1.5 million people were working in the city's factories. Since then, employment in its manufacturing has declined sharply. Between 1971 and 1981, Greater London lost 36 per cent of its manufacturing employment. By March 1985, the number of manufacturing jobs had been reduced to 554,000. One result was high levels of unemployment. In 1986 some 400,000 people were seeking work in the Greater London region, 11 per cent of the male working population and 6 per cent of the female.

Total employment in Greater London has, however, continued to grow although unsteadily. Employment growth has been due entirely to the expansion of services; industrial employment has been declining. Table 3.1 shows that between September 1984 and March 1989 manufacturing employment fell by nearly 25 per cent. The overall pattern of change in employment over the past years has been characterised by a major shift from manufacturing to services.

Table 3.2 provides a detailed breakdown of employment trends in manufacturing in Greater London between March 1985 and March 1986. In the sectors associated with defence engineering, such as electrical and electronics engineering and mechanical engineering, there has been a significant employment decline.

This decline in the engineering industry dates back to the 1960s and 1970s. Engineering output was seriously affected by falling demand for capital goods and the increased market share taken by imports. The industry's investment and its market share fell rapidly and competitiveness declined. Companies cut production costs by reorganising output. Typically this was achieved by mergers and takeovers, followed by closing older and more labour-intensive plants and concentrating production into larger and more capital-intensive units employing a smaller workforce. According to the London Regional Manpower Intelligence Unit (1986), 3,276 redundancies were served in the engineering industry between October 1985 and June 1986, representing roughly 40 per cent of all redundancies in manufacturing for the same period.

A major component of this trend has been the introduction of new technology-based production systems which have reduced the need for skilled operatives and cut the share of labour inputs in production costs. The introduction of modern methods such as CAD/CAM has led companies to be less dependent on certain types of skilled labour.

Relocation of production has been a central element in London's industrial decline since the 1960s. High land prices and rents, poor access, archaic production facilities and highly paid, organised labour have discouraged production. An added incentive to close sites in Greater London has been the high value of land for redevelopment; land sales have then financed investment elsewhere.

Table 3.3 provides a profile of job vacancies notified within the Greater London area between March 1985 and March 1986. It shows a decline in the number of vacancies available in such manufacturing occupations as machine operators, toolmakers, fitters, electronic technicians and welders. However, the demand for electricians, painters and maintenance workers appears to be growing. But few of these categories are employed at defence plants. In addition, there has been a decline in apprentice training opportunities, due to the cut in the intake of craft and technician apprentices.

Table 3.1. Employment in Greater London by sector (in thousands)

	Services	Manufacturing	Other	Total	Of which female, per cent
Sep. 1984	2 703	569	191	3 463	43.1
Mar. 1985	2 719	554	187	3 460	43.4
Mar. 1986	2 758	520	182	3 460	43.9
Mar. 1987	2 780	467	180	3 427	44.4
Mar. 1988	2 913	460	184	3 557	45.1
Mar. 1989	2 965	431	185	3 581	45.6

Source. *Department of Employment, Employment Gazette*, Oct. 1989.

Table 3.2. Manufacturing employment in Greater London, by sector

	March 1986	Change from March 1985
Chemicals	42 611	41
Electrical and electronic engineering	116 986	− 3 921
Food and drink	60 237	− 2 376
Footwear, clothing and leather	33 910	− 2 131
Instrument engineering	15 792	386
Mechanical engineering	65 532	− 2 108
Metal goods	28 493	− 683
Metals, minerals and glass	19 285	− 505
Motor vehicles and parts	17 342	− 3 818
Other transport and equipment	4 486	− 1 991
Paper, printing and publishing	112 056	− 974
Rubber and plastics	12 325	− 343
Timber and furniture	18 332	− 1 617
Other manufacturing	14 081	− 620
Total manufacturing	561 468	− 20 660

Source. London Regional Manpower Intelligence Unit (1986). (Note, this total differs from that of the Department of Employment given in table 3.1.)

Many of Greater London's defence workers are in electronic engineering. Defence employment represents a high share of the total in data processing, electronic instruments and controls, radio and capital goods and components sectors. Apart from components production, employment within these sectors has not fallen as sharply as in the purely civil sectors such as consumer electronics, office machinery and telegraph and telephone equipment.

In 1984 there were 55,750 people working on the hardware side, manufacturing electronic equipment, telecoms and instruments in Greater

Table 3.3.   *Occupational analysis of vacancies notified to London job centres, March 1985 to March 1986*

Occupational category	Total vacancies	Percentage share of total	Change since 1984	
			No.	Percentage
Managerial and technical	10 691	2.3	7	0.1
Nursing	2 858	0.6	−93	−3.2
Typing and secretarial	16 428	3.5	−1 298	−7.3
Clerical	82 962	17.6	1 387	1.7
Selling (distribution)	50 049	10.6	4 221	9.2
Selling (other)	5 924	1.3	−448	−7.0
Security	7 170	1.5	1 880	35.6
Catering	83 470	17.7	−11 459	−12.1
Cleaning and personal services	47 760	10.1	1 193	2.6
Horticulture	2 435	0.5	81	3.4
Materials processing:				
Food	2 789	0.6	11	0.4
Others	1 391	0.3	138	11.0
Making and repairing:				
Clothing	6 146	1.3	−495	−7.5
Other	7 401	1.6	220	3.7
Machine operators:				
Skilled	3 058	0.6	−177	−5.5
Unskilled	545	0.1	−23	−4.0
Toolmakers/fitters	1 142	0.2	−128	−10.1
Electric technicians	1 104	0.2	−214	−16.2
Electricians	3 222	0.7	163	5.3
Installation and maintenance	5 167	1.1	203	4.1
Welding and fabrication	5 255	1.1	−153	−2.8
Painting	6 490	1.4	511	8.5
Construction:				
Skilled	7 912	1.7	−676	−7.9
Unskilled	7 591	1.6	326	4.5
Drivers	4 609	1.0	−455	−9.0
Other transport and warehouse workers	47 560	10.1	−1 502	−3.1
General hands	51 251	10.8	2 311	4.7
Total	472 380	100		

Source. London Regional Manpower Intelligence Unit (1986). (Note, during this period the stock of notified vacancies – perhaps itself one-third of all vacancies – outstanding at any time was around 27,000. Evidently in the course of one year a far higher number of vacancies is notified. Most are filled quickly.)

London. Some 12,000 of these workers were employed in electronic consumer goods and electronic data processing. In the software industry there were a further 15,000 employees. London's electronics industry has a higher proportion of white-collar workers than the country as a whole. This reflects, among other factors, the rapid shift of employment from less-skilled production to white-collar work that has taken place throughout the London economy in the past few years.

The skill profile of the electronics workforce is more polarised than the rest of the engineering industry. There is a low proportion of craft workers and a high proportion of scientists, technologists, managers and administrators relative to semi-skilled production workers.

The general decline of manufacturing employment means that many manufacturing workers are forced to seek work in other parts of the south-east region. Alternatively, they may seek service sector employment. But what opportunities can services offer skilled manufacturing labour?

Many of London's large industrial estates are being transformed into warehousing and large retail outlets. These developments offer few skilled employment opportunities. In warehousing little skilled labour is involved. Most of the labour is either administrative, semi-skilled or unskilled. Similarly, Heathrow airport has been one of the largest developments in the London economy. However, it offers little scope for increases in employment in skilled engineering occupations. According to the West London report (GLC, 1986), employment at Heathrow fell between 1979 and 1983 by some 13,500. The increase of roughly 9,000 jobs, which resulted from the opening of Terminal 4, was insufficient to compensate for the previous job losses.

Office employment is another major area of expansion. But it offers few opportunities to skilled operatives and unskilled or low-skilled workers.

According to the London Strategic Policy Unit's report, *A city divided* (1986), there were 161,000 long-term unemployed (over one year) in Greater London and 94,000 of these had been out of work for over two years. Of the under-25s, 35,000 had been out of work for a year or more in the Greater London region. In April 1986, 31 per cent of London's unemployed female labour force had been out of work for over one year. Sixteen per cent had been out of work for more than two years. The proportion of women registered as unemployed has increased sharply in Greater London and represents roughly 30 per cent of the total, with a far higher rate amongst Afro-Caribbean and Asian women. However, the absolute growth in the number of women employed in London (+ 140,000 from September 1984 to March 1989) is almost entirely due to women's full-time employment in the service sector (part-timers rose by only 7,000). By mid-1989 unemployment rates in Greater London had fallen to 6 per cent from males and 3.5 per cent for females.

The distribution of non-White workers across manufacturing industry is fairly wide but there is a concentration both geographically and in manual unskilled and semi-skilled jobs. These ethnic minorities, which have the highest rate of unemployment, form a much higher proportion of the population in the boroughs of Ealing and Brent than elsewhere. Overall, London's proportion of ethnic unemployed to total ethnic employment is approximately one in eight. In Brent and Ealing ratios had reached one in three in 1982.

The ability of London's labour market to absorb displaced manufacturing workers would seem to depend largely on the skill of the individual. There is little difficulty for highly qualified, graduate and mobile workers such as electronic, software and aerospace engineers to find alternative employment. Although they may be forced to leave Greater London they may prefer to do so. Also, carpenters, plumbers and electricians should have few problems finding alternative employment. It is the semi-skilled and unskilled workers who face difficulties, particularly if they are women and/or Black.

III. The demand for defence employment

In the long run, the level of defence employment depends on defence procurement. Until the mid-1980s total defence spending had been increasing in real terms but the United Kingdom's commitment to NATO for a real increase in expenditure of 3 per cent per year ended in 1986. Subsequently, defence expenditure fell both as a share of GDP and when deflated by the consumer price index (by 4.5 per cent in real terms in the following two years). Within the overall defence budget, expenditure on defence equipment is expected to decline as a share of the total, but without major procurement cut-backs. The slow-down in procurement growth is unlikely to be evenly spread across the defence industry. Before the defence review of mid-1990 avionic systems were expected to grow by 30 per cent, sea weapons by 14 per cent and air electronic equipment by 14 per cent. But other segments will certainly suffer from reduced spending, for instance land-guided weapons, land communications and air-guided weapons. In the long term the growth areas are expected to be command, control, communication and intelligence systems (C3I), surveillance, guided weapons and semi-intelligent munition systems.

Furthermore, the Ministry of Defence (MoD) is aware that the cost of successive generations of weapon systems rises faster than the rate of inflation as defence equipment becomes more technically sophisticated. As a consequence less equipment is procured, leading to shorter production runs. These in turn remove the advantages of large-scale production and place upward pressure on costs. This has encouraged longer gaps between the replacement of each generation of equipment, causing the average age of in-service equipment to rise.

To overcome the constraints on the procurement budget the Government has introduced a number of measures to increase competitiveness in defence contracting. In the past the defence industry was generally one of low risk and high reward. Cost-plus contracts created an easy consumer-producer relationship for well-established contractors and it was difficult for new entrants to break into the defence market. Rigid product specifications allowed for constant product revisions and rising development costs. MoD funding included R & D costs, working capital and progress payments. Most contracts involved little risk. Sales, margins and profits were effectively assured. However, all this has changed and the industry may well become increasingly characterised by high risks but high rewards. The stronger and more experienced defence companies may force the weaker ones out of the defence market.

The major United Kingdom defence contractors naturally have different experience and characteristics. Thus, among those also operating in Greater London, GEC has been criticised for a lack of a long-term strategy and for a failure to invest in key high-technology areas in telecommunications and information-technology systems. This may have resulted in the closure of some plants and the loss of a number of jobs. In 1979 GEC's total workforce was 206,000 but by 1986 it had been reduced to 165,000. In the defence field GEC has had to face tougher competition. In response, the company attempted to increase its stake in defence production, partly through a number of takeover bids for major defence contractors in the United Kingdom and in the United States. Although two initial takeover bids were unsuccessful (for Decca in 1980 and for British Aerospace in 1984) GEC made a successful bid for the Yarrow Warship Yard in April 1985. Its most significant bid was for its major defence electronics rival, Plessey, in December 1985. Although this was first rejected by the Monopolies and Mergers Commission, in early 1990 GEC and Siemens jointly took over Plessey while GEC alone took over Ferranti's defence division.

Dowty, another London enterprise, in response to the depression in the engineering sector, has been attempting to restructure. This has involved a move away from its more traditional markets, such as mining and industrial engineering, towards electronics and aerospace. Investments were made in advanced manufacturing technology to facilitate expansion in the civil aircraft market. The company also has plans to develop information-technology operations. An expansion into defence markets was adopted as a strategy to maintain both capacity and profitability.

Defence constitutes some 40 per cent of the company's sales. Dowty has contracts with military establishments in over 80 countries and acts as a subcontractor to over 80 prime contractors from 17 countries. The company produces a wide range of subsystems for military aircraft, tanks and naval vessels, such as engine control systems, torpedo launching equipment, hydraulic systems and aircraft landing gear. It also has considerable capacity in underwater warfare, notably in the production of signal processing and communications equipment.

The high cost of product development for defence equipment has led Dowty to enter into collaborative projects with other companies, including one of its rivals, Smiths Industries. The two companies are at present working on the development and production of the digital engine control for the Rolls-Royce Pegasus engine. Dowty is also collaborating internationally with Messer-Hispano-Bugatti on the development of landing gear for the Airbus A320.

British Aerospace is extremely dependent on major military projects such as the Tornado and the Jaguar aircraft, and is therefore susceptible to fluctuations in demand. Troughs are normally associated with the displacement of labour, mainly in production and assembly, as took place at Weybridge while the Tornado project ran down. Despite its all-round capability, the British aerospace industry has difficulty in competing with other aerospace nations, particularly the United States, which dominates the world market. This has led BAe into an increasing number of collaborative programmes both with European and with United States partners. Restructuring may lead British Aerospace to become largely an R & D company with few production facilities.

Plessey is highly dependent on the MoD and very vulnerable to changes in procurement practices. The contraction in the defence market has adversely affected the largely defence-oriented Electronic Systems Division of Plessey. To compensate for the shortfall in domestic orders Plessey has been attempting to increase its overseas sales through an extensive marketing drive of its system 4,000 combat net radio. In recent years, Plessey has made two acquisitions to enhance its defence capability – the Italian company Electronica and Ameeco Hydrospace. Both have a substantial interest in electronic warfare and sonars, fields with above-average growth prospects. Both the company's acquisition policy and its internal development policy indicate its reluctance to diversify out of defence. Rather it has opted to entrench itself further into defence production by attempting to move into product areas which it has identified as growth markets.

The Royal Ordnance Factories (ROFs) had been under government control for 400 years, until their sale to British Aerospace in April 1987. The creation of Royal Ordnance plc brought into the private sector a large engineering and chemicals group specialising in ordnance manufacture with world-wide military sales. The future for the ROFs is bleak because of trends in the MoD's procurement policies and in the international market for small arms and ammunition. In particular, MoD cut-backs have affected the ammunition, mines and explosives section of the ROFs' operations. In early 1986 the Royal Ordnance plc announced redundancies at its ammunition plants at Chorley and Birtley. Some weeks later, 500 workers were given their notice at the ammunitions plant at Radway Green. More redundancy announcements are likely.

The companies mentioned are among the top defence contractors in the United Kingdom and yet all of them are being forced to restructure and streamline their operations, partly as a result of changes in the MoD's procurement policies. In theory, an obvious solution for many of these companies would be to transfer the resources released from defence production into the manufacture of civil goods. Conversion of defence production is no more than a form of economic restructuring, as new processes are developed and diffused. This may necessitate the retooling of factories, new investments, retraining workers and even closing old production plants and opening new ones. When an economy is expanding, firms have less difficulty in adjusting, but with slow growth, industrial contraction and high unemployment, adjustment measures are more difficult.

Trade unionists have argued that since the Government is the main customer of the defence industry and has created a system whereby companies have become accustomed to having a guaranteed market for a large proportion of their output, the Government should assist those facilities affected by cut-backs in procurement. However, the present environment is one of uncertainty and risk for many high-technology firms in the United Kingdom. Defence contractors have been reluctant to branch out into civil commercial markets and have tended to retrench themselves further into the defence market as a strategy for survival. This response is reinforcing the trend towards concentration within the defence industry, and an internationalisation of the United Kingdom's defence companies through acquisition or merger with foreign firms or the setting up of joint ventures abroad.

IV. Defence dependency in Greater London

The Greater London Council (GLC) estimated that about 95,000 jobs were supported by defence spending within the Greater London region in 1984. There were 16 Ministry of Defence offices inside the GLC boundaries, which employed 20,000 industrial and non-industrial civil servants, 20 barracks with 14,500 armed forces personnel. A wide variety of military products is manufactured in Greater London, from missiles to medals, sandbags to Sea-Harriers, sentry boxes to sub-machine-guns, busbies to bullet-proof cars.

Greater London hosts a significant proportion of the South-East's defence industry. About 70 companies, both prime contractors and subcontractors, were identified as MoD suppliers by the Greater London Council (1985). They are scattered throughout London with the larger weapon systems suppliers located in the industrial estates in Outer London, e.g. Ealing, Enfield and Brent. In 1986 roughly 32,000 workers were employed in defence production, some 6 per cent of manufacturing employment. Two-thirds of defence manufacturing jobs, some 22,000 workers, are located in nine major companies: GEC-Marconi, British Aerospace, Plessey, Thorn-EMI, Muirhead Vatric, Racal, the Royal Small Arms Factory, Lucas Aerospace and Dowty. These are among the largest manufacturing employers left in London. In addition, the GLC estimated that hundreds of small- to medium-sized companies, employing some 43,000 employees, were sustained partly by defence production in the area or by the defence workers' spending.

In Greater London the major defence companies are invariably the main employers in their localities, including Plessey's military communications factory in Ilford, British Aerospace in Kingston, the Royal Small Arms Factory in Enfield and GEC in Wembley. In her study of the locational impact of defence procurement in the United States, Markusen (1985) noted how defence companies have shaped the labour market for certain occupational groups and skills. In Greater London defence plants have created a relatively advantaged core of workers who tend to form a prosperous élite group, in contrast to other workers in their local labour markets.

Employment trends in the defence industry reflect the increasing technical intensity of defence production. The major characteristic of the defence labour market is scarce skilled labour, which is flexible and enjoys generous salary levels. The current restructuring of the defence sector amounts to an "upskilling" of the defence labour force exaggerating its male bias. The noticeable lack of women in defence employment in Greater London reflects the highly qualified nature of the workforce, most of whom are engineers, concentrated in the aerospace and electrical engineering sectors. The women employed in these industries tend to be concentrated in semi-skilled assembly work.

Skill scarcity and social mobility enable defence employees to be geographically selective, which has affected the locational preference of many defence companies (Lovering, 1986). In the past ten years there has been a trend to relocate defence production out of London to more attractive sites. Alternatively, companies are positioned on the outskirts of London thus enabling employees to commute from the more pleasant areas.

Defence industrial workers have a long tradition of white-collar union membership, e.g. in the Technical Administrative and Supervisory Section (TASS), the Amalgamated Union of Engineering and Foundry Workers (AUEW) and the Association of Scientific, Technical and Managerial Staffs (ASTMS). Unionism in the industry is by tradition relatively strong and it has not been politically challenged as in other highly unionised industrial sectors such as steel, mining or printing. However, the relative stability and security of the defence industry's workforce may be coming to an end with the changes in the MoD's procurement policy.

Table 3.4 provides a brief outline of the major defence companies' location, employment and manufacturing activities. The companies in table 3.4 are all prime defence contractors mostly with annual sales to the MoD exceeding £100 million. GEC is the largest employer; its three main sites for defence-related work, Stanmore, Wembley and Borehamwood, employed roughly 5,000 defence workers in 1986. British Aerospace was the second largest employer at its Kingston plant in Surrey, with about 4,200 defence workers. In 1987 some 20,000 of London's defence workforce were employed in electronics. Few of these workers were engaged in research and development, which is usually carried on outside Greater London.

A significant number of smaller companies operate as defence subcontractors in Greater London, supplying a wide range of components and subsystems. On the whole, subcontractors do not employ more than a hundred employees and many have as few as 20 workers. Some of the subcontractors operating in Greater London are listed in table 3.5.

Subcontractors have become increasingly vulnerable to the cut-backs in defence procurement. They have no direct relationship with the MoD, while the prime contractors are undertaking an increasing proportion of work on subsystems and components, thus squeezing out many subcontractors. Unfortunately, the scale of job loss at the subcontracting level has not been recorded and without detailed study it cannot be estimated.

Table 3.4. *Major defence contractors in Greater London*

Company and divisions	Location	Workforce	Products
British Aerospace	Kingston	4 200	Harrier jump jets
Royal Small Arms Factory	Enfield	1 165	Small arms and sub-machine-guns
	Waltham Abbey	320	Explosives R & D
GEC			
Marconi Underwater Systems	Wembley	850	Underwater defence systems
Hirst Laboratories	Wembley	1 021	Military R & D
GEC Avionics [1]	Stanmore Borehamwood	} 3 500	Avionic systems, headup displays, radar
Marconi Defence Saxtems Ltd.	Stanmore	1 500	Development work on electronic warfare and missile guidance systems
GEC computers	Borehamwood	540	Military computer systems
Plessey			
Military Comms. Div.			Tactical military radios
Plessey Marine	Ilford	} 2 000	Torpedo casings
Plessey Wound Products			Military radio components
Thorn-EMI			
Defence systems	Hayes		Weapon fuses, telemetry
	Feltham	} 4 400	Thermal imaging
Radar	Hayes		Ground and airborne radar
Racal			
Racal Avionics			
Racal Marine	New Malden	1 300	Avionics, radar
Racal Defence Systems			
Racal Simulation			Simulators
Racal Safety	Wembley	450	Military communications
Racal Acoustics			
Racal Automation	Ruislip	n.a.	Automatic test equipment
STC			
Defence Systems	Greenwich	1 171	Military radio components Missile components
Dowty			
Control Systems	Acton	323	Engine controls
Marine Division	Greenford	n.a.	Underwater defence systems
Gresham Lion	Feltham	900	Defence components

n.a. = not available.

[1] The GEC Avionics plant at Borehamwood is not strictly inside the Greater London region; it has been included because of its close proximity to the Greater London border and the fact that many of the workforce actually live in London. The same applies to GEC computers.

Source. GLC Defence Company reports, 1985-86.

Table 3.5. Subcontractors tendering for MoD orders in Greater London

ABMTM, London W1	Consultancy/management services on marine projects
Aircraft Materials, London NW1	Parachute equipment/cargo pallets
P. W. Allen, London N1	Visual inspection equipment for ships, aircraft and fighting vehicles
Avimo, London W1	Military optical/electro-optical systems
Bonaventura International, London SW1	Mine detectors/night observation devices
G. E. Bradley, London NW10	Defence electronic and navigation equipment
J. I. Case, Feltham	Land vehicles
CAP Scientific Ltd., Lambs Conduit Street, WC1	Operational signal tracking, navigational tracking and C3I systems
Chernikeff Instruments Ltd., Station Road, Chiswick	Electromagnetic speedlog systems
Evershead and Vignoles Ltd., Electro Dynamics Division, Acton Lane, Chiswick	Sensors and display for wind, compass and other data
Fairey Hydraulics, Hounslow	Flight control actuators
Graseby Instruments, Surbiton	Sonar systems
Kelvin Hughes, Ilford	Navigation equipment
Muirhead Vatric, Morden	Optical shaft encoders and systems for guided missiles
Redfon, London SW18	Radio communications and navigation equipment
Rockwell Collins, Hounslow	Ground airborne and marine radio communications
Saunders Roe, Hayes	Optical devices
Smiths Industries, London NW2	Aviation and naval flight deck displays
Sicon Ltd., Berners St., W1	Military software systems for the BATES and PHOENIX projects
Sterling Armaments, Dagenham	Small arms/sub-machine-guns
United Scientific Instruments, London W1	Weapon sights/periscopes/mine detection equipment
Magnesium Electron, Twickenham	Electron alloys
Laser Engineering, London WC2	Tank suspension systems/transit containers guided missiles

Source. Greater London Conversion Council data, 1987.

V. Case studies

For this section, the employment trends and structure of six establishments of the five larger defence contractors in Greater London were reviewed. The companies, selected to reflect the diversity of the defence sector, were: (1) GEC Hirst Laboratories, a major R & D establishment, located in north-west London; (2) Dowty Controls, in the West London Park Royal industrial estate; (3) the two Royal Ordnance sites in the north of London, Waltham Abbey, an explosives research centre and the Royal Small Arms Factory at Enfield (the latter was subsequently closed); (4) the British Aerospace plant at Kingston in the south-west of the city, which produces the AV-8B Sea-Harrier; and (5) the Plessey military communications plant at Ilford in north-east London.

The amount of detail concerning the workforce and skills at each site reflects the degree of co-operation of management and trade union officials. Reluctance to provide information is largely the result of the Official Secrets Act, which all employees at a defence plant are obliged to sign, whether working on defence products or not.

1. GEC Hirst Laboratories

GEC Hirst Laboratories is the company's main research laboratory studying silicon and compound semiconductor technologies, material science, systems research, infra-red devices, opto-electronics, optical fibres and display technology. In the past few years the centre has been extensively involved in major collaborative research programmes. The MoD is a major source of funds and much of the centre's work is defence-related.

The centre's employment increased from 679 in 1981 to 1,021 in 1986 and in 1987 it employed about 600 graduate research staff (see table 3.6). However, there have been considerable problems in recruiting skilled staff, reflecting growing skill shortage at the top end of the labour market. The major skill shortages are in silicon, communications and radar technologies. In 1986 GEC had vacancies for five electrical engineers, 25 electronics engineers, 25 physicists, 20 material scientists and chemists and 16 mathematicians and software scientists (91 in all). Linked to the skill shortage is a rapid staff turnover. On average, there is a 10 per cent annual turnover, as employees seek better opportunities in smaller, more dynamic companies, in particular, software houses.

Amongst the professional staff, only 10 per cent were women, some 50 physicists.[1] The maintenance staff were all male except the cleaners, and there were 12 women employed in catering. On the administrative and clerical side, all the secretarial staff are women with a few female accountants. Most technicians are Asian; 10 per cent of the professional staff are non-White. The few Afro-Caribbeans tend to be unskilled, mainly female cleaners. The majority of the professional staff do not live locally while the lower technical grades, the secretarial and maintenance staff all tend to live in Wembley.

The buildings are old but there has been extensive modernisation with a £5 million investment in clean rooms for chip production. There has been speculation that GEC may move their laboratories to a more pleasant location outside the Greater London region to overcome their increasing difficulties in recruiting graduates. In 1987 the company was building a new research centre in Cambridge.

2. Dowty Controls Division

Dowty's business is still based on its original activities, aircraft components and subsystems. Dowty bought its site in Acton from Ultra Radio

---

[1] The proportion of women in the total of professional and technical workers nation-wide was 40 per cent in 1981.

Table 3.6. Occupational structure of GEC Hirst Laboratories, 1987

Category and qualification	Job description	Numbers employed	% distribution
Professional and technical staff	Product engineers	200	19.6
	Physicists	300	29.4
Graduates and post-graduates	Computer scientists	77	7.5
Subtotal		577	56.5
Technical staff	Electrical and electronic engineers		
Higher national diploma	Laboratory operators		
Higher national certificate B. Tech	Draughtsmen/women		
Subtotal		140	13.7
Administrative staff	Managers		
	Accountants		
	Personnel department		
	Library		
	Purchasing department		
Subtotal		34	3.3
Secretarial and clerical	Secretaries		
	Typists		
	Library assistants		
	Office machine operators		
Subtotal		126	12.4
Workshop and maintenance	Machine toolists		
Skilled, semi-skilled craftsmen	Supervisors		
	Lathe operators		
	Building maintenance		
Subtotal		84	8.2
Apprentices and trainees		60	5.9
Total		1 021	100.0

Source. GEC, Hirst Research Centre (1987).

and Television in 1970, in order to expand into engine controls, in which Ultra had a small operation. In 1970 the site was a relatively large television assembly plant employing roughly 600 workers. Dowty relocated the production of televisions to Portsmouth and finally sold off the TV business. The workforce was reduced to 400-500, and output specialised in electronic components and subsystems for aircraft, tanks and missiles. In 1980 the site was refurbished to provide the dust monitoring and strict temperature control needed for the production of highly sensitive electronic equipment. By 1987 Dowty Controls was a highly sophisticated plant utilising all the latest CAD and computer information and stock control systems, and employing 323 people.

The plant is highly specialised in the development, design and manufacture of engine control, launch control, health monitoring, general purpose displays and test equipment for use in the air, on the ground, on the

Table 3.7. *Occupational structure of Dowty Engine Controls, 1987*

Department	Activities	Numbers employed	Skills
Product support department	Service and repair	29	Semi-skilled assembly workers Test engineers Electrical engineers
Engineering department	Engineering design, development and production	41	Hardware engineers Software engineers Research engineers Electronics engineers Development engineers Design engineers Component engineers
Production department	Assembly, test, control and inspection	71	Semi-skilled assembly workers
Drawing office	Product design	17	Design engineers Draughtsmen
Factory services	Building maintenance	7	Painters, repairers
Financial control	Firm's accounts	13	Accountants
Inspection	Product inspection	7	
Marketing	Marketing management	7	
Personnel	Public relations	7	
Project management	Management	7	
Purchasing	Buying materials	9	Administrators, clerks
Quality	Quality control	9	
Test methods	Developing accurate methods of testing equipment	11	Engineers, test technicians
Training department	Apprenticeship scheme Student placements	23	Day release B tech. apprentices, student engineers
Management	Plant management	17	
Administration	Office support	48	Clerks, typists, secretaries, etc.
Total		323	

Source. Dowty plc.

sea and underwater. A significant amount of R & D is conducted on-site. Dowty produces the engine control systems used in the Tornado, Harrier and Boeing 747 aircraft. It supplies the engine control system for the tanks manufactured by SAAB. For over 25 years Dowty has been providing components to Rolls-Royce for the Spey engine. While this is coming to the end of its life, Dowty will continue to service the related engine control systems. The torpedo launch controller for both the Upholder and Trident classes is produced on-site as is communications equipment for avionic systems.

The breakdown of the workforce is given in table 3.7. The average age of the workforce has been rising, although the company does occasionally recruit younger people. To reduce the workforce gradually, the company has used natural wastage – not replacing people when they leave. As a result there have been few redundancies, but the workforce declined from 450 in 1982 to 323 in 1986.

There is a very low level of unionisation on-site. The company formally recognises TASS and AUEW, however they both have only around 20 members. In 1987 there was only one shop steward in the plant, from TASS. At that time, there was a demand for a greater AUEW presence but no leadership. The previous two AUEW shop stewards had left Dowty's and not been replaced. The company's policy of non-discrimination is confirmed both by the numbers of non-Whites employed, roughly one-third of the workforce, and the relatively high number of non-White skilled engineers, technicians, accountants and administrators. The major groups represented include Asians, Chinese and Afro-Caribbean. Although there have been one or two female engineers in the past, there were no highly qualified female workers in 1987. Of the 57 women at the plant, only one had a supervisory position, the rest were clerks, typists, secretaries and semi-skilled production workers.

Until shortly before 1987 Dowty ran an apprentice scheme. The apprentices went on day release to local colleges and were absorbed into the workforce on completion of their training. In 1987 the company had one Youth Training Scheme (YTS) trainee in the Financial Control Department who was to be hired on a full-time basis. The YTS programme, however, is no substitute for the company's apprenticeship scheme in providing technical training.

The skills required at Dowty's are fairly specialised and there have been some problems in recruiting skilled engineers, particularly in the electronics field of servicing and fault finding.

While the plant had a full order book in 1987 several of the major contracts for which the plant provides subsystems, such as Tornado and the Harrier, were already past peak production. Servicing of the subsystems will continue but this cannot guarantee employment for all employees. The company's hopes for the future are linked to the European Fighter Aircraft and the EH101 helicopter built by Augusta and Westlands.

3. Royal Ordnance plc

Greater London has been host to two Royal Ordnance factory sites, Waltham Abbey and the Royal Small Arms Factory at Enfield. The two factories back on to each other and are located on a 400-acre site on the northern outskirts of Greater London. Waltham Abbey is the oldest Royal Ordnance factory in existence, established in 1560. The plant has been systematically run down and was expected to be closed in January 1989. The takeover of the Royal Ordnance factories in April 1987 by British Aerospace increased the vulnerability of the Enfield site to its subsequent closure.

Waltham Abbey

Waltham Abbey was the Royal Ordnance Research and Development centre for rocket propellents, gun propellents and explosives. Substances such as TNT, gun cotton and RDX were fabricated on site. The MoD had invested £4 million in the development of computer-aided equipment to improve the efficiency of explosive manufacture. However, the equipment is to be transferred to the Bishopton explosives plant in Scotland when that plant is ready. The equipment will allow 50 workers to produce what 160 workers manufactured in 1987.

The site's activities were progressively scaled down in the 1970s. The plan to close the site in 1989 involved the gradual transfer of activities to the newly privatised company's other major explosives R & D plant in Westcott, Hampshire. The Waltham Abbey site also had a considerable land value and could be profitably sold off.

In 1987 there were 320 employees on site, 160 industrial workers and the rest scientists, technicians and administrative staff. In 1963 the site had employed 1,800 people, one-half women. The reduction came about mainly through natural wastage and many who retired were women who had been taken on during the Second World War. Later recruits tended to be men. In 1987 only 30 of the industrial workers were women and of the rest there were only 20 female workers, mostly secretaries.

The industrial workers consisted of:
(i)   machinists making production equipment;
(ii)   maintenance staff, including carpenters, plumbers and bricklayers who also built structures for test explosions;
(iii) machine fitters to fit and service equipment and steam pipes; the latter maintained the high temperatures required to keep explosives stable;
(iv)   process workers, who produced the explosives. These workers were semi-skilled, with three months' training mostly concerned with the health and safety procedures necessary for handling dangerous and volatile substances.

The non-industrial staff included scientists, about 60 in the research laboratories, three nurses and one doctor, firefighters, administrative and secretarial staff, management and Ministry of Defence police. The major union on site is the Transport and General Workers' Union (TGWU), which has about 100 members.

Enfield Royal Small Arms Factory

This factory is part of the Royal Ordnance Small Arms Division, which also includes an ammunitions plant at Radway Green in Cheshire and a factory in Powfoot near Dumfries, which is the sole source of base propellent in the United Kingdom.

In 1987 the main products manufactured at the Enfield plant included:
–   Aden cannon: A 30-mm aircraft-mounted cannon designed shortly after the Second World War. The Mark 5 version is still in limited production.
–   Arwen 37: An anti-riot weapon originally developed for the British Army, but also sold abroad.
–   Hughes 7.62-mm chain gun: Produced under licence for fighting vehicles.

- Rarden cannon: The main armament for the Scimitar, Fox and MCV-80 vehicles.
- Rifles and machine-guns: Including the SA80 rifle, the Light Support Weapon (LSW), and the General Purpose Machine Gun (GPMG).

The central programme was the SA80 rifle. The first contract for this was awarded to Royal Ordnance without competitive tenders. One hundred and seventy-five thousand rifles were ordered which started coming off the line in July 1985. The production rate was unexpectedly slow as the equipment purchased had a fixed-timing mechanism making it almost impossible to increase the rate of production. The net effect was to quadruple the original price estimate. Management responded by cutting back staff to reduce costs. In 1987 over 70 staff were about to go, including trainees. But these measures could not solve the central problem of productivity.

The MoD opened up the second contract to competition with three other companies bidding.

In 1986 there were 1,165 people employed at the site – 835 industrial production workers and 330 white-collar workers (see table 3.8). The latter comprise clerical, administrative, management and R & D staff. The engineers operate as skilled piece-workers. Most of the skilled workforce has a four-year engineering training to Tech 3 standard.

Of the 535-strong semi-skilled workforce, 10 per cent are women and 3 per cent are non-White. Until shortly before 1987 the semi-skilled workers received one week's training in the local government training centre, but training later took place on the job.

Enfield had a good record for training apprentices. In 1986 all 26 apprentices who were taken on were offered employment at the site. The plant had its own training centre and apprentices were sent out on day release to a local college once a week. However, in 1987 a Manpower Services Commission scheme had been introduced in place of company training.

The workforce is predominantly White and male. There was one skilled female worker, a viewer, and three non-White skilled piece-workers. Roughly 3 per cent of the semi-skilled workers were non-White, mainly Afro-Caribbean. These figures suggest that the ROF recruitment policy had discouraged women and Black people from applying for jobs at the plant.

The factory was the main production plant in the Enfield region and, therefore, the major source of local employment. Some local families could trace back three or four generations who had worked at the plant.

4. British Aerospace, Kingston

The Kingston plant is the largest defence plant in Greater London. It is part of the company's Military Aircraft Division, producing the Sea-Harrier, jointly with McDonnell Douglas. The Hawk transonic jet ground attack/trainer is also assembled at Kingston. There are about 4,200 workers employed at the Kingston plant and this has been increasing in the 1980s. In 1986 roughly 400 workers, including 150 design staff, were transferred to Kingston from the

Table 3.8. **Occupational structure of Enfield Royal Small Arms Factory, 1987**

	Numbers	Percentages
Production workers of which:	835	71.7
Multi-skilled craftsmen	300	25.8
setters	130	25.8
toolmakers	60	5.2
inspectors	40	3.4
engineers (Tech 3 standard)	70	6.0
White-collar workers	330	28.3
Total	1 165	100.0

Source. Data communicated by Royal Ordnance plc.

Table 3.9. **Occupational structure, British Aerospace, Kingston, 1987 (partly estimated)**

	Numbers	Percentage distribution
Production staff of which:	2 000	48
Machinists	200	5
Toolmakers	40-50	1
Fitters	400	10
Skilled workers in smaller workshops	c. 60	2
Other production workers	c. 1 300	30
Design staff	c. 1 000	24
Managerial and clerical staff	1 200	28
Total	4 200	100

Source. Data communicated by British Aerospace.

Weybridge BAe site which was due to close. A further 70 workers (mostly skilled metalworkers) were recruited from the now closed Hangers' artificial limb factory. In April 1987, 100 new fitters were hired.

Of the 4,200 full-time staff at Kingston, 2,000 are manual workers and roughly 1,000 design staff (see table 3.9). The skilled manual workers include metalworkers, engineers, toolworkers, machinists, copper workers and lathe operators.

Making the Sea-Harrier, the main item produced at Kingston, is extremely craft-intensive. The production process is broken down into a number of different stages utilising different skills and working methods. This is reflected in the layout and organisation of the plant. The most labour-intensive part is the machine shop, which operates day and night, servicing the machines for the rest of the plant. This involves milling, turning and grinding, and each stage is divided according to individual tasks and skills. The machine shop is surprisingly low-tech, although the company has just begun to introduce CNCs and CAD.

Union officials at the plant expect job losses following the introduction of new equipment. They are attempting to negotiate a guarantee for staff retraining and redeployment rather than displacement. Some 40-50 workers are engaged in toolmaking. These are among the most highly trained of the manual workers. Most skilled manual workers are fitters (about 400) who work on aircraft assembly riveting.

The site also includes a number of smaller workshops, each employing between five and ten workers. These are:

– the electrical pen, which employs electricians producing some of the basic electrical equipment incorporated into the aircraft;

– the paint workshop, which sprays aircraft parts with anti-corrosion paint;

– the metal-pressing workshop, where pieces of metal are pressed into the desired shapes and sizes. The workshop employs largely foundrymen and metal cutters;

– the aluminium workshop moulds and cuts the aircrafts' aluminium frame, ready for assembly;

– the plastics workshop moulds and forms all plastic parts required for the airframe;

– the R & D test rig conducts a rigorous testing procedure on each aircraft before the final assembly stage. The R & D unit mostly consists of professional, highly skilled, aerospace engineers;

– the product control unit monitors the specifications for each item which is manufactured and incorporated into the aircraft.

The design staff (about 1,000 altogether) are all graduate engineers with qualifications including aerospace engineering, electronic engineering and software engineering.

Roughly 30 per cent of the workers are non-White, both Afro-Caribbean and Asian, which is a relatively high percentage for a skilled workforce. This is partly the result of an equal opportunities policy followed by the company. The company has also made an effort to recruit more women into the workforce by accepting female apprentices.

British Aerospace has a remarkable training record. The Kingston site has a large training school which takes 60 apprentices each year. Usually, apprentices are recruited at age 16 and given a four-year training, both in the class-room and on the shop-floor. In-house training is supplemented with day release to a local technical college.

Unionisation of the manual workers is strong as a closed shop is in operation. The recognised unions on site include AUEW, TASS, the Furniture, Timber and Allied Trades Union (FTAT) and the Association of Professional, Executive, Clerical and Computer Staff (APEX). Roughly 50 per cent of the professional staff are union members, a high percentage.

Although full order books seem to indicate a secure future for Kingston, the shop stewards' committee is concerned about long-term prospects. The whole future of the Military Aircraft Division rests on securing launch aid for the European fighter aircraft and on the sales of the Hawk 200 series. Neither of these aircraft is built at Kingston, but if the company should fail to secure these major programmes, the company would inevitably be restructured. Other plants at Preston and Wharton are more modern and the Kingston site has a high land value.

5. Plessey Military Communications, Ilford

The main production plant of Plessey Military Communications (PMC) produces tactical military radios and ship-to-shore communications systems.

The major items manufactured at the site include:

- the 400 tactical military radio, produced for export markets;
- the PV 5300, a high-performance HF patrol radio;
- the PVS 5400, a rugged hand-held VHF/UHF transceiver;
- the system 4000, an integrated combat net communications system which is being developed as part of the Australian Army's Project, Raven;
- the 730 shipborne communications system, developed for the Royal Navy;
- Ptarmigan, the largest project undertaken by PMC, is an advanced battlefield communications command and control system designed under an MoD contract for the British Army. It has been in service with the British Army since 1967. So far, the contract has been valued at an estimated £800 million and is expected to reach £1 billion by 1990.

Although PMC relies to a significant extent on MoD orders, roughly 60 per cent of its output is destined for overseas markets. Because of the relatively high dependence on foreign demand, the failure to secure the United States Army's Multiple Subscriber Equipment Programme in 1986 placed the future of the plant in jeopardy.

In the early 1970s, at the height of Plessey's operations in Ilford, there were roughly 8,000 employees working in seven or eight plants. But, since the mid-1970s, the company has been systematically winding down its presence and only the Vicarage Lane site is left. The workforce in 1986 stood at a little over 1,300. As a result of the decline in export orders, 280 redundancies took place in November 1984 (*Financial Times*, 24 Nov. 1984). In July 1985 there was a further reduction of 380 workers and in June 1987 another 60 workers were served notice.

Of the total workforce, about 600 workers are semi-skilled or unskilled, engaged in manual activities (see table 3.10). This category includes assembly workers, wiremen, packers, porters and janitors. Only one-eighth of the workforce is qualified professionals (test engineers, electrical engineers, chemical engineers, etc.), a comparatively low share for a defence plant. There are roughly 250 technicians, including 150 laboratory workers.

*Table 3.10. Occupational structure: Plessey Military Communications, Ilford, 1987
(partly estimated)*

Category	Percentages
Manual workers, semi-skilled and unskilled	46
Technicians	19
Graduate engineers and other professionals	13
Managerial, clerical and other staff	22
Total	100

In the past, Plessey had a good record for in-house training, training apprentices as electrical engineers and providing an opportunity for skill diversification. However, the training facilities at Ilford have largely ceased to operate and the training school has been closed. Many jobs previously performed by the full-time workforce have been subcontracted to small local companies, e.g. cleaners, as well as electricians who undertake some semi-skilled activities such as wiring and machining. Rationalisation has led to the increasing use of specialist consultants, engaged for short periods on specific tasks.

Plessey has dominated the Ilford labour market for at least three generations. There is a strong community identity with the company, not only because the company is the major employer in the area, but also because many small businesses and services depend on the site for their existence.

There are six formally recognised trade unions on site, the Electrical, Electronic, Telecommunication and Plumbing Union (EETPU), ASTMS, TASS, APEX, the TGWU and the AUEW. The unions have been engaged in a struggle to keep the plant open. However, the frequent redundancies have left a greatly reduced and demoralised workforce. In July 1986, with the help of the Greater London Conversion Council, the unions produced a joint report on future prospects for the plant partly as a result of GEC's takeover bid for Plessey. The report considered that diversification of production was the only long-term solution and identified digital cellular radios as a commercially sound alternative to military radios. The company finally decided that instead of closing the plant a modern production facility would be built on a part of the site. The company claims that the new plant will provide 2,000 jobs and that civil production will constitute a large proportion of the work. The rest of the old site will be sold off to fund the new investment.

* * *

These six case studies suggest that London's defence workers cannot depend on the defence market to provide job security. Most of the defence plants face an insecure future due to inter-related factors, including defence budget restraint, restructuring of the defence industry and the relocation of production. If the defence sector continues to shed labour there will be an increasing number of ex-defence workers looking for employment in Greater London's labour market.

VI. Conclusions

Clearly it will be very difficult for workers displaced from defence plants in Greater London to find other forms of employment in manufacturing. While no doubt service sector employment may be available, as may be other semi-skilled work, there will be an inevitable waste of skills. One reaction to this dilemma is to investigate the possibilities for the conversion of defence facilities.

In the United Kingdom proposals for diversification and arms conversion have been mainly put forward by the trade union movement and the Labour Party. Undoubtedly the best known conversion initiative was the Lucas Aerospace Corporate Plan developed by the workforce through their Combined Shop Stewards Committee. The plan had many strengths, including the concept of socially useful production, using skills and scarce resources for the production of goods for social rather than for military ends. Although the plan was never implemented, it brought the debate on arms conversion firmly into the trade union arena.

The Lucas plan inspired other plant-based initiatives. The workers at Vickers in Barrow identified 54 different products which could be made using their skills and the shipyard's resources, ranging from wave and tidal-power generators to submersibles for undersea exploration. As with the Lucas plan, many of the products identified required a guarantee of public procurement. None of these plans has been implemented because strong government measures would have been required to achieve the effective co-operation of the companies involved. Yet they operate as blueprints for positive action against redundancies in the defence industry and have substantially influenced the national debate on the need for defence conversion.

Perhaps the best known initiative was that taken by the Greater London Council which saw arms conversion as a central element in revitalising the local economy and creating employment. Subsequently, a number of borough councils have examined ways to support conversion plans. Ealing, for example, has reviewed defence operations in its area as a preliminary to identifying measures which could help displaced defence workers find alternative employment.

Apart from the growing role of local government in the conversion debate, the major lobbying force has been the trade union movement. All the major trade unions with members in the defence industry now have policies on arms conversion and at the 1985 conference of the Trades Union Congress a comprehensive motion was passed that "Congress reaffirms its commitment to a programme of arms conversion which will fully protect the employment of defence workers whilst permitting their labour and skills to be used for the production of socially useful goods and services". However, the emphasis of trade union policy on defence conversion has rightly been on securing a commitment at the national level for defence conversion rather than supporting plant-level initiatives.

In 1987 a number of unions, including the Society of Civil and Public Servants (SCPS), the Institute of Professional Civil Servants (IPCS) and the

TGWU, supported a conversion initiative at a naval stores depot in Wales, where some 350 workers faced redundancy. An alternative employment committee, "Alterplan 87", was set up by the workforce to investigate other possible jobs at the site. Support was secured from local and regional bodies, including the Welsh Co-operative Development Agency and the Welsh Development Agency. Alterplan received a grant from the EEC to fund a major feasibility study on the prospects for a number of small businesses organised as co-operatives. A unique aspect of this initiative was the co-operation of the Ministry of Defence, which provided two full-time workers for Alterplan and office space on site.

There is a long way to go before defence conversion becomes an acceptable aspect of economic and industrial policy, but present trends have established and formulated a national and regional structure and a strategy which could be activated if the political will existed to promote a national conversion programme.

References

General Electric Company. 1986. *Hirst Research Centre.*

Greater London Council (GLC). 1985. *Arms conversion in the London Industrial Strategy.*

———. 1985. *The West London report.*

London Strategic Policy Unit. 1986. *A city divided: London's economy since 1979.* July.

Lovering, J. 1985. "Defence expenditure and the regions: The case of Bristol", in *Built Environment*, (London) Vol. II, No. 3.

Markusen, A. 1985. "The military remapping of the United States", in *Built Environment*, op. cit.

Chapter 4

The regional and occupational dependence on defence contracting in the Greater Munich area

BURKHARDT J. HUCK

I. The defence economy and defence industry in the Federal Republic of Germany

According to the budget data of the federal Ministry of Defence, DM51,700 million were spent on national defence in the Federal Republic of Germany in 1985 (roughly US$21,000 million). This represented approximately 6 per cent of total government expenditure. By NATO criteria, which include in defence expenditure certain spending on military security that in the Federal Republic of Germany are listed in the budgets of other ministries, this sum would increase to about DM60,000 million. Of the total defence expenditure of DM51,700 million, DM24,026 million (i.e. 46 per cent) represented procurement contracts, of which DM15,816 million worth were placed with domestic firms and DM8,210 were imports.[1] These sums include procurement contracts for arms and military equipment, contracts for servicing and maintenance, for military R & D, as well as contracts for purchases of civilian goods such as clothing (uniforms), food and office supplies.

Besides the country's own armed forces, numbering over 500,000 (1986),[2] allied forces of almost the same size are stationed in the Federal Republic of Germany. The volume of the defence economy is thus enlarged by the expenditures of the allied forces on procuring goods and services in the West German economy. Full information on the procurements of the allied forces in the Federal Republic of Germany is not available. According to data published in the United States, the sums spent by the United States armed forces amounted to US$5,452 million in the fiscal year 1985, but the great majority of this expenditure was non-military.[3]

---

[1] Bundesamt für Wehrtechnik und Beschaffung: *Auftraggeber Bundeswehr: Die Vergabepraxis der Beschaffungsbehörden*, Appendix 2 (Koblenz, 1986).

[2] OECD: *Labour Force Statistics, 1966-1986* (Paris, 1988).

[3] Deputy Chief of Staff Host Nation Agency: *Financial and employment impact of the US forces on the German economy in FY 1986* (Washington, DC, Government Printing Office).

In order to evaluate the output of the West German defence industry, arms exports would have to be added to the value of procurements by the West German and allied armed forces. However, official data on arms exports are not available, although according to the Stockholm International Peace Research Institute, the Federal Republic of Germany ranks fifth among the world's arms exporters.[4] The United States Arms Control and Disarmament Agency data series put West German arms exports at US$520 million in 1985, a considerable fall from the annual average for 1981-85 of US$1,555 million.[5] Thus, in 1985, the total sales of military equipment by the West German industry, including supplies to the allied forces and including arms exports, could be roughly estimated at DM22,000 million or US$9,000 million. This represented about 2 per cent of the total manufacturing output. All the supplies, however, did not originate in the manufacturing sector, some services were also included. Thus, the above percentage provides only a rough order of magnitude. But it shows, nevertheless, that the importance of military production for the West German economy is relatively moderate.

Procurements of military (and other) equipment for the West German armed forces are carried out by a number of different organisations, the most important of which is the Federal Agency for Military Technology and Procurement (Bundesamt für Wehrtechnik und Beschaffung). The agency is responsible for about 80 per cent of defence contracting inside the Federal Republic of Germany. The amount and distribution by industrial branches of the contracts placed by the agency with domestic firms in 1981-87 is shown in table 4.1.

Apart from the relative importance of the different manufacturing branches for defence supplies, table 4.1 also illustrates recent procurement trends in the industrial branches concerned. It shows the rapid expansion of supplies of military aerospace and of electronic goods at the expense of most other types of equipment. While in 1981 mechanical engineering was the branch with the highest amount of defence contracts, in 1987 it ranked only third, after electronics and aerospace. Procurement of military vehicles declined in both absolute and relative terms during the period reviewed.

Information on the regional distribution of defence contracts placed by the West German procurement agencies is provided in table 4.2. The data need a number of caveats: they refer to the orders placed with enterprises having their headquarters in the states mentioned, and not to the actual shipments of military goods from these states. Furthermore, they refer to the total volume of all procurements, including non-military items, and including services such as R & D. For this reason, the last column of table 4.2, which shows military procurement orders as a percentage of total manufacturing sales (domestic manufacturing and mining sales), has to be taken only as a rough indication of

---

[4] Stockholm International Peace Research Institute: *World Armaments and Disarmament: SIPRI Yearbook, 1988* (Oxford, Oxford University Press), p. 177.

[5] US Arms Control and Disarmament Agency: *World military expenditures and arms transfers* (Washington, DC, United States Government Printing Office, 1987).

Table 4.1.   *Defence contracts placed by the Federal Agency for Military Technology and Procurement, by industrial branches (DM million)*

Branch of industry	1981	1985	1986	1987
Aerospace industry	1 342	1 307	1 594	2 161
Mechanical engineering	2 087	2 822	3 214	2 144
Electrical engineering and electronics	1 538	2 156	2 506	2 628
Road vehicle manufacturing	1 122	1 275	1 072	941
Shipbuilding	674	698	651	851
Other capital goods industries	552	925	881	813
Other industries	821	1 139	1 035	1 141
Total	8 139	10 325	10 955	10 684

Note. The coverage is more restricted than in table 4.2 and decimals have been rounded up to the next significant figure.
Source. Data of the Ministry of Defence.

the importance of military contracting in each region. Nevertheless, the data in the last column of table 4.2 make it possible to identify the regions with the highest relative weight of defence contracting. These are the city of Bremen, the State of Schleswig-Holstein and the State of Bavaria: Bavaria, which is the second largest state in terms of population and labour force, gets by far the highest share of defence contracts (38 per cent, in 1987), and the volume of these contracts represents a percentage of manufacturing output which is 2.4 times higher than the national average. Thus, Bavaria is considerably dependent on defence contracting, and the district around its capital, Munich, seems especially appropriate for a study of the regional dependence of defence contracting in the Federal Republic of Germany.

Regional data (data broken down by state or district) on any defence-related matters are extremely rare in the Federal Republic of Germany. For example, there is no officially published information on defence contracts by industrial branches for individual states. One of the reasons is that the West German arms industry is largely oligopolistic, and that such information would make it possible to derive the value of defence contracts of the few aerospace companies implanted in the area, for example. There is also no information on the production capacity or on the total sales of the defence industry in various regions; and finally there is no information on regional defence industrial employment. In fact, only rough estimates exist on defence industry employment even at the national level. Nation-wide, employment in the defence industry (direct and indirect) can be estimated at approximately 480,000 (1984), i.e. about 6 per cent of the manufacturing workforce. Direct defence industry employment represents about 2 per cent of the manufacturing workforce, which corresponds to the share of military supplies in manufacturing production mentioned earlier.

Table 4.2.   Regional distribution of defence contracts in the Federal Republic of Germany, 1984-87 (DM million and percentages)

State	1984	Per cent	1985	Per cent	1986	Per cent	1987	Per cent	Defence contracts as percentage of manufacturing sales, 1987
Schleswig-Holstein	876.3	5.7	1 391.0	8.8	1 501.1	8.6	1 042.1	6.6	3.7
Hamburg	418.3	2.8	586.0	3.7	391.3	2.2	394.1	2.5	0.7
Lower Saxony	561.8	3.7	663.5	4.2	639.6	3.7	653.9	4.2	0.6
Bremen	645.7	4.2	2 283.0	14.4	1 262.3	7.2	906.1	5.8	6.4
North Rhine Westphalia	3 253.7	21.3	2 402.8	15.2	2 437.5	14.2	2 220.0	14.1	0.8
Hesse	547.8	3.6	1 333.9	8.4	755.6	4.3	875.5	5.6	1.1
Rhineland Palatinate	373.6	2.3	350.9	2.2	456.0	2.6	335.3	2.1	0.6
Baden Württemberg	3 144.6	20.6	2 622.2	16.6	3 861.6	22.2	3 130.5	19.9	1.7
Bavaria	5 327.0	34.8	3 980.2	25.2	5 900.6	33.9	5 914.6	37.7	3.6
Saarland	153.7	1.0	202.3	1.3	192.1	1.1	234.8	1.5	1.3
Domestic total	15 302.5	100.0	15 815.8	100.0	17 397.7	100.0	15 706.9	100.0	1.5

Note. Because of data collection difficulties, the following contracts with domestic firms are not included:
– direct orders from NATO agencies;
– subcontracts from German and foreign contractors;
– compensation contracts from abroad.
Source: Ministry of Defence, direct communication; Statistisches Bundesamt, *Statistical Yearbook of the FRG, 1988* (Wiesbaden).

II. Dependence of the Munich area on the arms industry

The "Greater Munich area" surveyed in this chapter corresponds to one of the 18 government planning regions composing Bavaria (region 14) and includes beside the City of Munich, the counties (Landkreis) of Munich, Dachau, Freising, Erding, Ebersberg, Starnberg, Fürstenfeldbruck, and Landsberg.

Since the Second World War, the City of Munich and its surroundings have been highly sought-after sites for the location of new industries, in particular of aerospace, automobile and electronics. The region underwent a rapid transformation of its industrial structure, characterised by an increase of automobile, aerospace, electronics and precision instruments manufacturing, at the expense of the traditional branches of metalworking such as steel mills, sheet-metal and hardware manufacturing. The change in industrial structure went hand-in-hand with rapid economic growth. This growth trend is expected to continue also in the future, prompted, among others, by the establishment of the Single European Market.

The metalworking industry, to which most defence industry production belongs, has been traditionally well represented in the Munich area. At present, the metalworking industry accounts for 71 per cent of total manufacturing employment, a share which is well above the national average of 52 per cent. The area has 529 establishments belonging to the metalworking industry, of which there are eight aerospace plants, 45 road vehicle plants, and 151 electrical/electronic engineering plants. Between 1980 and 1986 the sales of the metalworking industry in the region increased by 62 per cent, i.e. by 8 per cent a year. Road vehicle manufacturing and electrical/electronic engineering achieved an even higher growth of sales, amounting to 10 and 9 per cent *a year*, respectively. The rapid growth of production in the metalworking industry has been achieved mostly with a slowly declining labour force, as industrial productivity has been rising. Only in electrical engineering/electronics and in aerospace did employment go up between 1980 and 1986, in the latter branch quite substantially (by 12 per cent), while aerospace sales, in Bavaria as a whole, are reported to have increased by 20 per cent. The overall decline of employment in the metalworking industry was part of the general shift of employment from industry to services, which, according to government forecasts, should continue at least until the year 2000.

While fairly detailed information exists on employment in different branches of industry in the Munich area, data on defence industry employment are not officially published, and even partial information on this topic is hard to find. In what follows tentative estimates are presented on defence industry employment in the area. These have been derived by adding up and by extrapolating the data on employment – defence industry and total – and on sales – military and total – available for companies known to be involved in defence production. Some companies, particularly the larger ones, provide information on the number of their workers engaged in the development and production of military goods. But many defence-contracting companies are reluctant to disclose the number of their personnel assigned to armaments production. It is generally somewhat easier, though, to obtain data on their sales of armaments and defence equipment. The information on defence sales can then be used to make rough estimates on the defence workforce in the companies for which such data are lacking.

Needless to say, this method of estimation is extremely imprecise and involves a wide margin of error. However, since at least partial data are available for a relatively large proportion of the companies, and since this seems to be the only way to determine an order of magnitude of the defence workforce in the region, it has been used to compute the figures presented in tables 4.3 to 4.6. Due to the methodological approach used, the data tend to represent lower limit values. Whatever their flaws, they indicate that the defence industry workforce represents about 8 per cent of manufacturing employment and 11 per cent of employment in the metalworking industry in the Greater Munich area. The dependence of the area on defence contracting is thus considerable.

Table 4.3 provides summary results of the estimates that have been made on defence employment in the Munich area, broken down by six industrial branches. The largest number of defence workers are to be found in the aerospace industry, where they represent as much as 58 per cent of total employment. The other industrial branches depend on defence contracting to a much lesser degree, apart, of course from ammunition production, which is entirely defence-dependent, but which is a relatively unimportant industry in the Munich region.

The dependence of *aerospace* on defence contracting is higher in the Greater Munich area than in the Federal Republic of Germany as a whole; the nation-wide share of defence employment in the aerospace total is 52 per cent, compared with 58 per cent estimated in the Munich area. In case of a significant defence cut, the aerospace industry of the Munich area would be seriously affected. A large part of its workforce would have to find alternative employment inside or outside the existing companies. Some of the aerospace companies of the region might have relatively fewer problems than others, namely those where military production represents a somewhat lower share of total sales, in particular Dornier GmbH (see table 4.4). But all the leading aerospace companies are highly defence-dependent and would face problems if defence expenditure were cut down.

The electrical engineering and electronics industry in the Greater Munich area is dominated by Siemens, which alone accounts for 57 per cent of the employment in the branch. Apart from Siemens, the industry consists of a large number of smaller firms. About one-fifth of these firms are engaged in defence production mostly on a subcontracting basis. Those which are known to have defence contracts and for which at least partial information is available, are listed in table 4.5. On the basis of the fragmentary data available, it has been estimated that of the 14,555 workers in the smaller firms with military contracts, about 2,500 work on defence assignments. If the 2,100 workers employed in the Siemens defence electronics establishment (Siemens Radio and Radar Systems

Table 4.3. *Employment and sales in armaments-producing industries in the Greater Munich area, 1986: Partly estimated*

Industry	Employment		Sales	of which: defence		Share of defence employment in total (4):(1)
	Total	Companies with defence contracts	Companies with defence contracts	Employment	Sales	
	(1) Numbers	(2) Numbers	(3) DM million	(4) Numbers	(5) DM million	(6) Percentages
Aerospace	24 000[2]	23 612	4 518	13 875	2 580	58
Electrical engineering/electronics	79 489	59 655	16 695	4 600	1 300	6
Vehicle manufacturing	50 195	17 043	4 428	2 000	1 700	4
Machine building	19 214	2 000	250	100	–	1
Ammunitions manufacturing	600	600	350	600	300	100
Precision instruments and optical engineering	11 712	1 200	700	1 000	100	8
Total	185 210	104 110	26 941	22 175	–	12
Total, metalworking industry[1]	204 185					11
Total, manufacturing industry[1]	283 424					8

[1] Calculations based on Landesarbeitsamt Südbayern, *Arbeitsmarkt Aktuell*, Nos. 12/81 and 8/88.   [2] Estimate.
Sources. Tables 4.4-4.6.

Table 4.4.   **Shares of defence sales and of defence-related employment in total sales and employment**
             of aerospace companies in the Greater Munich area, 1986

Company	Employment	Sales, DM million	of which: defence			
	Numbers		Sales, DM million	Share of total	Employment numbers	Share of total
Dornier GmbH	2 803	1 100	495	45	1 260	45.0
Dornier Reparaturwerft	1 691	260	175	67	1 120	66.2
Messerschmitt-Bölkow-Blohm (MBB), Ottobrunn	8 969	1 350	715	53	4 770	53.2
MTU, Munich	7 282	1 260	882	70	5 040	69.2
Total	20 745	3 970	2 267	57.1	12 190	58.8
All aerospace companies with defence contracts [1]	23 612	4 518 [2]	2 580 [2]	57.1	13 875 [2]	58.8

[1] The firms belonging to the aerospace industry in the Greater Munich area which are known to have defence contracts and which are not listed by name in the table, are: AOA-Apparatebau Gauting, employment 249; Astronautics, employment 45; Walter Dittel, employment 150; Hanns Häusler, employment 90: In all 534 workers. If the high technology composites-producing firm MAN Technology is also included, the aerospace-related employment of the Munich region increase by a further 1,333. Finally, the German Aerospace Research and Development Institute DFVLR (Deutsche Forschungs- und Versuchsanstalt für Luft- und Raumfahrt) employs about 1,000 workers in the Munich region. The total employment of all these establishments amounts to 2,867. The share of their workforce engaged in defence-related activities is not known. However, their total employment represents only 14 per cent of the employment of the four market leaders listed above. It thus seems legitimate to estimate their defence employment share on a pro-rata basis, since the average for the branch would not be fundamentally changed, even if their defence employment shares were different.   [2] Estimate.

Sources. Company information.

Division) are added to this number, the total of defence workers in the electrical/electronics industry in the area can be estimated at 4,600. This number represents less than 6 per cent of the total workforce in the electrical/electronics industry in the area. It appears, therefore, that the electrical/electronics industry in the Greater Munich area depends on defence contracting to a rather limited extent. The firms working exclusively or largely for defence are few. In this industrial branch, conversion to civilian production could be expected to proceed relatively smoothly, without undue negative impacts on employment.

The road vehicle industry in the Greater Munich area had, in 1986, 50,195 workers, almost a fifth of the manufacturing industry in the region. Of this number, only about 2,000 workers were engaged in the production of military vehicles. Output of military vehicles expanded considerably between 1963 and 1985, mainly due to the successful sales of the Leopard Mark 1 and Mark 2 main battle tanks, and also of all-terrain trucks. In the past few years, however, production of military vehicles declined. Employment in the companies concerned did not go down, because the reduction in military vehicle production was compensated by an increase in output of civilian goods thanks to the boom in the motorcar industry. Table 4.6 lists the companies producing military vehicles in the Greater Munich area, and shows their employment and sales. Only Krauss-Maffei can be said to be defence-dependent. On the basis of the data assembled in the table, a rough estimate – or rather informed guess –

Table 4.5. **Employment and total sales of leading electrical engineering and electronics companies producing defence equipment, in the Greater Munich area, 1986**

Company	Employment total numbers	Total sales (DM million)	of which: defence	
			Sales (DM million)	Employ- ment numbers
Base 10	100	20	16	80
Bentron	25	4		
Comp. Deutsch	45	40	32	36
Comtronic	45	5	4	36
Digital	2 663	810		
Eurosil	300	60		
Grill	104	9		
Hörmann	370	50		
Kabeltechnik	50			
Keltronic	66	10	10	66
Kollsmann	90	10		
Kontron	500	160	80	250
Laser-Optr.	92	40		
Litton	225			180
LRE	250	50	20	100
F. Merk	1 400	163		
Motorola	310	600		
Raychem	700	250		
Rohde & Schwarz	2 000	400	80	500
Schaltbau	450	60		
Schlumberger	170	45		
Siemens GB F + R (Radio and Radar Systems Division)	2 100	600	600	2 100
Siemens UB K + D (Telecommunications & EDP)	29 000	10 300		
Spinner	700			
Steinheil	500	45	22	250
Texas Instruments	700			
Thomson	1 000			450
Zettler	1 700	164		
Total	59 655	16 695		

can be made that about 2,000 workers of the vehicle manufacturing industry work on defence assignments, including defence exports.

The *machine-building industry* in the Munich area employed 19,214 workers (7 per cent of the manufacturing total) in 1986. Four companies in this branch are known to produce military equipment, namely Bauer Kompressoren (210 workers), Carl Hurth Maschinen- und Zahnradfabrik (1,500 workers), Junkers Maschinen- und Metallbau (43 workers), and Linde AG. Their combined workforce thus represents about 2,000, of which only a small proportion work in defence production.

Table 4.6.   Employment and total sales of military land vehicle manufacturing companies and leading subcontractors in the Greater Munich area, 1986

Company	Employment numbers	Sales, DM million	of which: defence		Share of defence employment in total
			Sales, DM million	Employment numbers	
Knorr AG	3 000	670	–	–	–
Krauss-Maffei	4 663	1 802	1 337	1 400	30
MAN Nutzfahrzeuge	5 000	1 000	100	250	5
Meiler	2 000	250	–	–	–
Steinbock	750	130	13	75	10
Webasto AG	1 630	576	–	–	–
Total	17 043	4 428	1 700	2 000	

Source. Company information.

The ammunition industry located in the area is not very important, as most ammunition production takes place in other parts of the Federal Republic of Germany. Ammunition plants work, of course, almost entirely for the military. In the Greater Munich area there are two ammunition-producing companies, namely RTG – Raketentechnik GmbH, a joint subsidiary of Messerschmitt-Bölkow-Blohm (MBB) and Diehl, and a publicity-shy company called Bayerische Metallwerke, producing bullets, moulded parts for artillery shells, tungsten granulates, spark-erosion electrodes, resistance-welding, etc. Employment in the two companies can be estimated at about 600 workers.

In precision engineering, optical engineering, etc., there is a certain proportion of workers assigned to defence production, which is difficult to estimate. The figure of 1,000 shown in table 4.3 is a minimum informed guess.

Adding all the metalworking branches together, there are about 22,000 defence workers in the Greater Munich area, which represent approximately 8 per cent of the manufacturing labour force of the region. It should be pointed out that the total of 22,000 does not include certain worker categories, such as chemical workers producing explosives and propellants.

In summary, the manufacturing sector in the Greater Munich area depends on defence contracting to a considerable extent, but this dependence is largely due to the weight of the aerospace industry. Outside the aerospace industry, dependence on defence contracts is relatively limited and defence cuts would not pose major problems, at least for most of the companies.

Besides the manufacturing sector, a certain part of the *service sector* also receives defence contracts. The service sector companies working for defence specialise in such fields as research and development, logistics, system management, software, radiation and decontamination, and various engineering services. However, the total personnel of the defence-related service companies only represent a few thousand in the Munich area. The high level of qualifications and the versatility of most of this personnel would facilitate its transition to civilian services in case of a reduction in defence contracts.

III. Case studies

In this section, three leading manufacturing companies and one service company engaged in defence activities will be studied in greater detail. Each of these companies is a market leader in its field: (i) Messerschmitt-Bölkow-Blohm is the largest aerospace company in the Federal Republic of Germany; (ii) Siemens, the well-known transnational corporation, is the leading company in the field of electrical engineering and electronics; (iii) Krauss-Maffei is an important manufacturer of heavy armoured vehicles; and (iv) IABG, or Industrieanlagen-Betriebsgesellschaft, is a large R & D establishment specialising in military technology.

The plants and other facilities of the four companies in the Munich area, such as the MBB's headquarters at Ottobrunn, or IABG's facilities also in Ottobrunn, have been built mostly in the past 20 or 30 years. The Siemens Radio and Radar Systems Division plant, specialising in defence production, was built very recently on a "green fields" site, north of Munich. Only the Krauss-Maffei factories are not absolutely new, although they have been recently expanded and modernised.

All the companies examined in this section are members of the Association of the Bavarian Metalworking Industry (Verein der Bayerischen Metallindustrie). The basic collective agreement concluded between this employers' association and the Union of Metalworkers is in force in all four companies. The collective agreement specifies a working week of 37 hours, an annual vacation entitlement of 30 days, and an additional vacation allowance of 50 per cent of the average earnings for each day. The rates of hourly wages for manual workers range from DM10.36 to DM18.13, depending on the grade. The standard monthly salaries for non-manual workers range from DM1,536 to DM4,924. In addition, there is a monthly contribution of DM52 under the Government Capital Accumulation Scheme, and performance supplements are paid according to merit. Despite the high hourly earnings, unit labour costs have risen only modestly since 1970, and price competitiveness remains good.

1. MBB Messerschmitt-Bölkow-Blohm, Ottobrunn

The history of the company can be traced back to 1909. It has been marked by a long series of mergers and takeovers. As a result of these, MBB emerged, in the mid-1980s, as the leading West German aerospace group, with only one remaining serious competitor, namely Dornier. MBB, however, could still not survive without substantial assistance from the Government, e.g. government subsidies for development costs, guarantees against exchange rate fluctuations, etc. In an endeavour to make the West German aerospace industry independent from large-scale government financing and government intervention, and in order to strengthen it before the creation of the Single European Market, the Federal German Government requested the Daimler Benz company, in 1987, to undertake the reorganisation of the industry. Daimler Benz was asked to take a substantial share in MBB, and to assume the leadership of the aerospace sector. After considerable negotiations, on 6 September 1989, MBB finally became part of a new company, Deutsche Aerospace AG, one of three independent public limited companies under the umbrella of the holding company Daimler Benz. The present corporate structure of MBB is expected to undergo yet another transformation, consisting of the transfer of the Airbus production – which has been a source of considerable financial problems for MBB – to a separate company called Deutsche Flugzeug-Gesellschaft, DFG, to be located in Hamburg. The separation from MBB of the Marine and Special Products Division has also been decided. MBB will hold 80 per cent of DFG. The headquarters of Deutsche Aerospace, of which MBB is now part, are in Munich.

MBB's total sales, which in 1987 amounted to DM6,098 million, are structured as follows:

	Per cent
Military aircraft division	27.5
Helicopter division	7.9
Space systems group	8.7
Transport aircraft group	27.1
Defence systems group	23.6
Diversification	5.2
Total	100

The sales of military aircraft, missiles and defence equipment represent 53 per cent of the total. Over half of the sales are exports.

MBB has a total workforce of 38,456 (1986) of which over 50 per cent is employed in divisions and groups making military equipment. It should be noted that only about one-quarter of the workforce is employed in Ottobrunn, which is the headquarters and main production site of the company. The rest of the workforce is employed in the 15 other establishments belonging to the company throughout the Federal Republic of Germany.

The total MBB workforce consists of 34 per cent manual workers, 61 per cent non-manual workers and 5 per cent apprentices. In the Ottobrunn establishment, however, which houses the company's headquarters and its R & D facilities, only 8 per cent of the roughly 9,000 employees are manual workers.

As far as the educational profile is concerned, about 21 per cent of the total MBB workforce hold university degrees, 67 per cent have completed a vocational education or an apprenticeship, and 12 per cent have an elementary or other education.

The female share of employment is 16.5 per cent, lower than the average in the West German metalworking industry, which is 23 per cent.

It is somewhat disappointing that the data available on the structure of MBB's employment are not very detailed. All that can be concluded is that they correspond broadly to the employment pattern generally found in the defence industry, characterised by an above-average share of university graduates, a below-average share of manual workers, and a relatively low share of women.

2. Siemens

The Siemens electrical engineering and electronics group, comprising Siemens AG and domestic and foreign companies in which Siemens has a voting majority, employs world-wide about 360,000 workers. In the Federal Republic of Germany Siemens employs about 230,000 workers and is the largest private employer in the country. Siemens is also the largest employer in the Munich region, where it has 45,000 workers. In terms of total sales, the Siemens group ranks fourth among the world's electrical engineering and electronics companies, after the United States corporations IBM, General Electric and AT & T.

According to information communicated by the company, sales for military purposes represent 2 per cent of the total. It may be assumed, however, that this percentage refers only to the sales of complete military systems and of equipment for exclusively military use and that it does not include sales of multi-purpose components supplied to other defence industry companies on a subcontracting basis.

Siemens is among the corporations which are reluctant to disclose information on their workforce. The data on its total employment in the Munich area originate from the trade union IG Metall, which has been concerned about the phasing-out of jobs in the manufacturing sector and which has recently announced that since 1986 Siemens reduced its workforce in the Munich area from 52,000 to 45,000.

Siemens has a number of different production groups and divisions. The Radio and Radar Systems Division of the Telecommunications Networks and Security Systems Group works almost exclusively on military assignments. It manufactures anti-aircraft, reconnaissance and guidance systems, systems for aircraft and ships, electronic combat guidance systems, etc. It employs altogether 3,400 workers, of which 2,100 are in the Munich area. Employment in the Radio and Radar Systems Division represents about 5 per cent of total employment in Siemens' plants in the Munich area.

Siemens' central personnel department could not provide data on the structure of the company's workforce in the Munich area plants, of which there are five. The reason given was that the facilities in the Munich area belonged to different divisions and that there was a considerable amount of personnel shifts between plants. The personnel department declared, however, that the occupational structure of the workers employed in the Munich area should not differ substantially from that of Siemens' personnel in the country as a whole. Nation-wide, the ratio of manual to non-manual workers changed from 2:1 in 1962 to 0.8:1 in 1987. Between these two years, the occupational structure shifted as follows:

	1962 (%)	1987 (%)
Manual workers	67	45
– unskilled and semi-skilled	44	25
– skilled	23	20
Non-manual workers	33	55
– engineers and technicians	18	33
– managerial, sales and clerical staff	15	22
Total	100	100

Women represent 28 per cent of the workforce. The proportion of male employees with university or technical college degrees is 28 per cent (1987), while 61 per cent have completed a vocational training school or an apprenticeship and 11 per cent have only a compulsory education. As far as the women workers are concerned, 59 per cent have only a minimal education, while 4 per cent are university or technical college graduates.

The company has a very good training programme and an important social benefits programme. Its non-compulsory expenditure on old-age pensions, health care, recreation and leisure activities, as well as on training courses amounted, in 1987, to about DM3,000 million. This sum also included the distribution of stock among the company's employees.

Because of the recent reshaping of the West German metalworking industry, and particularly because of the strengthening of the position of Daimler Benz, which already controls Siemens' chief competitor AEG, the Siemens management has been putting special emphasis on buying shares of foreign electronics companies, in order to secure a good position on the future Single European Market. For this reason, it bid for Plessey, the United Kingdom electronics firm. It also intends to improve its standing on the lucrative United States market for both civilian and military equipment.

3. Krauss-Maffei

Krauss and Maffei, two companies which originally specialised in locomotives and railway carriage production, merged in 1931. Maffei had been involved in the armaments trade since 1928. Between 1933 and 1939 the Krauss-Maffei company developed and produced half-track vehicles and during the Second World War it developed and manufactured armoured personnel carriers. After 1945 it produced engines and buses. In 1955 it started to make armaments again, particularly the KM 12 full-track vehicle. In that year Friedrich Karl Flick took over the company and until 1986 Flick's Buderus AG held 96 per cent of the stock. In 1986 the company was reorganised, as a result of financial difficulties caused by declining sales. The State of Bavaria stepped in and took over about 25 per cent of the stock. The Diehl-MBB subsidiary RTG (Raketentechnik-Gesellschaft) of Unterhaching near Munich holds another 25 per cent through Buderus, which thus retains a minority control of the company. Feldmühle Nobel, whose subsidiary Dynamit Nobel is the largest West German ammunition manufacturer, holds 15 per cent. The remainder is held by three big banks, Dresdner Bank, Deutsche Bank and Bayerische Vereinsbank, which each have about 10 per cent of the stock. From early 1990 the company has been owned by Diehl and Mannesmann.

Krauss-Maffei is prime contractor for the development and production of battle-tanks, combat support vehicles and anti-aircraft systems. The company manufactures the Leopard Mark 1 and Mark 2 tanks, the Cheetah and Wildcat anti-aircraft tanks, the Puma armoured multi-purpose vehicle, etc. However, it has been estimated that only some 10 per cent of the value-added embodied in their tanks is contributed by the Krauss-Maffei factory. The rest is bought in from elsewhere, e.g. steel, communication equipment, etc.

Total sales of the Krauss-Maffei group declined between 1985 and 1987, from DM2,003 million to DM1,277 million, i.e. by 36 per cent. Sales of military equipment went down during the same period by as much as 47 per cent, dropping from DM1,538 to DM807 million. In 1988 they declined further to an estimated DM550 million. Civilian sales increased between 1985 and 1987 by about 1 per cent and their total share went up from 23 to 37 per cent, but this was totally insufficient to offset the cuts in military contracts.

The proportion of exports in total sales went through considerable fluctuations. In the early 1980s it oscillated between 17 and 30 per cent, in 1987 it amounted to 50 per cent. This means that the decline in sales was caused mainly by a drop in domestic demand.

The Krauss-Maffei group employed 4,848 workers in 1987. During the 1985-87 crisis years the workforce was reduced by 7 per cent, i.e. much less than output. It is possible that Krauss-Maffei's suppliers were harder hit than the company itself.

Only a small amount of information is available on the structure of the company's workforce: 44 per cent are manual workers, 49 per cent non-manual workers and 7 per cent are apprentices and trainees. The composition of the workforce has been shifting in favour of non-manual workers, away from manual workers.

The measures the company took in order to mitigate the impact of the recent crisis on its workforce offer some remarkable features and are of real interest for the study of defence industrial conversion. The company, where the average length of tenure has been 15 years, and where 75 per cent of production workers have been trained craftsmen who mostly served their apprenticeship in the house, applied a series of measures destined to safeguard as much as possible the workers – and its own – future interests. It devised an early retirement scheme, of which about 100 workers took advantage in 1986-87. Of the total 150 jobs cut back in 1987, the majority concerned office and other service workers, who are supposed to be more versatile and find jobs more easily than craftsmen with specific skills, and who could also be more easily replaced should business pick up again. Other cuts concerned quality control units, where about half of the 220 jobs were eliminated. In the production departments, workers in shops with insufficient orders were transferred to other units. Workers for whom no work could be found inside the company were paid lump-sum redundancy compensation. In spite of the employment cuts, 80 apprenticeship agreements were signed in 1987. In-house training courses have been provided to help workers acquire new skills and to master new techniques, enhancing their chances of employment inside or outside the company. Particular attention was also paid to personnel promotion policies, which had been carefully worked out during the years of the company's prosperity.

4. IABG – Industrieanlagen-Betriebsgesellschaft, Ottobrunn

The R & D establishment IABG was founded in 1961, at the initiative of the West German aerospace industry and in particular of Mr. Franz-Josef Strauss, the then Minister of Defence. The original aim was to provide central R & D facilities for aircraft and missile production. Gradually, further tasks of military R & D were added to the company's assignments.

Three-quarters of IABG's stock are held by the Government of the Federal Republic of Germany, and the remainder by a Munich company, Flugtechnik GmbH, which in turn is owned by the leading West German aerospace and electronics firms.

IABG has a turnover of DM291 million. Its budget is determined by the financial plan laid down by the Ministry of Defence. About two-thirds of the funds originate from the defence budget, while the rest is supplied by the Federal Ministry of Research and Technology. Military R & D accounts for 60 to 80 per cent of the company's activities.

IABG has a staff of 1,798 (1987), of which 43 per cent are engaged in research, 43 per cent in technical services, and 14 per cent in administrative, commercial and general services. As much as 55 per cent of the staff are graduate engineers and scientists, 33 per cent are technicians, 11 per cent are manual workers and 1 per cent are apprentices.

The activities of IABG depend largely on the guide-lines of the Ministry of Defence. Because of this, and because of the lack of financial reserves, there have not been any plans to expand the civilian side of activities, which in addition, would face severe competition from other research establishments operating in the Munich region.

IV. The employment structure in the four companies compared to the employment structure in the Munich area as a whole

A study prepared by the West German Metalworkers' Union (IG Metall) identifies the main characteristics of the manufacturing industry in the Greater Munich area as follows:

The focal points of manufacturing production are the branches producing high technology goods requiring large outlays on R & D. These branches depend to a considerable extent on government funding, particularly aerospace and electronics. The manufacturing industry in the Munich area has a proportion of scientific and technical workers which is above the national average. The share of non-manual workers is 47 per cent, compared to 31 per cent in the Federal Republic of Germany as a whole. Manufacturing production is highly concentrated, with two-thirds of firms having a workforce of over 500.[6]

As far as the four defence industry companies are concerned, they all have a share of non-manual workers which is above the regional average of 47 per cent. This share amounts to 61 per cent in MBB; to 55 per cent in Siemens; to 49 per cent in Krauss-Maffei; and to 88 per cent in IABG. Conversely, in all four firms, the share of manual workers is below the regional – and still more the national average. All four companies have a total workforce exceeding 500. The labour market in the Munich region is said to be more polarised than in the Federal Republic of Germany as a whole, in the sense that there is a fairly large proportion of highly qualified workers, and also a relatively important number of workers, often immigrants, with a low level of qualification. However, in the four companies highlighted above, the share of workers with no training and belonging to minority groups is low.

It is not possible to establish a precise comparison of the skill and educational profiles of the workforce in the four companies and in the Munich area as a whole, because of a lack of data. All available sources stress, however, that the defence industry companies in the region employ an above-average proportion of highly qualified workers, both in R & D departments and in production divisions. The arms industry's motto that its jobs are skilled jobs is said to be particularly true in the Greater Munich area. For example, the already high degree of qualification of the aerospace workforce reaches an even higher level in military aircraft and missiles production. A similar pattern is also found in the electronics and vehicle-producing branches. The institutions of higher education in Munich, especially the technical university, form a large pool of specialists for the entire economy of the region and particularly for the defence industry. It may be worth mentioning that 13 of the 25 Max Planck Institutes, specialising in plasma physics, five institutes of the Frauenhofer Gesellschaft, with research emphasis on solid-state physics and several institutes of the DVFLR (Deutsche Versuchsanstalt für Luft- und Raumfahrt, i.e. the German Aerospace Research Institute) are located in the Greater Munich area.

V. Problems and perspectives of defence industrial conversion in the Greater Munich area

Given the specific characteristics of the defence-related workforce in the Munich area discussed in the previous section, how would employment be affected in the case of defence cuts? How easily would defence workers find

---

[6] IG Metall Verwaltungsstelle: *München in der Wirtschaftskrise* (IGM, Munich, 1985), p. 17.

alternative employment? The answer to this question would depend on the labour market situation and on the unfilled vacancies in occupational categories involved in defence production, e.g. the metalworking occupations. Table 4.7 provides information on employment trends in occupations of the metalworking industry, in the Greater Munich area, between 1980 and 1987. Given the general decline in manufacturing employment, it is worth noting that the metalworking total did not go down. But, while there was a rapid increase in employment of scientists, engineers and technicians, the number of manual jobs was mostly cut down.

Unemployment increased between 1980 and 1987, for all occupational categories, skilled and unskilled; but engineers and scientists were the only category of workers where unfilled vacancies exceeded, in 1987, the number of unemployed, as illustrated in table 4.8. The gap between unemployment and unfilled vacancies was widest in the case of fitters and of unskilled labourers. The latter category also had the highest unemployment rate, while technicians had the lowest.

The fragmentary information presented here suggests that defence industry conversion would be helped along by the recent shift in the structure of labour demand. Defence cuts would affect mainly industries employing an above-average proportion of highly qualified personnel, for which there is considerable demand on the labour market.

With the exception of aerospace, the majority of defence-contracting industries – and firms – in the Munich area depend on arms production to a fairly limited extent. For this reason, they would not need extensive government subsidies in order to compensate for the loss of military contracts and to make a smooth adjustment to civilian production. Aerospace, which is largely involved in defence production, represents a special case and would have to be dealt with separately since it could not survive without substantial government assistance. But, outside aerospace, the few companies with a high proportion of defence production seem to possess the technological capacity and have enough qualified staff to develop and produce new civilian goods which could hold their own on world markets.

In general, the armaments industry in the Greater Munich area has most of the features commonly considered favourable for a successful defence industry conversion, namely an orientation towards high technology products; a close relationship between military and civilian production; a relatively low dependence on highly specialised personnel and equipment; the existence of a market organisation oriented towards the civilian sector; and a low level of dependence on the production of defence equipment at both the corporate and the plant level.[7]

In view of the existing industrial resources and the possibilities of government intervention, a cut in military demand that was government

---

[7] Inga Thorsson: *In pursuit of disarmament: Conversion from military to civilian production in Sweden* (Stockholm, Liber, 1984).

Table 4.7. Employment by occupational category in the metalworking industry, 1980-87, Greater Munich area (excluding Landsberg County), June of end year

Occupational category	1980 (Nos.)	1986 (Nos.)	1987	Index 1980 = 100	
				1986	1987
Metal makers	20 072	16 005	15 159	79.7	75.5
Mechanics and associated trades	58 833	58 573	58 039	99.6	98.6
Electricians	24 479	26 487	25 553	108.2	104.4
Fitters and other metal-working trades	12 974	12 012	11 436	92.6	88.2
Unskilled labourers, unspecified	5 215	5 059	4 096	97.0	94.1
Machinists and associated trades	6 465	5 548	5 415	85.8	83.8
Engineers, physicists, chemists and mathematicians	32 116	39 955	41 862	124.4	130.4
Technicians	35 652	37 017	38 421	103.8	107.8
Other technical specialists	11 073	11 351	11 245	102.5	101.6
Total	206 879	212 007	212 036	102.5	102.5

Source. Author's calculations based on Landesarbeitsamt Südbayern, *Arbeitsmarkt Aktuell*, Nos. 9/81, 2/87 and 2/88.

Table 4.8. Employment, unemployment and unfilled vacancies in selected occupations in the metalworking industry, Greater Munich area, 1987

Occupational category	Employment	Unemployment	Unfilled vacancies	Unemployment rate	Number of unemployed per unfilled vacancy
Metal makers	15 159	963	81	6.0	12
Mechanics and related workers	58 039	2 691	541	4.4	5
Electricians	25 553	928	423	3.5	2
Fitters and related workers	11 436	1 315	31	10.3	42
Unskilled labourers	4 906	2 163	76	30.6	28
Machinists and related workers	5 415	263	50	4.6	5
Engineers, physicists, chemists and mathematicians	41 862	1 325	1 365	3.1	1
Technicians	38 421	987	216	2.5	5
Other technical workers	11 245	564	98	4.8	6

Source. Landesarbeitsamt Südbayern, *Arbeitsmarkt Südbayern*, June 1987 and table 4.7.

promoted and accompanied by appropriate measures for industrial adjustment, would offer more advantages than disadvantages to the Greater Munich area. The increase in unemployment which would most likely occur in the short run would be reduced again below the previous level in the medium run. A few cases of industrial adjustment in the Greater Munich area, which took place as a result of a fall in demand for non-military as well as military products, while not always comparable, prove the feasibility of conversion, and provide examples from which useful lessons could be derived.

Trade unions in the Federal Republic of Germany advocate disarmament measures strongly. They have opposed the recent reorganisation of the West German armaments industry, particularly the Daimler Benz and MBB works councils, on the grounds that it increased the dependence of the industrial sites on a continuous flow of government contracts, which tied them more and more to one customer.

Inspired partly by the British initiatives, the workers and the unions have increasingly raised demands for an alternative production. In order to spell out these demands, they established in the early 1980s "alternative production working groups" in various plants, which demand an extension of the production range, or a diversification of production, or a change in output and a partial conversion, in order to safeguard jobs and production sites. To understand fully the standpoint of the trade unions on defence industry conversion, it is necessary to see it in the wider context of the unions' policy. The unions intend to push through an alternative model of growth, which would take into account the existing technical possibilities, and which would specify the development of socially desirable and ecologically adapted products. The demands for an alternative model of growth involve concepts of regional restructuring, including defence industry conversion, and a general job-orientated diversification of production.

The increased use of new networking techniques, new logistics, and with it the diversification and optimisation of the site capacities, should present significant challenges to the unions, as well as to decision-makers at the enterprise, regional and state levels, for the years to come.

Chapter 5

Regional and occupational dependence on defence contracting in the Rome area

FABRIZIO BATTISTELLI

I. Degree of dependence on defence contracting: The defence industry in the Rome area

1. The defence industry in Italy

Half way through the 1980s the Italian defence industry had a total workforce of about 86,000 and a turnover of US$5,000 million (1986 prices), of which over half was exported (see tables 5.1 and 5.2).

.   In 1979 a survey of all larger enterprises engaged in defence production was carried out in Italy (Battistelli, 1982). A total of 300 companies was surveyed, belonging to five industrial branches, namely aerospace, electronics, shipbuilding, other engineering and the chemical industry. The 300 companies were found to have a total of 64,250 employees. Employment in medium and small establishments acting as subcontractors to the larger companies was estimated at 11,000. Total defence-related employment was thus evaluated at 75,250. Data for the more recent years shown in table 5.1 are extrapolations based partly on employment trends communicated by the major defence-industrial firms.

According to table 5.1, defence industry employment in Italy increased between 1977 and 1982 by as much as 23 per cent. Total manufacturing employment has had a generally declining trend.

Employment in the metal manufacturing and engineering industry (NACE 3), to which most defence manufacturing belongs, seems to have resisted the overall declining trend better than in other manufacturing branches (EUROSTAT, 1986a). The extent to which the slightly better performance of the metal manufacturing and engineering group was due precisely to the growth of the defence industry is difficult to judge in the absence of detailed information. But this is suggested by some of the evidence presented later. Symptomatically, the report on the 1979 survey of the Italian defence industry (Battistelli, 1982) was entitled *Armaments: A new type of development? The defence industry in Italy*.

It is interesting to notice that the growth of the defence industry was largely export-led. The share of exports in total sales increased from 36 per cent

Table 5.1. Employment in the Italian defence industry and in total manufacturing, 1977-86

Year	Defence industry employment		Total manufacturing employment	
	Numbers	Trend, 1977 = 100	Thousands	Trend, 1977 = 100
1977[1]	70 000	100.0	5 444	100.0
1978[2]	73 500	105.0	5 387	99.0
1979[1]	75 250	107.5	5 369	98.6
1980[2]	78 600	112.3	5 439	99.6
1981[3]	81 500	116.4	5 333	98.0
1982[2]	86 000	122.9	5 233	96.1
1983[3]	86 000	122.9	5 080	93.3
1984[3]	86 000	122.9	4 881	89.7
1985	..	..	4 766	87.5
1986	..	..	4 719	86.7

[1] Based on data for 300 defence industry companies.   [2] Extrapolation of above.   [3] Based on data from leading firms.
Sources. Battistelli (1982), and updating by Archivio Disarmo; and ILO: *Year Book of Labour Statistics, 1987* (Geneva).

Table 5.2. Total sales and exports of the Italian defence industry, 1977-84

Year	Sales value ($ million current prices)	Of which: exports		Sales trend 1977 = 100 (Derived from data at constant prices)
		($ million current prices)	Percentage share	
1977	2 200	790	35.9	100.0
1978	3 200	1 240	38.8	135.0
1979	3 800	1 560	41.1	144.1
1980	5 200	1 990	38.31	173.7
1981	5 000	2 020	40.4	151.3
1982	5 500	2 030	36.9	156.9
1983	5 300	2 650	50.0	146.5
1984	5 000	2 860	57.2	132.5

Source. Battistelli (1982), and updating by Archivio Disarmo.

in 1977 to 57 per cent in 1984 (table 5.2). Italy now belongs to the principal arms exporters in the world. Although the arms exports have been criticised in domestic political debates, and some deals even became the source of political scandals, such as the illegal arms supplies to the Islamic Republic of Iran and Iraq, the fast growth of arms exports has been generally considered a success for Italian manufacturing.

Nevertheless, following the boom year of 1982, there has been a significant decline in Italian arms exports. This turn-around was due both to the introduction of stricter controls and to changes in international markets (decrease in Third World purchases and increased competition from other industrialised and newly industrialising countries) (SIPRI, 1987).

Not only foreign but also domestic demand for military equipment rose in the period 1977-82 and domestic demand continued to rise also after 1982. Separate data on government military procurements are not available. However, total budget expenditure for national defence purposes increased between 1977 and 1985 by 47.3 per cent (at constant prices), which corresponds to an average annual growth rate of 5.7 per cent. This trend was in line with the growth of total government spending, the share of national defence in government budget expenditure remaining more or less constant at slightly over 4 per cent (ISTAT *(a)*). Table 5.2 indicates that arms production increased very fast in the late 1970s. Between 1977 and 1980 the volume of total arms sales grew by an average annual rate of 20 per cent. However, in the early 1980s arms production declined or stagnated.

Of the 300 firms covered by the defence industry survey of 1979, 40 were in aerospace, 109 in electronics, 66 in mechanical engineering, 67 in shipbuilding and 18 in chemical. These numbers reflect the distribution by manufacturing branches of Italian defence production: relatively few chemical firms are engaged in basic military production. Most aerospace enterprises are so engaged but their average size is large and the number of companies is limited. On the other hand, the electronics branch is characterised by a large number of enterprises. In this branch the amount of investment required is relatively low, while labour intensity and R & D input are high. The result is a proliferation of electronics firms in Italy. Even if only a certain proportion of them work for defence, their number is, nevertheless, important.

The contribution of different manufacturing branches to defence industry output and employment is shown in table 5.3. In 1979 aerospace accounted for over one-third of total sales and the electronics industry for one-quarter. Aerospace and electronics each accounted for about a third of defence industry employment.

Since the 1979 survey was completed, considerable expansion has taken place in the electronics branch. For example, the index measuring the output of electrical goods and electronics stood, in 1984, 55.4 per cent above its 1980 level, which means that between 1980 and 1984 output in this industry grew at an average annual rate of 11.7 per cent (ISTAT *(b)*).

Computer output *(macchine per informatica)* expanded even faster, at an average rate of 18 per cent a year. Although this growth rate may be partly due to a low starting base, it is nevertheless impressive. Employment trends for the same grouping of the electrical and electronics industry are not available. Employment in electrical engineering and electronics as a whole (NACE group 34) declined in the first half of the 1980s (EUROSTAT, 1986a). But the overall trend may cover considerable shifts between individual industrial subgroups.

The growth of the aerospace industry was also extremely fast. Between 1980 and 1984 output grew by an average annual rate of 18 per cent, prompted particularly by foreign demand. Employment in the aerospace industry increased at a slow rate – by an average of 1.2 per cent a year (Commission of the European Communities, 1986). But even the slow growth of employment may be considered as significant, because in all the other branches of manufacturing of means of transport, employment declined during the period considered.

In mechanical engineering, both employment and output declined in the first half of the 1980s. This industry is said to have maintained its size and relative importance almost entirely thanks to the large-scale production of military vehicles. Small arms and ammunition production declined, but within this group output of some types of arms, such as machine-guns, increased considerably (ISTAT *(b)*).

The shipbuilding industry has been undergoing a crisis, as in all European countries. The boost provided by the 1975 modernising Italian "naval law" and by a certain number of export contracts was insufficient to offset the long-term structural decline. Shipbuilding was once a leading sector of the defence industry, and of Italian heavy industry in general, while today it is technologically outdated and no longer economically viable.

As far as the chemical industry is concerned, its defence output consists mainly of explosives, fuels and propellants. It is dominated by one large company, SNIA-BPD, which manufactures, among other things, space rocket and missile high technology propellents. Total output of explosives declined in the first half of the 1980s, but again the manufacture of some products increased (ISTAT *(a)*). Employment in the chemical industry as a whole declined rapidly in the first half of the 1980s, but SNIA's defence workforce did not.

The trends just described indicate that in the 1980s the aerospace and electronics industries further increased their shares in total Italian defence production and employment. Thus, the structure of the defence industry illustrated in table 5.3 for 1979 has become even more dominated by aerospace and electronics, while the relative importance of the other three branches declined.

It may be noted that in spite of the important changes in demand for the products of the five defence-related industries considered, relative levels of earnings (average hourly earnings of manual workers in these industries as a percentage of those in total manufacturing) remained generally unchanged between 1978 and 1985 (EUROSTAT, 1986b). In electrical engineering and electronics (where incidentally the female employment share is relatively high) average hourly earnings were 3 per cent below the manufacturing average both in 1978 and 1985. On the other hand, in the aerospace industry they were 7 per cent above the manufacturing average in both years. Earnings in the chemical industry were the highest: 14 per cent above the manufacturing average in 1978 and 11 per cent in 1985.

Thus, the two industrial branches which dominate the Italian defence industry, namely aerospace and electronics, have certain widely different characteristics: The first one is highly capital-intensive, composed of a few large enterprises, with a mainly male workforce, paid above average. The second one

Table 5.3.   *Number of enterprises, size of employment and the value of sales in the Italian defence industry, by industrial branches, 1979*

Industry	NACE Code	Enterprises		Employment		Sales value	
		No.	%	No.	%	Lire (bn.)	%
Aerospace	364	40	13.3	21 400	33.3	970	35.7
Electronics	33-34	109	36.3	20 400	31.7	655	24.7
Engineering	32-35-36*-37	66	22.0	10 060	16.0	610	22.5
Shipbuilding	361	67	22.3	7 950	12.4	320	11.6
Chemicals	25	18	6.0	3 900	6.1	165	6.9
Total		300	100	64 250	100	2 720	100
Induced employ- and sales				11 000		450	

* Excluding 361 and 364.
Source. Battistelli (1982).

is characterised by low capital intensity, is composed of a large number of often small enterprises, employing a relatively high proportion of women, and pay is below the manufacturing average (EUROSTAT, 1981).

2. General features of defence industry enterprises in the Rome area

The defence industry is generally characterised by a high degree of geographical concentration and specialisation. Arms production is not uniformly distributed throughout Italy, but is concentrated in certain areas. There are areas with specific "vocations": for light arms, Brescia in Lombardy; for aircraft and helicopter production, Varese, also in Lombardy; for ground and naval artillery, La Spezia in Liguria.

The 1979 survey established that the Rome area was specialised in electronics. This was confirmed by a new survey carried out in 1987 specially for the purpose of this study, which focused exclusively on the Rome area and which revealed that electronics accounted for three-quarters of the defence industry companies and for almost 80 per cent of the defence industry workforce in the region. All the leading national electronics companies are represented there. The results of the 1987 survey are summarised in table 5.4.

The 1987 survey revealed the presence of 52 defence industry companies in the area, large, medium and small, which together employed almost 12,000 workers in defence-related activities. Adding a further 2,000 workers to account for the estimated numbers employed in small subcontracting establishments not covered by the survey, the defence employment in the Rome area was evaluated at just under 14,000 workers, or 16 per cent of the total Italian defence workforce. A rough estimate would be that defence industry employment represented about 8 per cent of employment in industry (ISIC 2-4). This was considerably higher than the proportion for Italy as a whole, which

Table 5.4. Survey of defence industrial companies in the Rome area, 1986

Company	Ownership[1]	Total workforce in Italy	Total workforce in Rome area	of which: defence workforce	Output
1. Electronics					
Aerochemie S.p.A.	SNIA-BPD 90% Wasagchemie Holding (USA) 10%	50	50	50	Missile motors (for SNIA-BPD)
Ansafone Elettronica S.p.A.		90	90	15	Telecommunication systems (TLC)
Assing S.p.A.		30	30	10	Electronic countermeasures
Autophon Italiana S.p.A.		118	118	10	Telephones; TLC
CEP – Centro Elettronico Professionale S.n.c.		10	10	5	Avionics maintenance
CISET – Compagnia Italiana Servizi Tecnici S.p.A.		900	900	400	Engineering; maintenance for TLC
CITEC – Compagnia Internazionale di Tecniche di Elaborazione e Computers		35	35	20	TLC
Contraves Italiana S.p.A.	Oerlikon-Bührle (Switzerland)	1 187	1 187	1 187	Radar; fire control systems TLC; satellite terminals
CSTM – Centro Studi Trasporti Missilistici		5	5	5	Design of rocket propulsion systems
Datamat Ingegneria di Sistemi S.p.A.	SMA 27%	140	140	70	System engineering
EIS – Elettronica Ingegneria Sistemi S.p.A.	Elettronica S.p.A.	60	60	60	EDP systems
Elettrofonica s.r.l.		10	10	5	TLC
Elettronica S.p.A.	Plessey (UK) 35%	1 328	1 300	1 300	Electronic warfare
Elmer-Industrie per lo spazio e le comunicazioni S.p.A.	Intl. Signal & Control Group (UK-USA)	900	900	900	Radio communications equipment and systems
Ericsson – Sistemi di Sicurezza S.p.A.	Setemer 100% (Sweden)	600	600	80	Anti-intrusion systems; fire-detection system; closed circuit TV systems
FATME – Fabbrica Apparecchiature Telefoniche Materiale Elettrico (Brevetti Ericsson)	Setemer 100% (Sweden)	4475	..	40	TLC
Franconi Antonio Costruzioni Elettromeccaniche		50	50	10	Generators

Company	Ownership				Activity
ISED – Ingegneria Sistemi Elaborazione Dati S.p.A.		50	50	50	Software
ITAL Elettronica S.p.A.	Contraves	50	50	20	TLC
LASPRE S.p.A.		85	85		TLC
LA.RI.MA.R.T. S.p.A.		135	135	135	TLC
Litton Italia S.p.A.	Copier business machines	430	430	410	Navigation systems for ships and aircraft; fire control systems; C31 systems
M.E.S. Meccanica per l'Elettronica e Opto-electronic Servomeccanismi S.p.A.		240	240	240	Precision mechanical and electronic equipment; fuses
NIMO S.r.l.		30	30	30	Overhaul and repair of power units and sundries for aircraft
Novatecnica – Telecomunicazioni sistemi elettronici S.r.l.		20	20	5	Beacons
OMI – Ottico Meccanica Italiana S.p.A.	Agusta 100%	458	458	430	Aircraft navigation systems; instruments for night vision; optical and mechanical components for missiles
Page Europa S.p.A.	Contel Page Inc. (USA)	180	180	150	System engineering in TLC; electronics; EDP
Radionica S.r.l.		20	20	5	Earth satellite stations; TLC
Rockwell – Collins Italiana S.p.A.	Rockwell Intl. Co.	961	961	130	Electronic equipment for air and maritime navigation; TLC
SOME – Sistemi Ottici Meccanici Elettronici S.r.l.		10	10	10	Electronic components
Selenia – Industrie Elettroniche Associate S.p.A.	IRI-STET 82% (es) Aeritalia 18%	7001	3220	2415	Radar; naval and ground command control systems
Sielte – Impianti elettrici e telefonici sistema	Setemer (Sweden)	3024	3024	40	TLC
SIMETEL – Societa impianti elettrici e di telecomunicazioni S.p.A.		50	50	20	TLC
Sintel Italia S.p.A.		20	20	10	Security systems
Sistel – Sistemi elettronici S.p.A.	Selenia 41% Otomelara 27% Contraves 18% Breda Meccanica Bresciana 14%	205	205	205	Projects in missile technology

(table continued overleaf)

Table 5.4 (*continued*)

Company	Ownership[1]	Total workforce in Italy	Total workforce in Rome area	of which: defence workforce	Output
Socorama S.r.l.			20	10	Radar equipment
SEIF – Società Elettronica Impianti Forniture		10	10	5	TLC
Technitron S.r.l.			40	15	Telemetry and avionics
Vitroselenia S.p.A.	Selenia-Elsa (IRI-STET) 100%		706	650	
2. Aerospace					
Giusti S.p.A.		20	20	10	Parachutes
Meteor – Costruzioni Aeronautiche ed Elettroniche S.p.A.	Aeritalia 50%		400		Remotely piloted combat vehicles
OML – Officine Meccaniche Latine S.p.A.		220	220	170	Airframe and engine components
Selenia Spazio S.p.A.			1 094		
3. Chemical and rubber industries					
SNIA-BPD S.p.A.	Fiat	15 000	2 400	1 940	Conventional ammunition; powders; propellants for rockets and missiles; rockets and unguided weapon systems; missile engines; warheads
Sekur S.p.A.	Pirelli	278	278	90	Gas masks; filters; fuel tanks
Tirrena Società Industriale S.p.A.		105	105	105	Flame throwers; ammunition; NBC defence
4. Mechanical engineering					
Fabbrica D'Armi Pietro Beretta S.p.A.		1 105	130	110	Small arms; guns for AMX fighters
Galeazzi Paolo S.p.A.		20	20	5	Disinfection equipment; decompression chambers

Mival – Materiali industriali valvole S.r.l.	20	20	5	Valves; bombs
Officine Meccaniche Galli S.p.A.	40	40	20	Practice bombs
Officine Viberti S.p.A.	781	140	10	Aircraft fuel supplies
5. Shipbuilding				
Canados Cantieri Navali di Ostia S.p.A.	20	20	20	Patrol boats in wood
Italcraft		130		Patrol boats

[1] Refers to ownership by other enterprises, where known.

Source: Own survey.

amounted to approximately 1.7 per cent (up from 1.4 per cent in 1979, due to the decline in total manufacturing employment).

The largest defence-electronics company in the Rome area is Selenia. In 1986 it had 7,001 employees nation-wide of whom 3,220 worked in the Rome area and 2,415 of the latter were engaged in armaments production. Selenia is a public company. The state holding group IRI-Finmeccanica owns the majority of the capital and Aeritalia, the state aircraft manufacturing company, owns the remainder. Selenia produces radar, naval and ground command and control systems and other advanced electronic equipment such as ECM (electronic counter-measure equipment). It also produces missiles.

Elettronica is the second largest electronics firm in the Rome area. Most of its 1,300 employees work for the military. Between 1979 and 1985 its employment increased by about 200 workers to reach 1,700, but in 1986 it declined again rapidly. Its production consists of various types of electronic warfare equipment, including ECM. Elettronica is privately owned, with Plessey, the British electronics firm, holding 49 per cent of the capital.

Contraves, which produces fire control systems, telecommunications equipment and satellite terminals, is third in order of importance among defence-electronic companies in the Rome area. All its 1,187 employees are engaged in military production. It is owned by Oerlikon-Bührle of Switzerland.

Of the 39 defence-electronic firms listed in table 5.4, ten are partly or entirely owned by foreign companies, with American and Swedish capital well represented, apart from British and Swiss interests just referred to.

About 20 per cent of the Rome area's defence workforce are in other industrial activities than electronics, mainly in the chemical industry. The largest Italian defence-related chemical company, SNIA-BPD, owned by Fiat, is situated near Rome. In 1986, 1,940 of its 2,400 employees in the Rome area worked for defence.

Other defence industry branches are little represented in the Rome area, even aerospace, in spite of its newly acquired importance nation-wide. Defence industry branches other than electronics and chemicals occupy about 400 workers. In the mechanical engineering branch just one establishment among those listed in table 5.4 seems worth mentioning: It is the Beretta plant, owned by Beretta of Brescia. Beretta took it over in the 1970s to produce small arms and guns for the AMX fighter. In shipbuilding a small yard, Italcraft, may deserve a mention. It is situated in the coastal area near Rome and has a limited military production.

Most defence contracting firms, particularly the larger ones, have offices in Rome, in order to facilitate contacts with the Ministry of Defence and the General Staff, which are in charge of military procurements and make decisions on defence contracts.

Table 5.4 includes a considerable number of small firms which depend largely or entirely on defence contracting, i.e. which have all or most of their workforce engaged in military production. These often act as subcontractors to the large- and medium-sized firms. Of the 39 electronics firms listed in table 5.4, 12, or about one-third, work exclusively for the military. In the other, non-electronic, defence industry branches only one of the 13 firms listed in table 5.4, namely Tirrenia – an ammunition-producing firm – also works exclusively for the military. These firms would be likely to face greater problems in case of defence procurement cuts than those mainly working for the civilian market. Clearly, the lower the proportion of the workforce on the military side, the easier the adjustment would be. Some of the companies with a small proportion of their workforce on the defence side, particularly the big ones like FATME, might be able to absorb their defence workforce into civilian production relatively easily. Table 5.4 includes five firms out of the total 52 where the defence workforce represents 10 per cent or less of employment. These should experience little difficulty, if demand for armaments were cut.

3. Notes on the methodology of the 1987 survey of the Roman defence industry

The 1987 survey covered defence contracting enterprises in the Rome area defined in the narrower sense, i.e. in the province of Rome (more about the possible definitions of the Rome area will be said later). In the initial phase the survey made use of published sources of information, such as published company results and balance sheets, directors' statements, industrial directories, specialised publications, etc. Thus, the companies contacted and covered by the survey were those which publicly declare their participation in defence production. It can be estimated that these companies represent about 85 per cent of the whole defence industry in the Rome area. The employment data communicated by the companies should therefore be increased by about 15 per cent, in order to obtain an estimate of the total defence employment in the region. Many small subcontracting firms do not publicise their military production, and they have not been included in the survey.

The 52 defence-contracting firms surveyed in the Rome area were divided in two groups: electronics and other industries. For each firm eight items were recorded:

(1) Registered name and legal form.
(2) Ownership: when this involved large industrial groups, state or private, or transnational companies, it was recorded.
(3) Headquarters: as a rule these were in Rome, although there are companies with headquarters in other cities operating plants in the Rome area.
(4) Plants in the Rome area: the number and location of plants in the Rome area was recorded.
(5) Plants outside the Rome area.
(6) Total workforce: the total number of the firm's employees, engaged both in civilian and military production, inside and outside the Rome area, was recorded.
(7) Defence workforce in the Rome area: the number of employees specifically employed in military production in the Rome area was asked for.

This information was provided by some of the large companies only. In all other cases, estimates were made on the basis of trade union information obtained from union federations or factory committees.

(8) Output: the surveyed firms were asked to provide data on the type of products manufactured and on the structure of output.

Among the 52 firms covered by the 1987 survey and on the basis of the information it yielded, a certain number of firms were analysed in depth for the purpose of the present study. Among the firms approached some refused to co-operate. Five were finally selected for closer examination, namely Selenia, Elettronica, MES, Sistel and SNIA-BPD. Interviews were arranged with managers and trade union officials of the firms, which produced some interesting information on the companies as well as on their workforce. As the survey indicated that the great majority of defence industry firms in the Rome area belonged to the electronics branch, four out of the five firms were selected in that branch, i.e. Selenia, Elettronica, MES and Sistel. The fifth, SNIA-BPD, seemed an obvious choice, as it is the leading Italian chemical company, it is situated near Rome and has quite important defence production.

Together the five companies account for over a half of the defence industry workforce in the area. Selenia and Elettronica are the first and second largest electronics firms respectively. The two together produce about 40 per cent of the total output of military electronics in the Rome region. MES, on the other hand, is a fairly small company. It mostly acts as a subcontractor to the large companies such as Selenia or Elettronica. Sistel, also a relatively small firm, speacialises in defence-electronic research and development.

The selected companies differ also in other respects. Different proportions of their production are for military purposes (100 per cent in the case of MES and a fairly limited proportion in the case of SNIA). The companies belong both to the public sector (Selenia, Sistel) and to the private one (Elettronica, MES, SNIA-BPD). In summary, the five companies can be considered as generally representative of the defence industry in the Rome area.

II. Analysis of employment characteristics in the five selected defence industry companies

1. Type and quality of information obtained

No specific problems arose in obtaining company information on the breakdown of the workforce by educational level, broad occupational classification and by sex. But difficulties appeared when it came to the definition of the type of job performed by detailed categories and to employees' exact qualifications. There seemed to be a certain lack of knowledge of the actual functions and jobs performed by employees, particularly in the smaller firms.

Among the five companies surveyed, only Selenia provided a detailed breakdown of its employees by occupation, cross-tabulated by sex. The list contained 50 occupational categories. These have been regrouped so as to follow, at least approximately, the ISCO classification of occupations, and are shown in table 5.5.

The reasons why the other companies failed to provide similar data are several:

(1) Many companies are reluctant to give information on personnel matters and the element of company secrecy is particularly strong in the field of defence production. Defence industry companies may provide detailed information on their employees in special cases, e.g. when needed for collective bargaining or when requested by government authorities for a statistical survey. But neither was the case here. On the contrary, the companies were assured that the purpose of the survey was purely academic.

(2) The reluctance of the companies to supply information on their occupational structure, in spite of long insistence and in spite of many informal interventions, may be related also to other factors, particularly to the actual availability of the data. The fact that the smaller companies supplied less information suggests that in the smaller companies all the information requested may not be available. In large companies the occupational structure is more rigid, which makes a fairly detailed occupational classification possible. The data are also more useful to the large companies themselves, because an overview of the tasks performed by employees can no longer be obtained by direct personal contact. This makes the collection of the data and the keeping of records on the subject justified. Small companies may find it difficult to draw up a detailed occupational classification of their employees, because of the much greater flexibility in the jobs performed. This flexibility may allow for only very broad occupational distinctions to be made.

(3) Finally, it may be noted that the collection of occupational statistics is not a well-established practice in Italy. Employment data in a detailed occupational breakdown are not published annually in Italian national statistics or in international sources such as the *Eurostat* statistical series. They are provided by the censuses. But census data are collected and published in the first half of each decade. Thus at the end of the decade they may look somewhat obsolete.

2. Presentation of the evidence

The information on employment which it was easiest to obtain for all five companies was the breakdown by sex. The sex composition of the workforce in the five companies is shown in table 5.6. The share of women in employment ranges from 18 per cent in Sistel and Selenia to 8 per cent in MES. The weighted average of the female employment share in the four defence electronics

Table 5.5.   Selenia: Occupational structure of employment, 1986 – Rome and Pomezia plants

Occupation	Men	Women	Total
Professional and technical workers			
Auditors	4	1	5
Financial officers	5	5	10
Fiscal officers	1	2	3
Legal advisers	2	2	4
Planning officers	1	2	3
Development and project planners	70	–	70
Graduate planners	382	29	411
Organisation analysts	11	–	11
Software analysts (graduate)	15	1	16
Programmers	26	2	28
Designers/coders/data technicians	80	18	98
Laboratory technicians	567	12	579
Laboratory operators	100	19	119
System expert surveyors/Workshop technicians	15	–	15
Quality control technicians	38	–	38
Electronics inspectors	92	2	94
Electronics and mechanical controllers	17	–	17
Components and environment testing technicians	24	–	24
Instrument setters	16	–	16
Communications specialists	23	–	23
Training and education specialists	9	3	12
Public relations officers	5	1	6
Advertising copy writers and graphic designers	7	1	8
Photographers	3	–	3
Subtotal	1 513	100	1 613
Administrative and managerial workers			
Higher level executives	62	–	62
Other executives	103	–	103
Budget inspectors	4	–	4
Administrative control officers	26	7	33
Programme managers and controllers	30	9	39
Co-ordinators, supervisors, production control officers	81	1	82
Administrative technicians	5	–	5
Personnel administrators	8	9	17
Personnel organisers	2	–	2
Other administrators	52	35	87
Subtotal	373	61	434
Clerical and related workers			
Data processing operators	12	14	26
Telex operators and telephonists	3	8	11
Clerks, photocopiers	18	3	21
Typists	–	186	186
Other office workers	69	86	155
Subtotal	102	297	399

Table 5.5. *(continued)*

Occupation	Men	Women	Total
Sales workers			
Commercial technicians	23	2	25
Internal supply officers	29	8	37
Subtotal	52	10	62
Service workers			
Service workers (caterers, cleaners, porters, guards, drivers)	114	56	170
Subtotal	114	56	170
Production and related workers			
Foremen and supervisors	249	–	249
Electrical/electronics operators, setters and repairers	101	31	132
Varnishers, galvanisers and chemical operators	21	–	21
Carpenters, construction and hydraulic installation workers	43	–	43
General labourers	28	2	30
Store keepers and warehouse workers	28	5	33
Packers	8	4	12
Subtotal	478	42	520
Other workers	24	–	24
Total	2 656	566	3 222

Source. Data made available by Selenia S.p.A.

Table 5.6. *Employment in five selected defence industry companies by sex, 1986 (numbers and percentages)*

Company	Males (a)	Females (b)	Total (c)	b/c (%)
Sistel	167	36	203	17.7
MES	219	19	238	8.0
Elettronica	1 156	158	1 314	12.0
Selenia	2 656	566	3 222	17.6
SNIA-BPD	2 170	246	2 416	10.2
Total	6 368	1 025	7 393	13.9

Source. Data communicated by the companies.

companies is about 16 per cent. Nationwide, the female employment share in the electrical engineering and electronics industry (NACE 34) is much higher, almost one-half according to the last available data (1975). Thus, women's employment share in the four selected defence electronics companies appears to be low. This is so even if account is taken of the below-average representation of women in manufacturing in the Rome area, of which more will be said later. It may be thought that the low share of women in employment is due to the particular need for highly qualified personnel in the defence industry, hired for engineering work, research, etc. But, among the four defence-electronics companies surveyed, Sistel – the specialised research and development establishment – has the highest share of women workers, whereas MES, which has the highest share of blue-collar workers and no research activities of its own, has the lowest. Thus, the low share of women in the workforce of the four defence-electronics companies seems little related to qualification or human capital factors. It may be more related to institutional factors. Sistel and Selenia, which have the highest female employment share, are both publicly owned. As such, they may follow equal opportunities policies better than the private companies. Finally, the low employment share of women is likely to be due to long-established recruitment practices and to a rather rigid job segregation along traditional lines. In Selenia, for which we have detailed information, almost two-thirds of women have either clerical or catering and cleaning jobs. Obviously, not many women are hired for other work although there are 100 professional and technical women workers, representing 6 per cent of the professional and technical staff. The smaller companies may follow sex segregation policies even more rigidly, perpetuating the image that the defence industry is a male preserve.

It was also fairly easy to obtain information on the educational characteristics of employees in the five selected companies. The data appear in table 5.7. The table shows that in Sistel – the R & D establishment – 26 per cent of the staff are university graduates and a further 36 per cent have a secondary advanced level certificate. In the two electronics manufacturing companies, Elettronica and Selenia, the educational level of the staff is broadly similar, even though the proportion of university graduates is somewhat lower. MES, on the other hand, employs only a few graduates and a relatively small proportion of secondary-school certificate holders, the majority of workers having little more than the compulsory level of education. SNIA-BPD collect data on education levels only from their white-collar workers: the large share in the "other" category (75.5 per cent) is certainly an exaggeration.

Table 5.8 shows the structure of employment in the five companies in a breakdown by four occupational categories, namely executives, professional, technical and office staff, production workers and labourers and other workers. A feature to be noted is the low share of production workers not only in Sistel, which could be expected, but also in Elettronica and Selenia, namely 24 and 21 per cent. (In the Italian electronics industry as a whole, the proportion of blue-collar workers is 52 per cent.) On the other hand, at MES, production workers represent the great majority of employees. This is linked to the largely traditional production methods prevailing in the company, whereas the bigger companies, e.g. Selenia and Elettronica, are more automated and technologically more advanced. SNIA-BPD employs a large proportion of blue-collar workers – 68 per cent – which exceeds considerably the average of 46 per cent for the Italian chemical industry as a whole. The high share of

Table 5.7. *Employment in five selected defence industry companies by level of education, 1986 (percentage distribution)*

Company	University degree	Secondary school certificate (matriculation examination)	Other	Total
Sistel	26.1	35.5	38.4	100.0
MES	2.5	17.2	80.3	100.0
Elettronica	17.0	41.0	42.0	100.0
Selenia	20.4	34.1	45.5	100.0
SNIA-BPD	8.8	15.7	75.5	100.0

Source. As table 5.6.

Table 5.8. *Employment in five selected defence industry companies by occupational category, 1986 (percentage distribution)*

Company	Executives	Professional technical and office staff	Production workers and labourers	Other workers	Total
Sistel	5.9	73.4	12.3	8.4	100.0
MES	3.8	24.4	71.8	–	100.0
Elettronica	7.5	68.4	24.1	–	100.0
Selenia	5.1	72.8	21.4	0.7	100.0
SNIA-BPD	1.8	26.8	68.2	3.2	100.0
Total	4.4	55.4	38.6	1.6	100.0

Source. As table 5.6.

blue-collar workers was attributed by the management, during the interviews held, to various moves towards diversification of production and to the resulting dispersion of machinery within the plant. However, the production of explosives tends to be relatively labour intensive, certainly more so than such types of chemical production as oil refining (Willett, 1988).

The absence of separate data for technicians and professional engineers in table 5.8 reduces considerably the informative value of the table, in view of the special importance of this category of workers for the defence industry. In Selenia (table 5.5) 57 per cent of male employees and 18 per cent of female employees belong to the professional and technical category. On the other hand, 52 per cent of female employees but less than 4 per cent of male employees belong to the clerical category. For both sexes together, the proportion of professional and technical employees is 50 per cent.

Table 5.9.   *Employment in five selected defence industry companies by type of occupational activity,*
              1986 (percentage distribution)

Company	R & D	Administration	Marketing	Services	Production	Total
Sistel	53.2	8.4	1.0	15.7	21.7	100.0
MES	–	3.8	2.1	2.5	91.6	100.0
Elettronica	20.0	17.0	4.0	–	59.0	100.0
Selenia	45.7	7.7	5.0	22.2	19.4	100.0
SNIA-BPD	21.1	11.0	2.1	20.7	45.1	100.0

Source. As table 5.6.

Table 5.9 provides some interesting complementary information on the structure of occupational activities in the five selected firms. It shows that at Sistel, 53 per cent of employees are engaged in R & D, which incidentally does not seem too high for a company specialising in the R & D field. But a surprisingly large percentage of the workforce is engaged in R & D also at Selenia, the electronics-manufacturing company, where production activities occupy only 19 per cent of the workforce. Such occupational structure, and particularly such a high share of R & D employment, does not correspond to the norm in the Italian electronics industry. The explanation lies in the fact that Selenia's research activities are concentrated in the Rome area, where well-qualified professional and technical personnel can be hired relatively easily. The company's research establishments in the Rome area (Tiburtina and Pomezia) cater for the other plants situated elsewhere in Italy (Naples, L'Aquila, Palermo). When the workforce of all Selenia's plants throughout the country is taken into consideration, the share of R & D employment is reduced to 21 per cent, which is similar to the share found in Elettronica. Conversely, the share of production workers at Selenia is considerably higher overall than in its Rome area plants. The small subcontracting firm, MES, stated that having no research activities of its own, 92 per cent of its workforce was on the production side.

Some information has also been collected on the breakdown by employment status of the Roman defence industrial workforce: only 9 per cent of the workforce in sectors concerned with military production is classified as "self-employed", compared with 20 per cent in industry as a whole. The self-employed, or artisan proprietors of small firms, are characteristic of a type of industrial production which is not common in the armaments industry.

To sum up, the study of the five defence industry firms in the Rome area has revealed the following characteristic features of their employment structure: (1) a below-average share of women workers; (2) a high proportion of university and high school graduates; (3) a high proportion of professional and technical workers; (4) a high proportion of the workforce engaged in R & D activities; and (5) an above-average share of salaried employees, with relatively few self-employed. These characteristics of the defence workers in the Rome area are similar to those found in other countries and regions.

III. Employment structure in the Rome area compared with the employment structure in the five selected companies

1. Structure of employment in the Rome area

There are several ways of defining the Rome area. The Italian administrative classification uses a larger concept which is the Rome region, or Lazio, and a narrower one which is the Rome province. The Rome region, Lazio, is one of 20 Italian administrative regions. According to the last Census (1981) it had a population of 5,002,000 and accounted for about 9 per cent of the population of Italy. The Lazio region is composed of five provinces: the Rome province – population 3,696,000; Viterbo province – population 268,000; Rieti province – population 143,000; Latina province – population 434,000; and Frosinone province – population 460,000 (ISTAT *(a)*).

The Rome province thus accounts for about three-quarters of Lazio's population. While the previous sections and the information in table 5.4 were limited to the Rome province, the present section mostly focuses on the Lazio region, for which data are readily available both in national statistics and in the statistical sources of the EEC.

In 1985 (the last year for which data are available at the time of writing) the gross activity rate (i.e. for all age groups together) in the Rome region (Lazio) for men and women together, corresponded to the national average of 41 per cent. It was slightly above the national average for men (56.1 per cent compared with 54.7 per cent) and slightly below the national average for women (26.7 per cent compared with 28.2 per cent). Between 1977 and 1985, a period for which there are comparable statistical series, labour force participation increased faster in the Rome region than in Italy as a whole. This was due to an above average growth in the labour force participation of women, which had been relatively low in the past, but also to a growth in the labour force participation of men, which nation-wide remained unchanged during the period considered. The growth in the male (and also female) labour force participation may be related to the fact that Lazio has been a region of net immigration, originating not only in Italy but consisting also of Italian workers returning from abroad (ISTAT *(a)*).

The unemployment level in the Rome region corresponds roughly to the national average. In 1987 the male unemployment rate, both in Italy and in the Rome region, was 7 per cent and the female unemployment rate was about 17 per cent (ISTAT *(c)*). In the past, unemployment in the Rome region was considerably above the national average. But it has remained unchanged since 1977, whereas unemployment in Italy as a whole had a fast-rising trend. Although the unemployment level is high, particularly for women, the fact that it resisted the overall rising trend and did not deteriorate may be considered as a positive sign, particularly since the total labour supply increased much faster in the Rome region than in the rest of Italy. Between 1977 and 1985 the total labour force increased in the Rome region by 15.5 per cent, and nation-wide by

Table 5.10.   **Employment in Italy and in the Rome region by industrial sector, 1985**
              (thousands and percentages)

	Total employment	Agriculture (ISIC I)	Industry (ISIC 2-5)	Services (ISIC 6-9)
Italy ('000)				
Both sexes	20 742	2 296	6 896	11 550
Men	13 986	1 484	5 270	7 232
Women	6 756	812	1 626	4 318
Employment share of women (%)	32.6	35.4	23.6	37.4
Percentage distribution by sector				
Both sexes	100.0	11.1	33.2	55.7
Men	100.0	10.6	37.7	51.7
Women	100.0	12.0	24.1	63.9
Rome region (Lazio) ('000)				
Both sexes	1 854	110	381	1 363
Men	1 278	71	326	881
Women	576	39	55	482
Employment share of women (%)	31.1	35.5	14.4	35.4
Percentage distribution by sector				
Both sexes	100.0	5.9	20.6	73.5
Men	100.0	5.6	35.5	68.9
Women	100.0	6.8	9.5	83.7

Source. ISTAT: *Rilevazione delle Forze di Lavoro*, Rome, 1985.

8.1 per cent. Total net employment increase amounted in the Rome region to 15.3 per cent, and nation-wide to 4 per cent. Thus, the Rome region has shown a considerable capacity for labour force absorption in recent years (ISTAT *(d)*).

New employment creation, both nation-wide and in Rome, was concentrated in the service sector, while agriculture, but also industry, were losing labour. Service employment grew at a faster rate in the Rome region than in the country as a whole (by 33.5 and 25.7 per cent respectively between 1977 and 1985). The importance of service employment in the Rome region is illustrated in table 5.10. The table also shows the low share of industrial employment in comparison with the national average, particularly for women.

The service activities which registered the fastest growth of employment nation-wide, between 1977 and 1985, were banking, insurance and business services, followed by community, social and personal services and by trade and public catering (ILO, 1987). These three service activities also accounted for a considerably higher employment share in the Rome area than nation-wide (ISTAT *(a)*). Thus, in the Rome region there was a rapid growth in demand for labour in three out of four main service activities during the period considered. This demand was insufficient, however, to absorb the fast-rising labour supply, and to reduce the unemployment rate, even partially. The absorption of labour into the relatively booming service sector may have been more difficult due to the fact that a part of the workforce had become redundant in the industrial sector, at home and abroad, and was not qualified or willing or sufficiently mobile to fill the available service vacancies.

In the case of a fall in demand for armaments and of a cut in defence production, labour made redundant in the defence industry would increase the numbers of those who lost their jobs in other manufacturing branches as a result of the de-industrialisation process, and who might have real difficulty in finding new employment. This difficulty would be aggravated in the Rome region by the fact that the industrial sector is relatively less developed than in the North, and the general reduction of industrial employment has been faster (at least as indicated by data for the period 1977-85).

2. Comparison of the employment structure in the Rome area and in the five selected defence industry companies

(a) Sex composition

In the previous section, women workers were found to be under-represented in the Roman defence industry, particularly as it consists mostly of electronics, which is a "female" branch nation-wide. But the share of women in industrial employment is generally low in Rome, as illustrated in table 5.10. There is, however, only a 10 percentage-point difference between employment share of women in Italy as a whole and in the Rome area, whereas the difference between women's employment share in Rome defence-electronics (16 per cent on the average in the four selected companies) and in the electronics branch nation-wide (50 per cent) is much bigger. Thus, women are under-represented in Roman defence electronics even if the special characteristics of the region are taken into account. If cuts were made in the defence industry workforce, women would not necessarily be the first to go, because of the high degree of occupational segregation and the continuing need for particular types of female workers. But those that would become redundant would have few chances to be rehired for another industrial job, in view of the general de-industrialisation process in the region. They would obviously have to seek employment in the service sector, where there might be openings for them, particularly for the clerical workers. Others would have to accept mostly unqualified, low-paid work, which, of course, many of them may be doing also in the defence industry, e.g. in cleaning and catering jobs. The hardest hit might be female professional and technical workers, because the number of industrial jobs in the Rome area has been shrinking, and given women workers' lower mobility, they would not be likely to move to another region in search of work. Thus, a fairly high proportion might swell the already large numbers of female unemployed.

Table 5.11.   Employment by educational attainment and by sex in the Rome region, 1985
            (thousands and percentages)

	University degree	Secondary school certificate (Matriculation)	Other	Total
Total	195	609	1 261	2 065
	9.4	29.5	61.1	100.0
Men	127	365	884	1 376
	9.2	26.6	64.2	100.0
Women	68	244	377	689
	9.9	35.4	54.7	100.0

Source. As table 5.10.

(b) *Educational profiles*

A comparison of the data presented in tables 5.7 and 5.11 shows that in the two large defence-electronics firms, Selenia and Elettronica, and in the electronics R & D establishment, Sistel, the educational profiles of employees are considerably higher than the average for the Rome region. In the medium-sized subcontracting firm, MES, on the other hand, the profile is much lower. (The data for SNIA-BPD only cover white-collar workers and are not comparable with the rest.) Since the chances of finding new employment grow, other things equal, with the level of education, a fairly high proportion of the staff of the leading defence electronics companies would be in a good position to find civilian employment, should defence production be cut down. But, as the qualified personnel consists often of narrowly specialised engineers, there might be few or no adequate vacancies for them in the Rome area's declining industrial sector. Many might have to move to the north where there are more industrial job openings. However, given the advantages of the cultural environment of a city like Rome, this might be considered as a real hardship and accepted with considerable reluctance.

(c) *Occupational structure*

Employment data for the Rome region are not available in the same occupational breakdown as that used in table 5.8. The available data indicate, however, that in the Rome area the average proportion of blue-collar workers in industrial enterprises is much higher than in the leading defence electronics firms. Blue-collar workers, particularly the semi-skilled and unskilled, usually have most difficulty in finding new employment, when they become redundant. Even if in the defence electronics companies the proportion of blue-collar workers is below average, the numbers involved are still considerable. If defence production were cut, the majority of these workers would probably join the dole queue. But so far, the defence industry workforce has been the one which best resisted the downward trend of manufacturing employment in the Rome area.

IV. Enterprise reactions to defence procurements cuts

An important part of the interviews conducted with the defence-company managers concerned the eventuality of a reduction in military procurements and their reactions to it. Six interviews were held altogether, five with management representatives of the five surveyed companies (Selenia, Elettronica, Sistel, MES and SNIA-BPD) and the sixth with two officials of the National Association of Electronics Industries (ANIE). The consultations took place between 6 July and 10 October 1987. The names of the managers and officials interviewed appear in the Appendix.

As already mentioned, some of the interviews were arranged with considerable difficulty. The notable exception to this was ANIE which, as an industrial association, is supposed to provide information on the electronics industry and which also has a public relations role to play. In the other cases, however, once the appointment for an interview was made, the managers proved very co-operative, ready to give detailed answers to all questions put to them.

The point of departure of the discussions was the hypothetical event of a reduction (for whatever reason) in military procurements. A clear consequence of such an event would be a cut in defence production, which may or may not be followed by a total or partial conversion to civilian production. The possibility and the extent of conversion from military to civilian production was discussed at length with all the managers interviewed.

The six interviews revealed a wide range of opinions held by Roman industrialists concerning the feasibility of defence output conversion. Selenia's representative denied outright any possibility of conversion of his company's defence industry activities. Sistel's management, on the other hand, accepted the idea without difficulty. Representatives of Elettronica, MES and SNIA-BPD expressed mixed feelings about conversion moves, accepting them with reservations or as a remote possibility. It can be said that outside Sistel a broad consensus emerged on the general difficulty of such a move, and basically also on its lack of desirability and useful purpose in the present circumstances.

The deputy director-general of *Selenia* made a number of interesting points when explaining his position. Apart from political considerations, he expressed two main objections to a reduction in defence output and to a conversion to civilian production. The first objection concerned the technological spin-offs from military production which are particularly important in the electronics field. The second objection concerned the advantages which a firm like his could derive from dealing with one main buyer, i.e. the Ministry of Defence, and from the resulting project stability and guaranteed volume of sales. These permit the introduction of the most up-to-date technology, which in turn makes the Italian defence industry competitive on international markets. The growth of exports leads to sufficiently large production series guaranteeing maximum efficiency.

On the point of technological spin-offs, Selenia's representative argued that in the military field the most advanced product was always sought after and thus large amounts had to be spent on R & D to maintain competitiveness. Military R & D, however, can later also profit the civilian production, since a large variety of electronic components can be used for both military and civilian products. He said that it was increasingly difficult to distinguish between various marketing fields, since there was a rising convergence. Due to the special characteristics of the electronics market, the spin-offs from military to civilian products were fairly rapid and important. Military R & D was financed largely by the Ministry of Defence, although some R & D was financed directly by the defence industry firms out of their (admittedly considerable) profits.

Selenia's representative also declared that the support of the Ministry of Defence was particularly effective, much more than that of other ministries. No other ministry gave as much help to industry, particularly in the R & D field, as the Ministry of Defence. In the event of a conversion to civilian production, MoD support would be lost. This would be a considerable set-back to the enterprises involved, because civilian ministries were much more difficult to deal with. Comparing military deliveries with supplies of electronics to state buyers other than the MoD, Selenia's deputy director-general stressed the main advantages of military contracts over civilian ones, particularly the standardisation, the single decision centre, the economies of scale and the resulting profitability. He explained that civilian state contracts, e.g. those involving sales of electro-medical equipment to the Public Health Service, suffered from a lack of standardisation. Purchases are carried out by a large number of regional or local health units, each with enough independence to make its own specifications and decisions as to the dates and terms of delivery. It was as if every military unit commander bought the cannon he liked best. Local health units were also entitled to import equipment from abroad, whereas in the case of armaments, of course, any import decisions are subject to highly restrictive, centrally defined, criteria. He said that "no industrialist would risk investing in sectors where not even the state demand was guaranteed". About 1,000 billion Lire worth of technologically advanced equipment was purchased by the Italian public and private health institutions each year. Such equipment could be produced entirely by the Italian industry and moreover a further 1,000 billion Lire worth of technologically advanced products could be exported. But medical electronics "does not exist as a national industry, because the Ministry of Health does not organise the market".

The advantages of military contracts over civilian ones were stressed by most of the interviewed industrialists. The manager of *Elettronica*, spoke of the constant evolution of military threats and counter-threats and the corresponding evolution of specifically designed weapons. He saw this as a continuous challenge, a never-ending chain of measures and counter-measures. As soon as the enemy realises that his striking capacity has been neutralised, he tries to find new ways of threatening. Hence the need for constant adjustment, in order to have an appropriate protection shield. For Elettronica the main problem concerning a switch to civilian production would be the market situation, both as far as demand and the adaptability of supply are concerned. In principle, there is nothing to stop Elettronica from producing medical electronics, for example. As a matter of fact, the company has already transferred some of the knowledge gained in military R & D to biomedical research. But demand in this field is now largely saturated, particularly the demand for the products where Elettronica has most to offer. Elettronica's manager admitted, however, that no market research had been done to analyse the real prospects of the company on the civilian market, as there was no need for it. At present the company does not have to worry about its future sales, because the major part of its production is procured by the Ministry of Defence, and the volume of procurement is guaranteed. This being so, the company's main preoccupations are the technological standards of its production and the performance level of its equipment, followed by the an optimal adjustment in the use of its production capacities. If the company switched to civilian production, it would have to concentrate mainly on the market situation, the considerations just mentioned becoming secondary. The company would have to re-think and reorganise its commercial network. As it is now used to dealing with a few large buyers, this would mean setting-up an entirely new distribution network, suitable for selling consumer goods through a large number of different outlets.

The last mentioned aspect was also considered to be the main problem of conversion by *MES*'s manager. MES was "born into and raised in military production". It does not "a priori" exclude the possibility of working for the civilian market, but it would have great difficulties in adapting to it. As MES's manager put it, "it would be necessary to reconvert all of us, not only the production".

The managing director of *SNIA-BPD* mentioned the lack of efficiency of the civilian state authorities in industrial contracting. The National Research Council is apparently very slow in financing research, and uses such cumbersome procedures that the funds granted have to be frequently returned for lack of agreement or progress reached within the statutory delays. There are certain exceptions, such as the European satellite project, a civilian programme administered by the Ministry of Foreign Affairs. But in SNIA's experience, the best working relationship is that established with the Ministry of Defence. The MoD is easiest to deal with not only for research but also for production and investment planning. To SNIA the continuity of procurements guaranteed by the Ministry of Defence is even more important than their volume (now ranging between 100-200 billion Lire per year). The conversion to civilian production would be extremely difficult for SNIA. In the field of propellants, for example, SNIA has reached such a degree of specialisation that its products could not be put on the civilian market, apart from the market for civilian satellites. But the civilian space market is relatively limited, with about 40 satellites launched a year, each having a ten-year working life. In addition, this market is practically saturated at present.

The only clear support for the idea of military output conversion came from the a spokesman of *Sistel*. The company's present situation and its history may provide an explanation to the difference in attitude. Sistel was founded in 1954 by Contraves of Switzerland. It was set up in its present form in 1967 and rapidly acquired a high reputation in the missile field. The firm reached the height of its success thanks to the design, production and export of the Sea Killer missile to the Shah of Iran. But its next project, called Mei, developed for the Italian armed forces, was cancelled and the company plunged into a long period of crisis. The crisis is still not over, although Sistel got financial help from a number of large, mostly publicly owned companies, such as Selenia, Oto, Melara and Breda, as well as from Contraves. Sistel continues to have a highly qualified workforce, but it has in fact become a design office and R & D establishment for the companies which took control of it. For these companies it is convenient to maintain a specialised R & D subcontracting establishment, drawing on its services only when required. Faced with this situation, Sistel's management and professional staff have been trying to find new outlets for their R & D activities, particularly on the civilian market. Sistel developed for example, a system of aerial tele-analysis of river basins for ecological purposes. But the project never got beyond the planning stage. More recently, Sistel developed a form of laser technology for the restoration of old paintings. This project looks quite promising, but is being held back by the shortage of public funds for civilian research purposes: a clear illustration of the difficulty of defence conversion. The laser-restoration technology is itself a spin-off from military research. Although considerable satisfaction has been expressed in some circles that "for once the military industry can do something useful for culture", the project would not have been undertaken if it was not for the knowledge gained in military R & D.

The two representatives of *ANIE* expressed support for a more balanced proportion between the military and civilian production in the Italian electronics industry. But they excluded the possibility of total conversion. The mere suggestion that the Italian defence industry could abandon its share of the international arms market, where it has gained such an unprecedented position, was dismissed as absurd. Italy would have to build from scratch a new position on the civilian market which would involve a lot of difficulty. ANIE could try prospecting the sections of the civilian market where some of the highly specialised and sophisticated defence industry production could find an outlet. But ANIE has not done any such research before.

In recent years, the growth of Italian arms exports ceased to be a matter known only to the industry (and to a few variously motivated pressure groups) and became public knowledge. All the managers interviewed considered the growth of arms exports as a welcome complement to the production for domestic needs, and the rising export trend was a source of great satisfaction to them. ANIE's representatives were particularly explicit on this topic. The production scale guaranteeing real profitability of defence electronics' output could be achieved only if sufficient foreign demand was added to the procurement needs of the Italian Ministry of Defence. Italy now occupies the seventh place in the world arms market (although its total share of this market was only 2.5 per cent in the period 1982-86 and 1.1 per cent in the year 1986 (SIPRI, 1987)). If the Italians withdrew from this market, "we would just be doing a favour to the other nations and absolutely nothing would change".

The general impression gained from the six interviews is that the Italian arms industry is now established on international markets, and is attempting a "technological jump" which would allow it to match the standards of production reached by the leading nations of the industrialised world. Its objective is to become "more competitive in industrialised countries' markets, ceasing to be limited to the petro-dollar area and to the Third World, which are markets for intermediate technology. But, of course, industrialised countries' markets are already largely saturated" (ANIE).

The alternative envisaged by Sistel, i.e. attempting a conversion to civilian production and trying to penetrate civilian markets, would require considerable imagination and a lot of good entrepreneurship. In all cases it would be difficult. The only chance of success would be strong and binding political support. But according to the industrialists interviewed the natural tendency for the Italian defence industry will be to continue improving its technology and increasing exports for as long as there is sufficient demand for them on international markets.

References

Battistelli, F. 1982. *Armi: nuovo modello di sviluppo? L'industria militare in Italia.* Turin, Einaudi; first ed. 1980.

Commission of the the European Communities. 1986. *The European aerospace industry. Trading position and figures,* doc. III/1950/86. Brussels.

EUROSTAT. 1981. *The economic and social position of women in the Community.* Brussels.

———. 1986a. *Employment and unemployment.* Brussels.

———. 1986b. *Earnings in industry and services.* Brussels.

ILO. 1987. *Year Book of Labour Statistics.* Geneva.

ISTAT *(a).* *Annuario Statistico Italiano.* Rome; various issues.

ISTAT *(b).* 1986. *Annuario di Statistiche Industriali.* Rome.

ISTAT *(c).* 1985. *Rilevazione delle Forze di Lavoro.* Rome; Media.

ISTAT *(d).* *Statistiche del Lavoro.* Rome; various issues.

KOMPASS. 1986. *Repertorio Generale dell'Economia Italiana,* 1985/86. Milan.

Stockholm International Peace Research Institute. 1987. *World Armaments and Disarmament: SPIRI Yearbook, 1987.* Oxford, Oxford University Press.

Willett, S. 1988. *The regional and occupational dependence on defence contracting in the Greater London area,* World Employment Programme Research Working Paper; restricted. Geneva, ILO.

Appendix

List of persons interviewed

6 July 1987 – Mr. Enrico della Chiesa, Selenia S.p.a. (Rome)

8 September 1987 – Mr. Giuseppe Grandi, Snia-BPD S.p.a. (Colleferro, Rome)

10 September 1987 – Mr. Enzo Brancaccio and Mr. Giuseppe De Micheli, National Association of Electronic Industries, ANIE (Rome)

6 October 1987 – Mr. Franco Bida, Sistel S.p.a. (Rome)

6 October 1987 – Mr. Francesco Incicco, MES S.p.a. (Rome)

10 October 1987 – Mr. Camillo Pariset, Elettronica S.p.a. (Rome)

Chapter 6

Defence manufacturing employment in Michigan: Possible effects of cuts in procurement

CHRISTOPHER A. GOHRBAND and
JEANNE P. GORDUS

I. Introduction

Research on the consequences of changing public policies has become a consistent feature of economics, sociology and political science, representing a fairly large part of the literature within those disciplines. This topic also interests a subgroup of professional disciplines, for example, administrative studies or urban and regional planning. Various policy decisions, such as the imposition or revocation of certain regulations concerning the environment or public health, have had significant economic effects and raised questions debated at the local, state and national levels. The economic and employment impact of a hypothetical cut in military spending appears and reappears in the literature.

Various currents within political science, economics and sociology have addressed the issue of defence contracting, beginning with the debate in which Kenneth Boulding took a major role (Boulding, 1973; see also, Melman, 1974, Dumas, 1982). The related literature frequently holds that using investment funds for purposes other than defence-related expenditures has more social value for economic reasons, since defence-related investment represents a useless consumption of resources. This area also captured some attention in the early days of the *Journal of Conflict Resolution*.[1] More recently, local impact studies and national impact studies have appeared in important North American journals and elsewhere (Smith, 1977; Glickman, 1977; Kahley, 1982; Thore et al., 1984; Royer, 1986). The general tenor of these articles has been that the removal of a significant portion of defence contracting would have serious negative effects with respect to local defence-based employment. Moreover, within a relatively short period, a ripple effect would be felt, since defence-related contracting is, by definition, not locally consumed. Funds flow

---

[1] Many of the most important issues covered in several years of this journal, particularly Rapoport's analysis of Richardson's theory of the arms race, can be found in Rapoport and Chammah (1965). See also McGuire (1965).

into a local area where production is completed and payment for the produced goods is drawn almost totally from outside the area, bringing in new moneys. The multiplier effect of such defence-related production business and jobs is quite large. Therefore the ripple effect in terms of loss of business, and ultimately jobs, in local suppliers of goods and services to the industry would be substantial and would take place after the first loss. Thereafter, another ripple effect, related to loss of employment and reduction of purchasing power of employees, would be felt in local service and retail establishments. Finally, the loss of public revenue through land and personal taxes, to which would be added the (probably) temporary dependency on some ex-employees on public unemployment adjustment funds would be felt.[2]

Some research on job loss associated with defence-related contract termination appears to reveal, however, that job loss is job loss regardless of the cause (Powell and Driscoll, 1973; Hepworth, 1980). Unfortunately, no research in this area appears to have addressed a crucial question with respect to defence-related job loss, namely whether those who continue career development on public contract work of any kind, which implies significant insecurity, were better able to cope with transitions to new careers, since the possibility of the contract ending and of subsequent jobs loss is ever with them. In a small study of permanent job loss at a major midwestern university, it was clearly demonstrated by the respondents that those who worked on "soft money" or contract-related research had different expectations of career development and were thus better prepared to make career transitions than were colleagues whose jobs had been more secure.

Another area of research addresses the personnel and labour and industrial relations aspects of defence-contracting firms (Hartung, 1983; Hartley and Lynk, 1983; Black and Rothschild, 1985). Defence-contracting firms are different in many respects from other firms and employers. Since United States Department of Defense contractors, like the DoD itself, tend to be rule-keeping organisations and bureaucratically and hierarchically different from other non-defence companies in the same types of enterprise, the results for industrial and labour relations within these companies are important. Finally, there is a genre of polemical literature associated with this field. Some materials, which are not quantitative in approach, have been produced by church and social service groups, particularly the "historic peace churches".

As far as the quantitative approach is concerned, in the 1960s Leontief and his colleagues (Leontief and Hoffenberg, 1961) estimated the effect of an arms cut on the structure of final demand and on the industrial distribution of the labour force in the country as a whole using input-output analysis. Later, a futher step was taken by dividing the country into 19 distinct subregions and

---

[2] There has been considerable debate on this point recently. For an exchange of views about the ripple effect, including costs incurred because of unemployment, see De Grasse Jr. (1983), and Bell and De Grasse Jr. (1983).

assessing the employment consequences of a cut in defence expenditure for each of them (Leontief et al., 1965). While such analyses were interesting at the time, the identification of specific occupations which were particularly vulnerable to reductions was not possible. Therefore, any estimates of the probable outcomes of potential unemployment generated by cuts in defence spending were impossible as well.

For nearly a decade, a small group of researchers has worked in this area, attempting to investigate the impact of increases in defence spending upon different industries, regions, states and demographic groups. Two recent efforts in this area require some mention. Anderson argued that potential positive employment impacts would result from the reallocation of $10,000 million from defence spending into several selected industries producing goods or services for civilian use.[3] The five industries chosen for reduction were those receiving the highest amounts of defence contracts: missiles, ordnance, communications equipment, aircraft and shipbuilding. These resources were theoretically redirected towards conversion projects such as solar energy, gasohol, fishing vessel production and alternative uses other than defence production. The major problem with this approach is that it assumes those alternative uses and assumes the existence of sufficient demand for those products and services.

In a more recent publication, Anderson et al. (1986) turned to a simulation model of the American economy by region. This methodology was an improvement over the earlier approach, and appears to produce a reasonable simulation of the employment effects of government spending. Once again, however, estimates provided by this methodology of the alternative policy impact focused on implausible forms of resource utilisation. Further, it is likely that the job gains forecast as a result of hypothetical reduced military spending were overestimated.

Generally speaking, the literature analysis – which began with one genre of qualitative research somewhat polemical in nature and biased against defence-related expenditures justified for economic rather than moral reasons – appears to have moved on to another sort of biased analysis, to demonstrate the evils of job loss associated with cuts in defence spending. A third stream of studies, not polemical, reviewed various subsets of defence or organisational activities, and narrowed down the analysis so as to prevent any generalisation. The work of Anderson et al. advanced the study of this problem by simulation, using national data, and making an overt case for an extension to regional economies. The analysis revealed that even a modest effort toward careful, detailed research in a specific region would be a major advance in this research area.

---

[3] Anderson (1986). For an occupational assessment by the same group, see Anderson (1979).

II. Rationale for a study of employment impact of defence production in Michigan

The possible impact of a cut in defence spending, rather than speculation on any gains which might be associated with alternative policies, has not been available for relatively small regions of the United States. Michigan is a particularly interesting example for several reasons. Some policy proponents, including Anderson et al., see this heavily industrialised state as a loser in the battle for Federal funds in a defence-oriented era. Certainly the state is no longer the "Arsenal of Democracy". Whether or not other states have been more successful in lobbying for defence funding, defence-related expenditures in Michigan are not nearly as visible as such expenditures in other areas, since contracts are awarded to firms which produce many other kinds of goods and many of the same goods for other customers. Another point of interest is that, over the past decade, Michigan has lost thousands of jobs in durable goods manufacturing. In an economy so hard hit by foreign competition, any potential job loss has serious consequences. Finally, Michigan attempted to develop and implement a local level economic development policy which focused on replacing civilian-related production jobs by government-related production jobs. This study was designed to address these issues.

III. The goals and objectives of the study

The aim of this chapter is to identify those occupational groups most likely to experience displacement as a result of reduced defence expenditure and to assess the difficulties experienced by these groups in adjusting to the employment shift.

The first objective was to determine the degree of dependence of the State of Michigan on defence contracts by identifying the companies in the defence sector and determining their levels of employment.

The second objective was to develop an occupational profile in a small number of selected companies. It was presumed that clerical employees and managerial personnel had a wider range of options available should employment be reduced, since their skills were less specifically tied to types of production. Therefore production and technical and professional personnel were to be the focus of the investigation. In fact, 11 companies were identified and case studies performed for the majority of them. The gender composition of the workforce in the companies which are unionised is known to have been 11 to 89 per cent in 1978 (Needleman and Tanner, 1987), and since women's seniority tends to be lower than that of male co-workers, women's employment share is likely to be somewhat less than 10 per cent now.

The next objective was to develop an occupational profile for the area in order to determine the capacity of the economy to absorb labour displaced from the defence sector.

A final objective was to determine the response of the defence contractor firms to possible reductions in defence spending and the resulting probability of surplus employees. The benefits available both through the companies and from the public sector were issues important to the adjustment of laid-off employees. The availability of special private, public or partnership programming to assist in adjustment was to be considered together with an estimate of potential efficacy. Other strategies for assisting with job replacement were to be considered as well.

IV. Description of the data

The manufacture of products for the United States Department of Defense in Michigan is well integrated into the strengths of Michigan manufacturing capabilities, which lie in the manufacture of car and truck parts and the assembly of finished cars and trucks. There are also significant defence manufacturing activities outside the car and truck industry. These products include components and accessories for aircraft, aircraft navigation equipment and other flight instruments, guns of various sizes, jet engines and turbines for aircraft and Cruise missiles, fire control equipment, communication and detection equipment, etc.

The diversity of products and the integration of defence production with civilian production at many firms are obstacles to the characterisation of the occupational profile of the Michigan defence industry, particularly when using occupational information only about a few firms. The sensitive nature of the companies' employment structure has made occupational data difficult to obtain.

The diversity of products means that a limited number of case studies of firms will inevitably fail to capture the occupational make-up of some branches. The integration of defence production with civilian production means that it is difficult to identify the vulnerability of workers to displacement as defence contracts are reduced. Integration increases the likelihood that workers will be retained to produce civilian products if defence production is cut. If defence cuts cause lay-offs, it is likely that workers will be laid off according to senority rather than occupations, resulting in the lay-off of low skill, low seniority workers. The more highly skilled workers will be retained, because of their ability to adapt to the production of new products. Thus, integration of defence and civilian production makes it impossible to identify precisely the workers who are "dependent" on defence production by the work they do, and complicates the prediction of the occupations likely to be affected by any cuts.

Occupational analysis of the workforce is considered sensitive and proprietary information by companies, even those which provide the total number of employees by detailed occupational category. As labour costs represent a significant part of operating costs, the knowledge of the labour force structure could help a competitor to underbid on contract work. Thus, many companies will not answer the questions of outsiders on this subject.

To cope with these difficulties, we have gathered information about employment in the defence sector and defence contracts in Michigan from a number of sources, including not only the companies, but also unions, federal government publications, and CACI, a private data base service. The Michigan Employment Security Commission (MESC) is our source for data about employment by occupation and region at the state level.

Because the availability of occupational information about firms is limited, the data on defence contracting and the estimated related employment obtained from CACI are particularly important. CACI obtains records of all contract actions between the Department of Defense and private contractors, and organises the data into a computerised data base. For a fee they can produce several kinds of reports. We have obtained two reports, one giving the names and addresses of contracting firms in Michigan and the amounts of their contract actions with the Government for fiscal years 1983 to 1986, in each of 118 product and service categories. The second report uses the data in the first report to provide a more detailed listing of products produced under the same contracts in fiscal year (FY) 1985. The second report lists the products and services produced by Michigan contractors, by the place where the product was made or where the service was performed in FY 1985. It also gives an estimate of the number of jobs supported, directly and indirectly, by the contract actions for that year, for each product, in each location. CACI does not estimate the breakdown of occupations corresponding to the number of jobs.

The estimates of defence-related jobs from CACI are not survey data, they are inferred, using various algorithms, from the data on contract actions. The derivation of these estimates must be explained, if their implications are to be understood. The explanation that follows is based on information provided by CACI.

As noted above, the job estimates are based on contract actions between the Department of Defense and its contractors. The contract data are as accurate as the Government's reporting allows. The contract data are not estimates, they are a record of all transactions (though contracts concerning certain secret products are probably excluded).

To obtain job estimates the contract data to be analysed must be specified. Our report reflects the data for all contractors with Michigan addresses in FY 1985. The contract data are first sorted by place of performance for each product/service code. This sort gives the contract amounts for each product or service in each location. Not all contracts with Michigan addresses are performed in Michigan, so with this sort we can identify the contract sums which were actually spent in Michigan by Michigan contractors. Contractors from outside Michigan also perform contracts here. However, this corresponds to a relatively small amount which can easily be omitted.

The next step is translation of the contract spending by product and service into spending by standard industry codes (SIC). This method of translation was developed by the American Small Business Administration. The contract spending is finally translated into jobs by deflating the spending figures to constant 1977 dollars and applying the deflated spending by SIC code to a matrix developed by the United States Bureau of Labor Statistics, which assigns a direct and indirect jobs impact to expenditure for the products of different industrial sectors. These jobs impacts are allocated back to Michigan defence products and locations according to their share in contract spending.

As a possibility for further research it should be noted that contract spending, translated into SIC codes could be used to study occupational impacts directly if they were linked to a matrix such as the MESC Occupational Employment Statistics (OES) matrix. This matrix is developed from a survey of employers' occupational staffing patterns, and is used to convert forecasts of industrial sales and employment growth by SIC code into occupational employment forecasts.

The direct job estimates from the CACI report are subject to three major limitations:

(1) They are based on contract spending which may show more fluctuation from year to year than employment levels.

(2) They are based on a matrix which gives job impacts across all occupations based on national data; consequently, these impacts must be thought of as averages and not strictly characteristic of the staffing practices of particular contractors.

(3) They are impact estimates and so cannot reflect full current employment, portions of which may be supported by payments received in previous periods or by payments expected in the future.

These estimates must be interpreted as the employment impact of defence spending by product sector, on relatively large labour markets. The most appropriate use for this job impact methodology is to estimate the employment impact of particular permanent increases or decreases in defence contracting. In this report the job estimates will be reported as approximations of the employment levels in locations and product sectors of the Michigan defence manufacturing economy (Appendix).

While these figures are probably an undercount, they should reflect the relative size of defence employment in different sectors, and the order of magnitude of employment in each sector. One advantage of using these estimates is that they are based on the only reliable measure of defence manufacturing activity available, the amounts of defence contract actions. Thus, the employment reported can be confidently used as a conservative estimate of the employment associated with defence spending. Using this methodology avoids the problem of separating defence production and the associated jobs from civilian production and jobs, which is very difficult when both activities are taking place in the same establishments. This report will use only the direct jobs impact, because the goal of this report is to understand the pattern of employment in defence manufacturing in Michigan.

V. Michigan defence manufacturing employment

In the last year for which these figures were published, 1983, the United States Census Bureau's "Shipments to Federal Government Agencies" reported that 15,400 people in all occupations were employed by private manufacturing firms which shipped US$1,800 million worth of goods to the Department of Defense. This employment figure is an estimate based on a random sample survey of manufacturers' staffing levels in different industries. This number (15,400) represents 1.8 per cent of the average 1983 fiscal year manufacturing employment for the State of Michigan, which was 858,000. The total number of people employed in all occupations, producing all categories of products and services in 1985 based on the CACI employment estimates was 19,200, of which 9,300 were considered to be employed in defence manufacturing. This estimate of defence manufacturing employment (9,300) is 0.95 per cent of the average fiscal year 1985 Michigan manufacturing employment of 978,000.

Considering that 15,400 in 1983 may have been an overestimate because it is based on the number of workers in each plant, whether or not all the plant's work is defence related, and that 9,300 may be an underestimate because it is based on one year's defence contracts, the number of workers in defence manufacturing in Michigan may be estimated to be between 1 and 2 per cent of manufacturing employment.

The focus of the main report and of the Appendix is on the production of manufactured goods for defence purposes. In FY 1985 this activity resulted in defence contracts with a value of US$2,170 million in Michigan. Compared with this, research and development activities in Michigan are small, with FY 1985 contracts totalling US$185 million. Ninety-five per cent of this research money goes to private companies for research which is closely associated with the products they make. Five per cent of this money goes to many relatively small research projects at Michigan universities in general science, medicine and other research areas.

The 95 per cent of Michigan research and development contracts to private research may be further broken down. Engine development for missile and space system accounts for 47 per cent of all research and development contract money. This research is associated with the production of gas turbines and jet engines which are not for aircraft. Twenty-seven per cent goes to the tank-automotive area. It is associated with the production of combat assault and tactical vehicles. The remaining 21 per cent goes mainly on electronics and communications equipment. In some cases, this research is less closely associated with specific products.

There is no information about the employment patterns at purely research establishments. The CACI estimates of employment resulting from service contracts are not reliable because of the general difficulty of quantifying activity in the service economy. Some of the professional and technical employment reported in the main body of the report may pick up some of the employment created by research associated with particular products.

VI. Occupations in Michigan's defence manufacturing industries

Additional data collected from seven companies which manufacture goods in 11 major product categories, permit us to make estimates of how Michigan's defence manufacturing employment is divided among five occupational groups. We estimate that defence sector employment consists of:

- 28 per cent managers and clerical workers;
- 16 per cent professional and technical workers;
- 19 per cent craft workers;
- 36 per cent operatives, who are sometimes referred to as general production line workers or semi-skilled workers; and
- 1 per cent unskilled sweepers and labourers.

These estimates are derived by combining the distribution of jobs across the 11 major product categories from the CACI data with the distribution of occupational categories at the firms we surveyed, operating in these product categories. The overall occupational distribution is the average of the firms' occupational distributions weighted by the size of the sector in which each firm operates. The sectors included in the occupational distribution weighting scheme covered 76 per cent of all employment in the defence manufacturing industry in Michigan reported in the CACI report. Thus 24 per cent of employment is in sectors where no company was surveyed.

Supposing a defence manufacturing workforce of the order of 10,000 in 1985, then we estimate that about 2,800 would have been managers or clerical workers, 1,600 professional or technical workers; 1,900 craft workers; 1,600 professional or technical workers; 1,900 craft workers; 3,600 operatives; and 100 would have been unskilled workers. The precision of our data cannot support a more detailed quantitative distribution of employment among occupations.

In table 6.1 the estimates of occupational employment levels in the defence sector are compared with estimates of average annual openings by occupations for the 1980-90 period, published by the MESC. In the first column in table 6.1, the defence employment figures derived above are presented. In the third column, the projected average annual number of openings from the MESC data is presented. The projected openings for each major occupational group is the sum of the openings listed for the occupations in the table. These occupations have been selected as relevant to defence manufacturing from the MESC data. The second column gives the ratio of estimated fiscal year 1985 defence manufacturing employment to the projected openings. The fourth and fifth columns break down the openings into those due to the average expected rate of economic growth and to attrition, respectively.

The ratio in the second column is a simple measure of the size of defence employment relative to annual openings in each occupational group. The ability of the Michigan economy to absorb market entrants from the defence sector depends on the number of other entrants competing for the openings and on

Table 6.1. **Occupational information comparison table**

Occupations	Estimated fiscal year 1985 defence employment	Ratio of defence employment to openings	Average annual projected occupational growth, 1980-90		
			Total annual job openings	Growth openings[1]	Replacement openings[2]
All occupations	10 000	n.a.	n.a.	n.a.	n.a.
Management and clerical	2 800	n.a.	n.a.	n.a.	n.a.
Professional and technical	1 600	0.44	3 610[3]	1 800[3]	1 810[3]
Crafts and related	1 900	0.24	7 910[4]	2 180[4]	5 730[4]
Construction [5]			2 880	870	2 010
Metalworking			2 090	380	1 710
Job and die setters			360	100	260
Machinists			340	90	250
Millwrights			310	80	240
Model makers			90	20	70
Sheet metal workers			220	50	160
Tool and die makers			590	30	560
Other			180	10	170
Mechanics and repair			1 400	560	840
Product inspection			1 550	370	1 180
Operatives	3 600	0.39	9 310[4]	2 700[4]	6 610[4]
Metalworking			3 630	390	3 240
Assemblers			3 180	1 640	1 530
Packing machines			720	20	700
Cutting machines			180	60	120
Painters, manufacturing items			170	− 20	190
Sewing machines [6]			610	280	330
Fork-lift drivers			750	320	430
Miscellaneous manufacturing operatives			70	10	60
Cleaning services	100	0.02	6 570	970	5 600

n.a. = Defence employment category is too broad for meaningful comparison to MESC data.

[1] Projected new openings.   [2] Projected openings created by death, retirement, disability or quitting for personal reasons.   [3] Includes only projected openings for engineers and engineering and science technicians.   [4] Includes only those occupations which are considered relevant to the manufacture of major Michigan defence products.   [5] Includes carpenters, electricians, painters and pipefitters. These crafts are employed in manufacturing plants for plant maintenance.   [6] Includes only non-garment production workers.

the maintenance of the rate of economic growth which underlies the projected openings. A large cut in defence spending could have an effect on the number of actual openings, as well as on defence sector employment. This simple descriptive analysis cannot simulate the labour market to give reasonable estimates of the excess supply of labour that might occur in different situations.

Some occupations may face more difficult circumstances than others in the event of defence cutbacks. Because of the national market for engineers, these professionals would not necessarily suffer due to the slow growth of this occupational category in Michigan. Engineering technicians, such as draughtsmen, would face a more difficult situation because they must cope with the encroachment of automation on their jobs, as well as labour market fluctuations.

The relevant occupations from MESC data on craft and operative occupations have been listed in some detail to describe the occupations included in the more general categories and to show the relative sizes of the openings at a more detailed level. Three factors make the metalworking crafts an object of particular concern. Defence manufacturing employers mentioned these crafts as the largest occupations employing craft workers in their establishments; these crafts require more specialised training than operative positions; thus it is more difficult to switch among these occupations and many of these occupations have a relatively small number of projected openings per year. A large sudden contraction of defence manufacturing could result in an excess supply of labour in some of these occupations.

Of course, the worst possible situation would be a simultaneous cutback in defence contracts in Michigan and a sharp reduction in car and truck sales in the United States. The defence-related displacements would only be a small part of the Michigan unemployment problem in such a case.

It is unlikely that wholesale lay-offs of defence workers due to defence cuts would occur in Michigan. In the largest defence manufacturing sector, combat assault vehicles and trucks, the CACI job estimates presented in the Appendix show that about 2,175 jobs are supported by defence contracts. Vehicular equipment and engine parts account for another 683 and 933 jobs, respectively. While these large concentrations of employment appear vulnerable, many firms in these sectors produce civilian products alongside defence products. In some cases, military vehicles, engines, and equipment are similar to civilian products. The major exception is tanks, which are not similar to civilian products. Much of this employment could be directed toward civilian production in the event of military cutbacks. The technical problem of converting this manufacturing capacity to civilian use would hinge more on appropriate capital equipment than on appropriate skills. The economic problem would be the existence of sufficient demand to justify the conversion of military production to civilian use.

Another factor protecting this sector is the basic need of the armed forces for these products. Trucks and other vehicles are so fundamental to modern armed forces that the number of men under arms in the United States Army would have to shrink significantly to reduce demand for them. The fact that these products are subject to constant use and wear creates a replacement demand which is only indirectly related to the growth of the United States armed forces.

The rest of the defence manufacturing employment in Michigan is spread among a great diversity of products. The Appendix gives a complete accounting of the distribution of employment and contract payments for fiscal year 1985 by product and location, based on the CACI data.

VII. Benefits available to displaced workers in defence manufacturing

The objectives of this section are:

(1) to consider the response of the largest firms to the reductions in the labour force required, were defence contracts to cease;

(2) to consider the response of local agencies of government to these lay-offs; and

(3) to assess the likelihood of economic development efforts to replace jobs.

In order to ascertain how firms holding defence contracts would respond to a surplus of workers should those contracts be terminated, a small survey instrument was developed and presented to personnel/industrial relations managers in 11 of the largest defence contractors in Michigan. These managers were contacted and nine agreed to participate, although only eight of those nine contractors had information of interest to us. The employees of the firms whose managers responded to the survey total more than 3,400 workers, ranging from high-level managers through engineers, technicians, administrators, skilled, semi-skilled, and unskilled workers. It is estimated that when managers, professionals, and clerical workers are excluded, about 2,600 workers remain.

Table 6.2 below provides information on the workers' union status, methods of lay-off, and amount of notice given.

In response to a specific question whether United States Department of Defense requirements imposed any special human resource activities around the lay-off, all respondents said no. The only constraint on the lay-off process of any responding firm was the collective bargaining agreement. It should be emphasised that the selection of the firms for interviewing was based solely upon the amount of their defence contracts and the associated possibility of large numbers of employees. No effort was made to match union and non-union facilities. However, since the majority of the responding firms are not solely defence-oriented and a good fraction of their output is purchased by original equipment manufactures (OEM) in the automotive industry, it is no surprise that the United Auto Workers represent so many unskilled workers in these firms.

VIII. Benefits for the displaced

An important issue in outcomes for unskilled and even skilled workers is the benefit level they can expect upon lay-off. Currently, individuals who have lost employment through no fault of their own are eligible for Unemployment Insurance, the state-federal programme, providing income maintenance for a period of 26 weeks under current circumstances. Depending upon the length of employment and wage level, various payments are made on a bi-weekly basis. On 1 December 1987 these benefits rose to US$223 per week from their previous level of US$197 per week.

Table 6.2. **Union status, method of lay-off and advance notification in defence contracting firms in Michigan**

Company	Union	Lay-off method	Advance notice
A	UAW	Reverse seniority by job class	3 days
B	UAW	Reverse seniority	24 hours
C	UAW	Reverse seniority	1-7 days
D	None	No reverse seniority	1 hour
E	UAW	Reverse seniority	? hours/unskilled 2 days/skilled
F	None	Criteria: 1. Performance 2. Seniority	2 weeks
G	UAW	Reverse seniority	24 hours
H	UAW	Reverse seniority	72 hours

Some workers represented by the UAW have severance payments due to them when there is a permanent lay-off. More common, however, is the Supplemental Unemployment Benefit (SUB), a company-funded addition to the American federal-state unemployment insurance system. Each worker entitled to SUB becomes eligible upon lay-off to cash in 52 weekly installments (52 SUB credits). SUB is intended to pay the difference in weekly income between unemployment insurance and the benefit the employee is eligible for under the SUB programme, for one year. Workers with at least ten years of seniority are guaranteed the maximum benefit. Under the maximum benefit each credit provides 95 per cent of the weekly base wage rate for a 40-hour week minus US$12, adjusted for unemployment insurance payments.

In contrast to high-seniority workers, workers with less than ten years of seniority draw from another fund which is variable, not guaranteed, and heavily dependent upon the prosperity of the company. The funding mechanism of SUB required by the collective bargaining agreements prescribes a certain sum to be allotted (now about US$0.35/hour) for every hour worked by every union-represented employee in the firm. Amounts drawn by low seniority employees on lay-off depend upon the condition of the fund, and can range from the maximum available to high-seniority employees (almost complete income replacement for one year) to just a few dollars per SUB credit.

Other issues of interest are whether health benefits continue for any period after termination and whether a vested or portable pension plan is present. In table 6.3 we show data from the responding firms on these issues.

The data in table 6.3 indicate that SUB is not available to all UAW-represented workers. Generally, only very large employers offer SUB. We estimate that about 20 per cent of the 5,600 craft workers, operatives, and cleaning service workers in table 6.1 are eligible for SUB.

The underlying rationale for SUB is that the employer has an important stake in retaining through that income maintenance a tie with the laid-off

Table 6.3.   Post-termination benefits reported by defence contracting firms in Michigan

Company	Severance payment	SUB	Health benefits	Vested pension	Portable pension
A	No	No	6 months	Yes if over 10 years	No
B	No	No	Several weeks?	Sometimes	No
C	No for hourly	No	Yes	No	No
D	Depends on service	No	Yes	No	No
E	No	Yes	Yes	Yes	Yes
F	Yes	No	No	Sometimes	No
G	No	No	Yes	Yes	No
H	Yes	Yes	Yes	Yes if over 10 years	No

employee which will make the employee available for work at a moment's notice. Income security and work availability are benefits of the SUB to the union and workers and to the employers as well. Generally, the probability of stability of employment within the company for those concerned by potential cuts in defence spending is higher in larger companies, with a larger product market, that also have collective bargaining agreements, including SUB.

Personal decision-making based upon post-termination income levels will differ, depending upon whether SUB is available or not. There are differences between communities where the majority of workers have SUB compared with communities where more limited income-maintenance is available to the majority of those laid off, since a community with a majority of SUB-supported unemployed individuals may feel little or no economic effect of the lay-offs for one year. The former income level of those individuals is nearly maintained, and purchasing power remains nearly the same as before. However, individuals with these levels of benefits, which can exceed the wages of available open jobs in the community, often do not look for new work until all benefits are exhausted. This delay often increases their difficulties in searching for and successfully finding new employment after such a long period.

It appears that the employees of many firms have their pensions vested after a specified period of time. Interestingly, the question of health benefit continuation uncovered some lack of knowledge on the part of some of our respondents regarding the provisions of a new federal law requiring that employees have the privilege of continuing their health coverage for a period of time at their own (reduced) cost.

Inquiries were also made about programmes the companies would plan to implement in case of major lay-offs due to discontinuation of a defence contract. With a few minor exceptions, no programmes were planned. The exceptions were for career counselling should there be a very large lay-off.

In summary, the companies involved in defence contracting in Michigan do not have special protective policies toward terminated employees.

Indeed, the length of notice provided and the absence of some lay-off benefits suggest that, although some firms mention that an upturn would result in their recalling some laid-off employees – a feature of collective agreements – no attempt would be made to retain this pool of workers for new defence contracts or for transfer to other departments within the establishment. Therefore, it seems clear that most employees laid off due to contract termination would face the normal unemployment situation encountered by most citizens. No special protection or programmes are available.

It is true, however, that Title III of the Job Training Partnership Act (JTPA) authorises the development and implementation of special adjustment programmes for which laid-off employees from these defence contractors would be eligible. However, not many local areas routinely operate such programmes on a scale to accommodate relatively large numbers. Unless either the company, the union, or both the company and union in a joint programme, join with local providers and request funds in case of large lay-offs, no programmes would be available for job retraining or placement. The UAW has recently been the most active of all United States industrial unions in such efforts. It is safe to estimate that, should all the contractors lose their defence work, some efforts would be made. Generally, however, the record of most recent United States job training programmes for the unemployed has been rather ambiguous. About 6-7 per cent of those eligible each year have been served and, nationwide, the placement rate has been 69 per cent (US General Accounting Office, 1987). This rate does not compare particularly favourably with the unassisted re-employment of dislocated workers across the United States. The Bureau of Labor Statistics of the United States Department of Labor arranged for the collection of survey data about those who suffered permanent job loss from 1979 to 1984. Among those who fell into this group who were questioned in June 1984, 60.1 per cent were re-employed, virtually all of them finding jobs without assistance (Pogursky and Swaim, 1987).

Although it seems likely that some of those who could lose employment might receive some special assistance, the degree to which that assistance would permit them to become re-employed much more rapidly and/or at a much better wage rate than they would have obtained without such assistance is not clear.

Another strategy to assist the general economic well-being of the local areas was much discussed during the trough of the 1980-83 recession, namely the support of active efforts to help local companies compete successfully to gain new federal contracts, including defence. This was planned as a dual marketing thrust, marketing new companies to the Department of Defense and other departments, and marketing the idea of becoming a federal or defence contractor to companies not engaged in that arena. Knowledgeable developers in Michigan indicate that this initiative has not been successful. The focus has shifted toward helping companies with such contracts to retain them or expand activities, not in bringing new companies and the Department of Defense together. Numerous barriers have already been mentioned by one recently surveyed group of employers in response to questions about defence contracting. The complexity of the bidding process, the burden of federal regulations, special rules thought to be associated with defence and other federal work, the disclosure of company information thought to be required, and new and different personnel policies are all mentioned as reasons to avoid dealing with any federal agency. Summed up as "red tape", these barriers, which are sometimes present in minds in Michigan rather than in agencies in Washington, have been a factor in limiting Michigan federal contracting mostly to those establishments which have long had such associations.

In summary, those whose employment depends upon defence contracts in Michigan would, should the contracts be terminated, receive less than a week's notification, would have Unemployment Insurance payments for 26 weeks, would have access to self-funded continuation of health benefits at a lower than average cost, and if they have ten years or more of service would have about a 60-75 per cent chance of having their pension vested and secure. One-fifth of them would receive Supplemental Unemployment Benefit payments. Otherwise, they would be required to compete without any special assistance for employment in an area with a surplus of semi-skilled and unskilled workers.

References

Anderson, M. 1979. *The impact of military spending on the machinists union*, in a Report of Employment Research Associates. Lansing, Michigan; 16 pp.

———. 1986. *Converting the work force*. A Report of Employment Research Associates. Lansing, Michigan; 16 pp.

Anderson, M., et al. 1986. *The empty pork barrel: The employment cost of the military build-up 1981-1985*, in a Report of Employment Research Associates. Lansing, Michigan; 17 pp.

Black, R.; Rothschild, E. 1985. "The effect of United States defense spending on employment and output", in *International Labour Review* (Geneva), Nov.-Dec., Vol. 124, No. 6, pp. 677-697.

Boulding, K. 1973. "The impact of the defense industry on the structure of the economy", in B. Udis (ed.): *The economic consequences of reduced military spending*. Lexington, Massachusetts, Lexington Books; pp. 225-252.

De Grasse, Jr., R. W. 1983. "Military spending and jobs", in *Challenge*, the magazine of economic affairs (Armonk, New York), July-Aug., Vol. 26, No. 3, pp. 4-14.

Dumas, L. J. 1982. *The political economy of arms reduction*. Boulder, Colorado, University of Colorado Press.

Glickman, N. J. 1977. *Econometric analysis of regional systems*. New York, Academic Press.

Hartley, K.; Lynk, E. 1983. "Budget cuts and public sector employment: The case of defense", in *Applied Economics* (London), Aug., Vol. 15, No. 4, pp. 531-540.

Hartung, B. 1983. "Would a nuclear freeze bomb the economy?", in *Business and Society Review* (New York), Fall, No. 47, pp. 34-39.

Hepworth, S. J. 1980. "Moderating factors of the psychological impact of unemployment", in *Journal of Occupational Psychology* (Letchworth, Herts.), Vol. 13, pp. 139-145.

Kahley, W. J. 1982. "Southern fireworks: Will defense spending light up the south?", in *Economic Review*, Dec., Vol, 67, No. 12, pp. 21-31.

Leontief, W., et al. 1961. "The economic effects of disarmament", in *Scientific American* (New York), Apr., pp. 43-52.

Leontief, W. et al. 1965. "The economic impact – industrial and regional – of an arms cut", in *The Review of Economics and Statistics* (Oxford), Aug., Vol. XLVII, No. 3, pp. 217-241.

McGuire, M. C. 1965. *Secrecy and the arms race*. Cambridge, Massachusetts, Harvard University Press.

Melman, S. 1974. *The permanent war economy: American capitalism in decline*. New York, Simon and Schuster.

Needleman, R.; Tanner, L. D. 1987. "Women in unions: Current issues", in K. Shallcross Koziara et al. (eds.): *Working women: Past, present, future*, Industrial Relations Research Association Series. Washington, DC, Bureau of National Affairs, p. 192.

Pogursky, M.; Swaim. P. 1987. "Job displacement and earnings loss, evidence from the displaced worker survey", in *Industrial and Labor Relations Review* (Ithaca, New York), Oct., Vol. 41, 1, pp. 17-29.

Powell, D. H.; Driscoll, P. J. 1973. "Middle class professionals face unemployment", in *Society* (New Brunswick, New Jersey), Vol. 10, pp. 18-26.

Rapoport, A. A.; Chammah, A. 1965. *Prisoner's dilemma*. Ann Arbor, University of Michigan Press.

Royer, J. 1986. "The long-term employment impact of disarmament policies: Some findings from an econometric model", in *International Labour Review*, Geneva, May-June, Vol. 125, No. 3, pp. 279-303.

Smith, R. P. 1977. "Military expenditures and capitalism", in *Cambridge Journal of Economics* (Cambridge, UK), No. 1, pp. 61-76.

Thore, S. G., et al. 1984. "Effects of defense spending on the Texas economy", in *Journal of Policy Modeling* (New York), Nov., Vol. 6, No. 4, pp. 573-586.

US General Accounting Office. 1987. *Dislocated workers: Local programs and outcomes under the Job Training Partnership Act*; Mar.; Washington, DC, GAO/HRD 87-41, pp. 15-19.

Appendix

Products of Michigan defence contractors by location, with contract payments and estimated jobs supported in order of the highest number of jobs supported to the lowest, 1985

Product	City	Estimated no. of jobs supported	Contract payments (US$'000)
Grand total, all locations and products		9 301.0	2 173 281
Ground attack vehicles, motor vehicles, trailers and cycles Total		2 175.3	1 442 813
Trucks and truck tractors, wheeled	Iron Mountain	25.3	3 775
	Pontiac	825.4	3 775
Combat assault and tactical vehicle	Warren	778.4	249 646
	Centerline	230.1	110 528
	Troy	275.1	653 668
Unattributed cities/products		41.0	4 963
Engines, turbines and components Total		1 436.0	273 501
Gas reciprocating engine (not for aircraft)	Farmington	15.5	1 605
Diesel engines and components	Roseville	66.2	7 716
	Muskegon	80.0	9 330
	Muskegon	257.5	146 508
	Romulus	133.3	15 531
	Detroit	396.3	46 180
Gas turbines and jet engines (not for aircraft)	Walled Lake	93.5	9 089
Gas turbines and jet engines for aircraft	Kalamazoo	18.9	1 837
	Grandville	32.9	3 202
	Muskegon	56.8	5 515
	Whitehall	109.2	10 604
	Troy	41.5	4 033
	Romulus	35.6	3 464
	Taylor	15.7	1 529
Unattributed cities/products		83.1	7 358
Weapons Total		700.2	27 969
Guns, up to 30 mm	Grand Rapids	14.0	1 236
	Lexington	13.6	1 201
Guns, from 75 mm to 125 mm	Warren	352.3	12 137
	Mount Clemens	38.9	1 342
	Sterling Heights	197.6	6 809
Unattributed cities/products		82.8	5 244

Product	City	Estimated no. of jobs supported	Contract payments (US$'000)
Vehicle equipment			
Total		683.0	66 528
Vehicle cab, body, frame, stuctural components	Mancelona	30.8	3 284
	Saginaw	12.8	1 365
Vehicle power transmission components	Sterling Heights	19.4	1 886
	Rochester	22.4	2 175
	Troy	30.7	2 989
	Garden City	56.5	5 489
Vehicle brake, steering, axle and wheel components	Warren	11.8	1 376
	Owosso	22.5	2 630
	Plymouth	22.6	2 638
Vehicle furniture and accessories	Tecumseh	39.4	3 244
	Roseville	21.0	1 732
	Detroit	40.4	3 326
Miscellaneous vehicle components	Mount Clemens	20.0	1 870
	Roseville	15.0	1 404
	Inkster	13.8	1 298
Unattributed cities/products		303.9	29 822
Instruments and laboratory equipment			
Total		627.6	51 732
Navigational instruments	Grand Rapids	272.7	23 177
Flight instruments	Grand Rapids	87.3	7 165
Auto-pilot mechanisms and airborne gyroscopes	Kalamazoo	31.9	2 863
	Grand Rapids	83.9	7 526
Electrical and electronic measuring instruments	Troy	44.7	2 958
Pressure, temperature, humidity instruments	Boyne City	24.2	1 874
Unattributed cities/products		82.9	6 169
Aircraft components and accessories			
Total		589.4	53 442
Helicopter rotor blades-drive mechanism	Warren	17.9	1 742
Aircraft landing gear components	Troy	13.4	1 296
	Livonia	20.1	1 946
Aircraft wheel and brake systems	Saint Joseph	15.7	1 680
Hydraulic de-icing equipment for aircraft	Kalamazoo	352.6	33 878
	Warren	21.9	2 107
Parachute recovery systems and tie-down equipment	Southfield	13.0	771
	Cadillac	81.8	4 832
Miscellaneous aircraft accessories components	Kalamazoo	13.9	1 337
	Grand Rapids	13.2	1 263
Unattributed cities/products		25.9	3 590

Product	City	Estimated no. of jobs supported	Contract payments (US$'000)
Engine accessories			
Total		325.5	27 964
Engine fuel systems components (not for aircraft)	Mancelona	31.9	3 089
	Roseville	21.0	2 038
	Romulus	23.5	2 281
Engine electrical system components (not for aircraft)	Bay City	23.5	1 620
	Roseville	14.7	1 011
	Farmington	23.9	1 645
Miscellaneous engine accessories for aircraft	Kalamazoo	20.6	1 937
	Dearborn	12.6	1 190
Unattributed cities/products		153.8	13 153
Fire control equipment			
Total		286.7	24 558
Fire control-computing equipment, sights and devices	Grand Rapids	23.3	2 018
Fire control systems, complete	Sterling Heights	139.2	12 121
Optical sighting and ranging equipment	Sterling Heights	46.2	3 919
Fire control radar (not for aircraft)	Grand Rapids	51.5	4 159
Unattributed cities/products		26.5	2 241
Furniture			
Total		278.0	17 983
Office furniture	Holland	37.3	2 584
	Grand Rapids	107.6	7 455
	Zeeland	65.2	4 519
Miscellaneous furniture and fixtures	Holland	28.5	1 309
	Grand Rapids	16.3	751
Unattributed cities/products		23.1	1 365
Modification of equipment			
Total		258.2	20 508
Modification of aircraft	Grand Rapids	28.6	2 757
Modification of aircraft components	Grand Rapids	168.4	16 175
Modification of miscellaneous equipment	Grand Rapids	42.2	2 202
Unattributed cities/products		19.0	107
Communications, detection and coherent radiation equipment			
Total		231.0	19 235
Communications and security equipment and components	Grand Haven	19.7	1 673
Aircraft radio navigation equipment	Grand Rapids	99.1	8 141
Radar equipment other than airborne	Jackson	43.4	3 625
Underwater sound equipment	Jackson	23.0	2 097
Unattributed cities/products		45.8	3 699

Product	City	Estimated no. of jobs supported	Contract payments (US$'000)
Aircraft launching, landing and ground handling equipment			
Total		185.6	15 205
Airfield special trucks and trailers	Mount Clemens	162.6	13 111
Unattributed cities/products		23.0	2 094
Maintenance and repair shop equipment			
Total		183.6	13 273
Motor vehicle maintenance equipment	Saint Joseph	46.9	2 982
	Troy	16.2	1 034
Aircraft maintenance and repair shop equipment	Grand Rapids	13.6	1 098
Lubrication and fuel dispensing equipment	Sterling Heights	41.5	3 348
Unattributed cities/products		65.4	4 811
Electrical and electronic equipment components			
Total		150.9	12 565
Circuit breakers	Jackson	12.8	923
Relays and solenoids	Troy	50.2	4 154
Antennas, waveguides and related equipment	Grand Haven	36.6	3 286
Unattributed cities/products		51.3	4 202
Automated data processing equipment, software, supplies and support equipment			
Total		123.5	7 268
Automated data processing equipment configuration	Benton Harbor	19.2	1 257
Automated data processing software	Ann Arbor	18.1	893
Automated data processing components	Grand Rapids	44.0	3 058
Unattributed cities/products		42.2	2 060
Aircraft and airframe structural components			
Total		121.1	11 690
Airframe structural components	Grand Rapids	108.9	10 488
Unattributed cities/products		12.2	1 202
Textile, leather, fur and other materials			
Total		112.5	7 241
Tents and tarpaulins	Standish	112.5	7 241
Unattributed cities/products		0.0	0
Mechanical power transmission equipment			
Total		107.3	9 403
Gear, pulley, sprocket and transmission chain	Warren	14.7	1 194
Miscellaneous power transmission equipment	Roseville	30.9	2 863
	Melvindale	19.5	1 815
Unattributed cities/products		42.2	3 531

Product	City	Estimated no. of jobs supported	Contract payments (US$'000)
Containers, packaging and packing supplies			
Total		103.2	11 866
Ammunition and nuclear ordnance boxes	Saline	33.2	4 366
Special shipping and storage containers	Livonia	65.0	6 920
Unattributed cities/products		5.0	580
Pipe, tubing, hose and fittings			
Total		81.3	6 361
Fittings-hose, pipe and tube	Jackson	45.7	3 746
Unattributed cities/products		35.6	2 615
Ammunition and explosives			
Total		81.0	10 724
Ammunition over 125 mm	Saint Joseph	22.2	3 056
	Port Huron	19.4	2 668
Torpedo inert components	Grand Rapids	14.9	2 048
Unattributed cities/products		24.5	2 952
Books, maps and other publications			
Total		67.0	4 279
Miscellaneous printed matter	Grand Rapids	65.4	4 164
Unattributed cities/products		1.6	115
Fire-fighting, rescue and safety equipment			
Total		66.6	6 036
Fire-fighting equipment	Grand Rapids	53.7	4 827
Unattributed cities/products		12.9	1 209
Medical, dental and veterinary equipment and supplies			
Total		62.9	6 930
Drugs, biological and official reagents	Kalamazoo	27.9	3 500
	Keego Harbor	15.5	1 951
Unattributed cities/products		19.5	1 479
Electric wire and power distribution equipment			
Total		61.9	4 626
Electrical generators and generator sets	Roseville	32.3	2 472
Unattributed cities/products		29.6	2 154
Bearings			
Total		51.6	5 270
Bearings, anti-friction, unmounted	Muskegon	38.2	3 879
Unattributed cities/products		13.4	1 391

Product	City	Estimated no. of jobs supported	Contract payments (US$'000)
Materials handling equipment			
Total		48.7	4 411
Winches, hoists, cranes and derricks	Iron Mountain	33.3	3 195
Unattributed cities/products		15.4	1 216
Hand tools			
Total		34.3	2 681
Hand tools non-edged, non-powered	Saginaw	12.6	1 021
Unattributed cities/products		21.7	1 660
Guided missiles			
Total		31.9	2 514
Guided missile handling service equipment	Ann Arbor	12.6	1 034
Unattributed cities/products		19.3	1 480
Household and commercial furnishings and appliances			
Total		21.8	1 959
Household and commercial utility containers	Bronson	11.9	1 072
Unattributed cities/products		9.9	887
Measuring tools			
Total		13.4	1 013
Gauges and precision layout tools	Livonia	12.3	920
Unattributed cities/products		1.1	93

Chapter 7

The INF Treaty and the United States experience: The industrial, economic and employment impact

GREGORY BISCHAK and MICHAEL ODEN

I. Introduction

The ratification of the Intermediate-Range Nuclear Forces Treaty (INF) represented a major breakthrough in East-West arms control efforts. For the first time two entire classes of nuclear weapons systems will be eliminated and an extensive and rigorous verification process put in place to ensure Treaty compliance. The Treaty received strong support in the USSR, in the NATO alliance and the Warsaw Pact countries, and even sailed through the normally contentious United States Senate ratification process with relative ease.

However, the immediate implications of the INF Treaty for significantly reducing military spending must be kept in perspective. Over 95 per cent of the United States and Soviet nuclear arsenals will be left intact after INF systems are dismantled. The United States will only reduce the number of its deployed nuclear warheads by less than 4 per cent[1] and rapid modernisation of strategic and tactical nuclear weapons systems continues. Demand for the manufacture of missile systems and support equipment remains robust. Also, the United States Pershing II and Ground-Launched Cruise Missiles banned by the Treaty were at the end of their production cycles, so the Treaty will have little direct impact on procurement demand from major missile manufacturing firms.

Given these realities, the economic impact of the INF Treaty on contractors and regions producing INF regulated systems is likely to be quite modest. Moreover, the continuing high demand for missile and weapons systems suggests that there will be little incentive to convert existing missile production facilities to civilian use in the near term. On the other hand, the ratification the INF treaty may pave the way for future agreements which could substantially reduce military forces and allow for major reductions in military

---

[1] Estimate based on the ratio of total warheads removed from INF regulated systems to the total number of strategic and and intermediate range nuclear warheads deployed in 1987 as reported by Robert S. Norris and William M. Arkin: "Nuclear notebook", in *Bulletin of the Atomic Scientists*, May 1988, p. 56.

expenditures. In this context, a systematic analysis of the economic impact of INF can provide useful insights into the effects of more extensive disarmament and highlight some important features of the conversion problem for United States defence sectors.

The aim of this chapter is to analyse the national and regional economic impact of the INF Treaty. Specifically, after detailing the basic requirements and time frame of the Treaty it will address five related issues: (1) how the implementation of the Treaty will affect military purchases from private sector firms; (2) what effects the cancellation of INF regulated weapons systems will have on the defence divisions of the principal private contractors; (3) how the reduced demand from INF contract cancellations will affect regional output, income and employment in states where the principal contractors are located; (4) the impact on occupational employment that can be expected from these cuts in expenditure; and (5) the lessons that can be drawn from the INF experience about the nature of the United States defence market and the barriers and possibilities for conversion to civilian activities.

II. The INF Treaty's implementation requirements and time frame

The INF agreement stipulates that the United States and the USSR eliminate all short-range missiles (500-1,000 kilometres) and intermediate-range missiles (1,000-5,500 kilometres), their launchers and certain support facilities. The Treaty, which was ratified by the United States Senate in June 1988, calls for the elimination of all missile systems in the 500-5,500 km range in periods varying from 18 months to three years.[2] Therefore, by June 1991, all INF regulated systems must be removed and destroyed; 1988-91 will be referred to as the implementation period, when the expenditure changes affecting the private sector and the related economic impact will be most pronounced. Once the elimination of these missile systems is completed, both procurement cost savings and costs incurred for verification will level off to a "steady state" in 1992, and should remain stable over the remaining ten years that active treaty verification is required.

The Treaty requires the elimination of three United States missile systems: the short-range Pershing IA, the intermediate-range Pershing II, and the intermediate-range BGM-109G or Ground-Launched Cruise Missile (GLCM). Since the Pershing IA was already scheduled for mothballing, and since none of its components can be reused, its elimination will have little impact on expenditures or procurement demand. The production and procurement of Pershing II systems was completed in fiscal year (FY) 1986 so the Treaty does not cause the cancellation of actual missile procurement outlays for this

---

[2] US Department of State: *Treaty between the United States of America and the Union of Soviet Socialist Republics on the elimination of their intermediate-range and shorter-range missiles*, Selected Documents No. 25, No. 9555, Dec. 1987, p. 3.

system.[3] Unlike the other two systems, the procurement and production cycle for GLCMs was not completed at the time the Treaty was signed. Funding was rescinded for 37 GLCMs scheduled for production in fiscal year 1988, as well as a large number of W-84 warheads being produced in the same year to arm the full GLCM force.

Under the Treaty, all of these completed missiles, launchers (both deployed and non-deployed), and support facilities must be destroyed or dismantled by 1991. However, what is obvious only from a close reading of the Treaty Protocol is that many components of the GLCM and Pershing II systems can be recovered and reused on other weapons systems. Components which can clearly be salvaged and reused before these systems are destroyed include:

– guidance, electronics and control systems from the GLCM missile, and Pershing II re-entry stage;

– the W-84 warheads from the GLCM and W-85 warheads from the Pershing II, including all nuclear materials which can be removed and reused;

– the 76 Launch Control Centres for use with the GLCM are not explicitly considered "support equipment" under the Treaty Destruction Protocol and can be reused or transformed.

A more controversial issue is the plan to transfer complete sets of unassembled missile parts produced under GLCM contracts to the production of nuclear armed Sea-Launched Cruise Missiles (SLCM). The status of these unassembled components is unclear at the time of writing and may have to be resolved by the Special Verification Commission, a special entity set up to arbitrate Treaty disputes.[4]

The Treaty's implementation and verification requirements also have implications for the level of defence expenditures and the economic effects flowing from these changes in expenditures. For the first time in the history of arms agreements between the United States and the USSR an extensive regime of inspection, verification and monitoring has been established.

The United States has established an On-Site Inspection Agency (OSIA) and funded a variety of additional activities to meet INF Treaty inspection and verification requirements. The OSIA has primary responsibility for all inspections in the Soviet Union and purchasing, operating and maintaining the monitoring station which is being installed at Votkinsk, near the Ural mountains.

Aside from OSIA costs, other existing defence agencies and services will receive funding to carry out other Treaty-related implementation and

[3] *Program acquisition costs by weapons system*, Department of Defense Budget for Fiscal Years 1988 and 1989, Jan. 1987, p. 53.

[4] Jeffery Smith: "Defense Department applies new math to missiles", in *Washington Post*, 8 Feb. 1989, p. A-25. More recently the referral of this matter to the Special Verification Commission was confirmed in a telephone conversation with Ronald Bartek of the US Department of State, the Politico-Military Affairs Branch, 17 March 1989.

verification requirements. By far the largest expenditure item outside of the OSIA budget is classified and unspecified expenditures which are probably related to the use of national technical means to monitor Treaty compliance.

III. The impact of the INF Treaty on military purchases from private contractors

An estimate of the net cost savings attributable to the INF agreement can be derived from a close analysis of the specific provisions of the Treaty, the production cycles of systems banned by INF and of those missile and weapons systems which could absorb components not eliminated under the Treaty. The purpose of deriving these estimates is to calculate the savings in military procurement and in operations and maintenance, relative to the baseline expenditures that would have been required had the Treaty not been implemented. These savings are then broken down further to isolate those concrete reductions in military expenditures in the United States which will lead to reduced final demand from the private firms producing the systems regulated by the INF Treaty. These calculations in turn allow us to estimate the impact on major systems contractors and to determine how the Treaty will affect regional economic activity and employment.

Table 7.1 below details the actual savings in terms of reduced military purchases from the private sector made possible by the INF Treaty. These cost savings are estimated for the Treaty implementation period, fiscal years 1988-91. This three-year implementation period includes the last six months of fiscal year 1988, the two full fiscal years 1989 and 1990, and the first six months of fiscal year 1991. Average annual cost savings are also estimated for the subsequent steady state period fiscal years 1992-2001. These estimates reflect the annual average savings that will accrue in each of the last ten years of active Treaty verification. All estimates in the following tables are expressed in constant 1987 dollars.

The first set of cost savings are the direct reductions in expenditure on weapons procurement attributable to the Treaty. As line 1 in table 7.1 indicates, savings on direct weapons procurement are concentrated in fiscal year 1988 when outlays were rescinded for 37 GLCMs and an estimated 155-191 accompanying W-84 warheads.

With the ratification of the INF Treaty, production of the W-84 warheads was officially terminated, but production probably ended with the signing of the INF Treaty by President Reagan and General Secretary Gorbachev.[5] The Natural Resources Defense Council estimates that between 150 to 200 were not produced out of a planned total of 500 W-84 nuclear

---

[5] The termination of the W-84 warhead production with the signing of the INF Treaty was indicated by David Stevens, Acquisitions Divisions, Office of the Secretary of Defense, as confirmed by the Atomic Energy Section of the Office of the Secretary of Defense, in a phone conversation of 17 March 1989 with Gregory Bischak.

Table 7.1. *Savings in military purchases from the implementation of the INF Treaty (millions of 1987 dollars, fiscal years)*

	Implementation period				Steady state, 1992-2001
	1988 (6 month)	1989	1990	1991 (6 month)	
1. Direct savings on weapons procurement					
A. *GLCM and Pershing II related procurement savings*					
GLCM missile procurement reductions (−37 FY 1988)	68.14	0.00	0.00	0.00	0.00
Cost savings from reduced W-84 warhead production (range based on 155-191 warheads cancelled)	243.13-278.03	0.00	0.00	0.00	0.00
GLCM research and development savings	4.81	0.93	0.00	0.00	0.00
GLCM modification and spares savings	28.87	27.93	27.93	13.96	27.93
Pershing II modification and spares savings	10.20	13.96	21.26	14.28	27.81
B. *Transfer of GLCM components to SLCM programme*					
Reuse of GLCM guidance, electronics and control equipment (from 442 missiles to be eliminated)	73.67	147.33	147.33	73.67	0.00
Transfer of unassembled GLCM parts to SLCM programme	0.00	109.72	0.00	0.00	0.00
Sub-total A and B	428.82-463.72	299.87	196.52	101.91	55.73
2. Savings on operation and maintenance and military construction					
A. *GLCM O & M and military construction savings*					
GLCM O & M savings	27.91	40.03	59.26	39.25	97.74
GLCM military construction savings	74.11	0.00	0.00	0.00	0.00
B. *Pershing II O & M savings*	6.74	17.69	30.41	21.56	55.85
Sub-total A and B	108.76	57.71	89.67	60.81	153.59
Total cost savings from reduced military purchases	537.58-672.48	357.58	286.19	162.72	209.32

Lines may not total due to rounding.

Sources: US General Accounting Office, *INF Treaty: Cost of weapons systems to be destroyed and possible savings*, Mar. 1988, pp. 1-6, and Congressional Budget Office, "Letter to Senator Jesse Helms from James L. Blum, Acting Director of the Congressional Budget Office", 28 Mar. 1988, table 1.

warheads.[6] Testimony in congressional hearings indicates that logistical planning for the GLCM was to provide support for only 464 of the 597 missiles which were to be produced.[7] Logistical planning might provide a reasonable ceiling for warhead production planning. Given that 309 missiles were deployed in Western Europe, this would imply that 155 warheads were not produced. However, warhead reliability testing requirements would probably call for some additional production, so a ceiling of 500 warheads might also be reasonable. Accordingly, these warhead production ceilings, less actual deployments, suggest that between 155 and 191 warheads were not produced.

The total programme cost for the W-84 nuclear warhead is reported to have been US\$630 million in 1983, or US\$727.8 million in 1987 dollars.[8] If the planned production ceiling for the W-84 was 464, this implies a unit cost of approximately US\$1.57 million per warhead. By contrast, if the production ceiling was 500, this implies a unit cost of US\$1.46 million.

Given this estimate, savings on missile procurement in fiscal year 1988 equal over US\$68 million and the cancellation of warhead production yields savings of between US\$243 and US\$278 million. Modest savings totalling US\$44 million in 1988 will also be obtained from cancelling planned outlays for GLCM research and development and contracts for modification and spare parts for the GLCM and Pershing II. Continued savings in these three areas will average over US\$50 million per year during the implementation period, and US\$55.7 million per year over the steady state period.

Another source of substantial savings in weapons procurement appears in the form of reduced procurement costs in the SLCM programme. In table 7.1 the first line of savings in this category stems from the reuse of GLCM guidance, electronics and control components in SLCM missiles currently under production. Discussions with United States and Soviet officials involved with arms control indicated that if these components from all 442 Treaty-regulated GLCMs are reused, this could amount to a total saving of approximately US\$442 million.[9] Since these components are removed and recycled as GLCMs are eliminated over the implementation period, these savings are averaged over 1988-91. Average annual savings would equal US\$147.3 million over the three-year period. The reuse of parts from unassembled GLCMs in the SLCM

---

[6] See Thomas Cochran, William Arkin and Robert Stan Norris: "Nuclear warheads and the INF Treaty", in *Summit Watch Background Brief No. 3*, Natural Resources Defense Council, Washington, DC, Dec. 1987.

[7] *Hearings on HR 1748* (National Defense Authorization Act, FY 1988-9), US House of Representatives, 100th Congress, First Session, Mar. 3-26, 1987, pp. 391-392.

[8] See *Department of Defense Appropriations, FY 1982*, Hearings Before a Subcommittee of the Committee on Appropriations, House of Representatives, 97th Congress, 1st Session, p. 749.

[9] A breakdown of the average cost of a GLCM guidance and control systems was estimated to be about \$1 million for each missile and was based on an analysis of the industrial distribution of GLCM outlays in W. Thomas et al.: *The defense translator*, Institute For Defense Analysis, Alexandria, Virginia, June, 1984, p. IV-83. In addition, the million dollar figure was verified in personal corespondence with Dr. Bryon Doenges of the Arms Control and Disarmament Agency and through conversations at the ILO Conference with Mr. Kromov, a Soviet representative at the INF negotiations.

programme would generate an additional US$109.7 million savings in 1987 dollars. Because the issue of reuse of these unassembled parts had to be settled by the Special Verification Commission, these savings would not accrue until 1989.

Adding up these categories, total direct weapons-procurement savings will be between US$428.8 and US$463.7 million in 1988. Average annual direct savings on procurement will amount to between US$342.4 and US$354 million over the three-year implementation period. Subsequently, annual procurement savings will be limited to the elimination of modification and spare parts contracts for the two systems. These savings will equal US$55.7 million per year over 1992-2001.

Savings are also generated in the second main category, operations and maintenance (O & M) and military construction. As table 7.1 shows, US$ 74 million savings in GLCM European military base construction occurs in FY 1988. The effects of these savings will be felt primarily in Europe and in the form of reduced demand for base construction. Savings from reduced O & M requirements increase over the implementation period as both deployed and non-deployed systems are retired. The sum of O & M cost savings for both systems averages about $81 million per year over the first three years of the Treaty and will climb to nearly US$154 million per year over the 1992-2001 steady state period.

As indicated on the bottom line of table 7.1, total savings in military purchases from all INF system contractors equalled between US$537.6 and US$572.5 million in 1988, and will average between US$448 and US$ 459.7 million over the implementation period. These savings will fall to an average of US$55.7 million over the remaining ten years of the Treaty.

Against these various military savings, or reduced private sector purchases, we also estimated the implementation and verification costs that will be incurrred as a result of the Treaty. These costs will be reflected in additional military personnel and procurement purchases which will increase economic activity. Because of limited information on the costs of implementation and verification, we examine below only the additional economic activity which will accrue from the design and production of the portal monitoring system which is to be installed at the Votkinsk missile facility. The start-up and contract cost for the production, transport and operation of the portal monitoring station in the USSR is estimated at US$16.29 million (1987 prices).[10]

We will now turn to examine the impact of these INF contract reductions on military purchases from private contractors engaged in the production of GLCM and Pershing II systems.

---

[10] *Department of Defense Appropriations for 1989*, Hearings Before a Subcommittee of the Committee on Appropriations, US House of Representatives, 100th Congress, Second Session, 1988, Part 7, pp. 754, 784-785. Initial start-up costs were confirmed by discussions with the staff of the US On-Site Inspection Agency.

IV. Economic impact of the INF Treaty's implementation on United States prime contractors for GLCM and Pershing II missiles

In the United States the military contractors that produced the INF-regulated missile systems experienced measureable losses in sales, and some employment dislocation due to lay-offs and reassignments directly related to the implementation of the INF Treaty. None the less, the losses of sales and jobs were quite small, both absolutely and relatively, given the size of their workforces and overall sales revenues. The Treaty verification requirements in the United States have not, to date, significantly disrupted production, nor has the intrusiveness of these inspections led to any apparent shift in production from military to civilian work. Indeed, there seems to be no real conversion from military to civilian production resulting from the INF Treaty.

This section reviews the major contractors for each of the INF missile systems, and examines the scale and scope of the economic repercussions attributable to the INF Treaty, drawing on government and corporate reports on contracts awards, sales and employment. However, given the inherent limitations of these data, they were supplemented by a mailed questionnaire and telephone interviews. Five of the 12 major contractors chose to respond to this questionnaire. Fortunately, all of the prime contractors responded and provided important details on the employment and verification impacts of the Treaty. Moreover, the questionnaires helped to identify the effects on the numerous plants of these multi-divisional, multi-plant firms.

1. Ground-launched Cruise missile contractors

The most visible effect of the Treaty's implementation was the termination of the last 37 of the originally planned 597 ground-launched Cruise missiles. The termination of these contracts resulted in procurement losses of about US$68 million for all of the contractors. In addition, the phased elimination of GLCMs in Western Europe meant a reduction in missile modification and repair contracts estimated at US$98.7 million and an additional loss of US$5.7 million in R & D contracts over the 1988-91 period. Reductions in operation and maintenance contracts would probably amount to US$166.4 million in losses over the implementation period. All of the principal contractors would experience contract losses, although some would be greater than others.

The principal prime and secondary contractors for the GLCM are shown in table 7.2. General Dynamics was the lead prime contractor, but it shared the role with McDonnell Douglas Corporation. In the production phase of the GLCM work, General Dynamics and McDonnell Douglas split the prime contract awards, with about 60 per cent going to General Dynamics. In 1987 the contract shares were reversed, but returned to the previous ratio in 1988.[11]

---

[11] See *Annual Report of McDonnell Douglas, 1987* (St. Louis, Missouri), p. 14.

Table 7.2. *Ground-launched Cruise missiles: Principal contractors, location of plants, value and nature of production contract*

Company	Production location	1987 contract award (US$ thousands)	Contract/products
General Dynamics	San Diego, California	26 000	GLCM, prime contractor airframes and transporters-erector-launchers
McDonnell Douglas	Titusville, Florida	21 858	Guidance, system hardware, complete guided missiles, launchers
Williams International	Walled Lake, Michigan	4 867	Gas turbines, engines modifications, RDT & E
Teledyne	Toledo, Ohio	1 439	Gas turbines and engines
Vitro Labs	Silver Springs, Maryland	997	Software, maintenance and repair
Atlantic Research	Alexandria, Virginia	n.a.	GLCM rocket motors
Honeywell International	Minneapolis	n.a.	Radar and altimeters

Sources. *Prime contract awards over $25,000 by major system* by the Directorate for Information Operations and Reports, US Department of Defense, 1987; and responses to mailed questionnaires.

General Dynamics reported that its Convair Division in San Diego was awarded contracts to produce a total of 340 GLCMs through 1987, while McDonnell Douglas accounted for the balance of the 124 GLCM airframe contracts.[12] This splitting of prime contract obligations had been promoted by the United States Air Force as a competitive mechanism for keeping costs down.[13]

Competitive dual contract awards were made to Teledyne and Williams International, with the two contractors splitting the work on the GLCM gas turbines and engines. Smaller contracts for the other major components and subcomponents were awarded individually, with the contracts going to the other companies listed in table 7.2 and to numerous other companies in over 22 different states. In addition to these production contracts, the prime and secondary contractors were awarded modification and spare parts contracts, as well as operation and maintenance contracts.

General Dynamics reported that it expected cumulative losses totalling US$85 million as a result of the cancellation of the 37 GLCM for FY 1988 and the related contract losses for modification, spares, and operation and maintenance contracts over the 1988-91 period. McDonnell Douglas did not report its estimated losses from these contracts, although officials did acknowledge that losses would probably amount to 35 to 40 per cent of all operation and maintenance (O & M) and modification contracts. Most of this would occur through the reduction of operation and maintenance contracts.

[12] Ibid., and *Annual Report of General Dynamics Corporation, 1987* (St. Louis, Missouri), p. 9.
[13] *Hearings on HR1748*, op. cit., pp. 376-378.

Over the 1984-87 period, General Dynamics had won 64 per cent of all domestic O & M contracts, while McDonnell Douglas had 34 per cent. Contracts for O & M work in Western Europe went to the Belgian firm SABCA S.A. which held 20 per cent of all O & M contracts in 1987.

These losses, however, constitute a very small share of the total revenues for their respective divisions. For example, the loss of 22 of the 37 GLCM production contracts for 1988 would amount to less than 3 per cent of General Dynamics' Convair Division's 1987 sales revenues. McDonnell Douglas' total estimated sales losses (assuming a 35 per cent share of these modification and O & M contracts) would comprise just 5 per cent of its Missile Systems Division's 1988 sales.

Because these losses comprise such a small share of sales, and because there are other contracts to maintain workloads, the employees of these firms will suffer few job losses due to the INF Treaty. General Dynamics reports that of the 4,500 employees at its Convair Division only 5.7 per cent (260) were still employed on the remaining GLCM contracts and only ten were directly laid off as a result of the termination of these GLCM contracts. Of the 250 workers retained, 200 were reassigned to other military contract work, while 50 workers were reassigned to civilian aerospace work. About 100 of the workers reassigned to other military work are now working on the Sea-Launched Cruise Missiles contracts, which currently accounts for a total of 3,000 jobs at the Convair Division.[14]

McDonnell Douglas reports a similar impact on employment, with only 10 to 15 per cent of its workforce being affected by the INF agreement, out of a total of 18,000 workers employed at the Titusville aerospace facility. None of these 180-270 workers was laid off. All were reassigned to other military production work, mostly to the Navy's SLCM and Harpoon missile contracts.

The experience of both these prime contractors illustrates the importance of parallel production of the SLCM for minimising the economic impacts of the INF Treaty. The SLCM has proved especially important for both the prime and secondary GLCM contractors because the airframes, engines, turbines, guidance systems and other components are virtually identical in both weapons systems. This allows the use of the same tooling and dies in production, and permits the ready transfer of personnel from one system to another.

Other current military contract work by these prime contractors illustrates the classic R & D follow-on from the GLCM contracts. For example, General Dynamics reported that it is studying follow-ons to Tomahawk production, including evolving designs for guidance, aerodynamics and propulsion for application in advanced air- and sea-launched Cruise missiles.[15] General Dynamics plans spin-offs in their bid for the NATO Long Range Standoff Missile and the NATO Modular Standoff Weapon programme. In addition, the GLCM transporter-erector-launchers' production capacity is

---

[14] Ibid.
[15] *Annual Report of General Dynamics, 1987*, p. 9, and *AR, 1986*, p. 8.

being developed for possible use in the Missile Launch Car (MLC) of the rail-garrison system for the MX ICBM strategic missile programme.

Neither of the prime contractors reported any conversion of military to civilian production as a result of the termination and reduction of the GLCM contracts. In large part, the lack of conversion to civilian work can be traced to the successful efforts of the contractors to develop follow-on military contracts. The implication of this follow-on imperative for conversion will be discussed in the concluding section of this chapter.

These are the main impacts on the prime contractors for the GLCMs. The secondary contractors undoubtedly experienced a lesser economic impact because of the smaller size of their contracts. For example, Teledyne, which produced gas turbines and engines for the GLCM, had contract awards of US$1.4 million in 1987, which was less than 1 per cent of its aviation and electronics division's sales in that year. Little other information is available from the secondary contractors because they did not respond to the questionnaire and their annual reports do not discuss their GLCM contract work.

There are, however, two other major impacts of the INF Treaty on the GLCM contractors which must be considered, namely the curtailment of the production of its warhead, and its possible reuse on other systems.

2. LCM nuclear warhead production contracts

With the termination of the GLCM programme, there was no further need for continued production of its warhead, the W-84, which was designed exclusively for use in the GLCM. The warhead was designed by Los Alamos National Laboratory, and produced at the "government-owned and contractor-operated" (GOCO) facilities comprising the nuclear weapons production complex. This complex is made up of six geographically dispersed facilities, each of which fabricates key components. Fabrication of nuclear components for warhead assemblies takes place at the Rocky Flats facility outside Denver, Colorado, managed by Westinghouse Corporation and at the Y-12 plant at Oak Ridge, Tennessee, managed by Martin Marietta. Non-nuclear warhead components are manufactured at: the Mound Laboratory managed by Monsanto in Miamisburg, Ohio; the Pinellas facility managed by General Electric in Pinellas, Florida; and the Kansas City facility managed by Bendix in Missouri. Final assembly of nuclear and non-nuclear components into the warhead takes place at the Pantex facility in Amarillo, Texas, and is managed by the Mason and Hanger-Silas Company. These production facilities are provided the fissile materials for nuclear warhead fabrication by a set of seven separate materials production facilities.

The main impact of the US$243 to US$278 million reduction in contracts will be felt in the six principal warhead production facilities, rather than the nuclear materials production plants. About two-thirds of these savings will probably be reflected in reductions in contracts for the warhead production complex, with the other one-third of the savings reflected in reduced demand for fissile materials. This distribution of the contract reductions assumes that the respective demands for warhead and materials production capacities bear a proportional relationship to the annual budget outlays for the warhead production and materials production components of the Department of Energy's Atomic Defense Activities Budget.[16]

While the end of W-84 warhead production will probably have repercussions throughout the production complex, its main effect will be realised first at the final assembly facilities at Pantex, where production capacity has been at full utilisation.[17] Labour and capacity within the warhead assembly bays could be reassigned to increase production rates of other warheads. Elsewhere within the production complex, resources will be released to produce the nuclear and non-nuclear components for other warhead designs. However, some of the generic components and other long-lead time elements of the W-84 warheads had probably already been produced for many of the 150-200 warheads on order. Some of these generic components can be reused, particularly the neutron generators, detonators and timers produced at Pinellas and Mound Laboratory. The specialised nuclear and non-nuclear components of the W-84, however, will have to be recycled or scrapped. None the less, the freeing of specialised production processes at Rocky Flats, Mound, Kansas City and the Y-12 plant will probably reduce the production constraints within the bomb factories.

The impact of the reduced demand for fissile materials from W-84 cancellations is impossible to measure directly. However, the overall effect of the lower demand and the use of these fissile materials in other warheads is likely to be negligible.[18] Indeed, since there is no current active production of any fissile materials, the impact of the reduced demand is best considered a reduced charge against inventories. It is for this reason that the impact on nuclear materials production facilities is not considered in this study.

The complete W-84 warhead, however, cannot be used for the SLCM programme because of the different operational requirements for the SLCM which are met by the W-80-0 warhead. For those W-84 warheads that were completed but not deployed, and the W-84s removed from the operational GLCMs before the missiles were destroyed, current planning calls for them to be stockpiled for possible reuse on new follow-on systems. Possible follow-on uses might involve the advanced intercontinental Cruise missile.

Officials within the US Department of Defense and the Office of Management and Budget have said that the termination of the W-84 warhead

[16] See, *Department of Energy, FY 1984-1989 Congressional Budgets, Estimates for Laboratories and Plant*, by US Department of Energy, Comptroller. See also Thomas Cochran et al.: *Nuclear weapons databook, Vol. II* (Cambridge, Massachusetts, Ballinger Books, 1987; Natural Resources Defense Council), p. 21, table 1.7.

[17] Thomas Cochran et al.: *Nuclear weapons databook, Vol. III, US nuclear warhead facility profiles* (Cambridge, Massachusetts, Ballinger Books, 1987; Natural Resources Defense Council), p. 78. Also see, *United States Department of Energy Nuclear Weapons Complex Modernization Report*, Report to the Congress by the President of the United States (Washington, DC, Dec. 1988).

[18] See Cochran et al., Vol. II, op. cit., pp. 72-88, 179-191. Also see, William Broad: "Vital gas for nuclear weapons lies untapped at reactor sites", in *New York Times*, 28 Feb. 1989, p. C-8.

Table 7.3. Pershing II missile contractors: Principal locations, value and type of contract awards

Company	Production location	1987 contract award (US$ thousands)	Contract/products
Martin Marietta (prime contractor)	Orlando, Florida Middle River, Maryland	55 016	Complete guided missiles; electrical and electronic equipment; RDT & E; engineering; maintenance equipment; launchers
Hercules, Aerospace Division	Magna, Utah	27 500	Solid rocket fuel, motors and propulsion
Loral Corporation, Defense Systems	Akron, Ohio	14 000	Guided missile components; terminal guidance systems; targeting devices; production engineering
Bendix Guidance Division	Teteboro, New Jersey	1 444	Launchers; guided missile remote control systems; production engineering
Singer Company, Kearfott Guidance and Navigation Division	Little Falls, New Jersey	1 328	Inertial guidance systems; guided missile components; vehicucular lights

Sources: *Prime contract awards over $25,000 by major system*, by the Directorate for Information Operations and Reports, US Department of Defense, 1987. Also, responses to mailed questionnaires.

will not affect employment levels within the complex.[19] The main effect will be to reduce the demand for new hires, overtime, and stretchouts of production schedules. These changes will be reflected in reassignments of the workforce to other production schedules. Finally, there will probably be some indirect employment effect because the income of the GOCO contractors will be slightly lowered and the composition of their inter-industry demand will be altered. These are issues which we will examine in section VI of this chapter.

3. Pershing II missile contractors

For the contractors for the Pershing II missile the Treaty will result in the loss of modification and spare parts contracts amounting to nearly US$60 million over the 1988-91 period, and operation and maintenance contracts amounting to US$76 million. Overall job losses reported by Pershing II contractors were very small. In addition, there was little apparent disruption of production due to the on-site inspection process. None of the contractors reported any conversion of capacity from military to civilian uses.

Table 7.3 shows the major contractors for the Pershing II system, the principal locations of production, the value of 1987 contracts and the types of contracts reported in contract awards.

---

[19] Telephone conversation with David Stevens, Acquisitions Branch, Office of the Secretary of Defense, 17 March 1989, and with Paul Cassidy of the Office of Management and Budget, White House, Washington, DC, 17 March 1989.

Martin Marietta, which was the prime contractor for the Pershing II, will sustain most of these contract losses. From 1984 to 1987 Martin Marietta accounted for nearly 90 per cent of all O & M and modification contracts. Corporate officials at Martin Marietta declined to estimate the anticipated losses due to reduced O & M and modification and spares contracts. However, assuming that the company did manage to win its historical share of O & M and modification contracts, this would amount to an average of US$40.8 million over the 1988-91 implementation period. Yet the loss of these contracts would only amount to 2.7 per cent of its Electrical and Tactical Systems Division's sales in 1987.

Loral Corporation's Defense Systems Division (formerly Goodyear Aerospace) is the secondary contractor which would lose the most from reduced O & M and modification contracts. Officials at Loral Corporation indicated that it could lose as much as US$15 million annually due to the reduction of O & M and modification contracts, with its cumulative losses over the life of the system amounting to as much as US$100 million. These estimated long run losses suggest that Loral expected to win a larger than historical share of O & M and modification contracts. These losses were probably connected to Loral's contracts in the Federal Republic of Germany for ongoing modification, maintenance and repair of the missiles. If Loral incurred these annual losses they would amount to 3.4 per cent of the division's 1987 sales revenues.

Hercules Aerospace reported that there were no identifable losses, but there were potential losses from follow-on contracts for Pershing II motors. The other secondary contractors either declined to respond to the survey, or reported no losses from the INF Treaty implementation. Data from contract awards and company reports indicate that there should have been very little, if any impact, since the contracts were completed by the time the Treaty was signed.

Not suprisingly, the immediate job losses due to the INF Treaty's implementation were minimal. Martin Marietta reported that there were no direct job losses attributable to the Treaty, primarily because it had already planned for the reallocation of its Pershing II workforce. Martin Marietta did not identify the product lines to which these workers were reassigned, but the total number involved in Pershing II work amounted to 600 full-time workers out of a total of 14,500 workers at the Orlando facility. Loral Corporation reported that 9.6 per cent of its 2,600 workers were involved in INF-regulated work. Of these workers, the company laid off 50 because of the termination of its Pershing II modification and O & M contract work. Another 200 workers were reassigned to other military contracts. Approximately 100 of these reassigned workers were shifted to work on Loral's SLCM contracts. Hercules Aerospace reported that 105 workers out of the 4,200 employees at the Bacchus Plant had been working on Pershing II rocket motor modifications. However, none of these workers was laid off. Hercules officials declined to say how these workers had been reassigned.

Finally, since the W-85 warhead for the Pershing II missile was fully deployed before the Treaty's signing, there was no impact on the nuclear weapons production complex. However, under the Treaty's provisions, the W-85 warhead is being removed from the missiles before the Pershing IIs are destroyed. Reuse of the W-85 warheads on other non-regulated missile systems is permitted under the Treaty. To date it has not been determined how these 125 warheads will be used. The Natural Resources Defense Council has suggested that the W-85s might be reused for the modernisation of the short-range Lance missile currently being considered by NATO.[20]

The foregoing discussion demonstrates that the major contracts for the Pershing IIs and GLCMs are held by few firms so that the direct economic effects from the implementation of the INF Treaty will tend to be concentrated geographically. As such, the regional economic implications of these impacts are of particular interest when assessing the total direct, indirect and induced effects on regional output, income and employment.

V. The regional economic impact of the INF Treaty

Geographical concentration of military industry is a well-documented phenomenon and the review of the INF-regulated systems illustrates once again the pattern of the regional concentrations of the military-industrial base. Over half of the GLCM contracts are concentrated in California, with 93 per cent of all the contracts in the top five states. The Pershing II contracts are even more concentrated, with 90 per cent in Florida alone.

While subcontracting by the prime contractors may disperse these contracts somewhat, the existence of well-developed subcontracting chains within the major military-industrial states tends to keep many of the subcontracts within the state. This is reflected in the well-known agglomerations of military industry in such areas as Southern California, with its military aerospace and defence electronics corridor running from San Diego to Los Angeles, and the military high-tech complex stretching from Florida's gulf coast near the Tampa-St. Petersburg area, through Orlando to the Titusville-Cape Canaveral area on the Atlantic. These concentrations tend to amplify the effect of changes in military spending as the indirect effects ripple through the regional economy, inducing further changes in regional income and employment. Thus, it is of some interest to examine the regional economic effects flowing from the implemenation of the INF Treaty.

In this section, we examine the regional economic impact of the changes resulting from the INF Treaty by using input-output generated multipliers for each of the major military contracting states. The Department of Commerce's RIMS II regional multipliers for 1987 are used to analyse the indirect and induced industry-by-industry effects on output, earnings and employment

---

[20] See Thomas Cochran, William Arkin and Robert Stan Norris: "Nuclear warheads and the INF Treaty", in *Summit Watch Background Brief No. 3* (Washington, DC, Natural Resources Defense Council, Dec. 1987), p. 2.

flowing from the contract reductions and cancellations.[21] The RIMS II multipliers are disaggregated to 39×39 sectors.

The analysis focuses on six distinct effects attributable to the Treaty. First, the regional economic effects of the reduction of GLCM procurement and modification contracts for the top five states are reviewed; second, the impact of the reductions in the GLCM operation and maintenance contracts for the same states; third, the effects of the pass-through of GLCM components to the SLCM programme; fourth, the effects of reductions in Pershing II modification contracts and operation and maintenance contracts in Florida and Ohio; fifth, the repercussions of the cancellation of the W-84 warhead contracts on the nuclear weapons production complex; and sixth, the economic impacts of the portal monitoring contract at the Sandia National Laboratory.

Clearly, many of the changes considered here are marginal in nature, and therefore it would be ideal if a dynamic input-output model could be used to evaluate the regional economic impact. Further, a more disaggregated industry analysis applied to smaller geographical units such as counties would be preferred. However, financial and time constraints do not permit the use of such dynamic input-output regional econometric modelling for this study. The use of the RIMS II multipliers will provide static measures of the average impacts flowing from the contract changes, rather than the marginal changes which are the most likely result. Hence, the use of these multipliers should provide measures of the maximum regional impacts attributable to the Treaty.

1. Regional economic impact of changes in the GLCM programme

The most immediate effect of the Treaty's implementation came through the cancellation of the order for 37 GLCMs in 1988 and the termination of contracts for modification and spares. These cancellation affected the demand for most of the major components of GLCM programme including the airframes for the missiles, the guidance systems, the turbojets, engines and radar. The transporter-erector-launcher vehicle (TELs) was probably the only major component not substantially affected because the orders for the TELs were already completed, but spare parts contracts for the TELs would be affected. Thus, a particular composition of industrial demands were affected by the reductions in these contracts.

2. Methodology

A defence weapon system "translator" is available from the Department of Defense, Defense Economic Impact Modeling System (DEIMS) which breaks down the industrial proportions for various major components of the GLCM and other major weapons programmes.[22] Drawing on this

---

[21] Thomas et al., op. cit., pp. IV and 82-84.

[22] *Regional multipliers: A user handbook for the regional input-output modeling system (RIMS II)* (Washington, DC, US Department of Commerce, Bureau of Economic Analysis, May 1986) for a discussion on the input-output model and the multipliers.

"translator" for the GLCM, we distributed the particular contract reductions proportionately according to the missile's basic industrial components. The industrial aggregation of the DEIMS translator was adapted for use with the more highly aggregated 39×39 industrial sectors of the RIMS II I-0 multipliers.[23] Using this approach the demand shock from procurement contract terminations was distributed among five basic industry groups: machinery, except electrical (21.4 per cent); electrical and electronic equipment (46 per cent); motor vehicles (6.2 per cent); transportation equipment, except motor vehicles (22.2 per cent); and instruments and related products (4.2 per cent).

The demand shock was based on the average annual reductions in procurement and modification contracts over the three-year period from mid-1988 to mid-1991. Since the RIMS II multipliers are for 1987, the dollar value of the contract reductions was deflated to 1987 dollars.[24] As noted above, the average annual reductions in GLCM procurement and modification contracts amounts to US$57.5 million in 1987 dollars.

This demand shock was distributed among the top five states based on each state's percentage of all GLCM contract awards over the 1984-87 period. California, Florida, Michigan, Virginia and Ohio were the top five states for GLCM contracts. Since the contracts and contractors in each state covered a wide variety of production activities, the same translator proportions were used to distribute each state's share of contract reductions. Based on this methodology, the direct, indirect and induced effects from contract reductions on output, earnings and employment for each state by industry were calculated.[25]

The use of contract award data to distribute the demand shock among the several states implicitly assumes that contract awards were fully expended by the contractor at their principal location in a particular state. The location of the contractors' main production operations was checked against the responses to the questionnaire. With the exception of those in Virginia, all contractors verified the location of their operations. The main adjustment was to shift all McDonnell Douglas GLCM and SLCM contracts from St. Louis, Missouri, where the contracts were awarded, to Titusville, Florida, where the actual production work was done.

---

[23] The translator was adapted to eliminate certain adjustments which were used in the DEIMS translator, particularly the inclusion of tooling and die costs which would not be relevant in case where a production line was being terminated.

[24] Procurement deflators for DoD purchases were drawn from the *National Defense Budget Estimates for FY 1987*, by the Office of the Assistant Secretary of Defense, US Department of Defense, Washington, DC, May 1986, table 5-8, and were updated using the series from the May 1988 edition.

[25] The direct employment multipliers were derived by taking the given industry's demand from itself for employment and dividing it by the industry's demand for its own output. These figures are from computer printouts from the 1987 RIMS II 39×39 multipliers by state, which are available from the Bureau of Economic Analysis, Regional Economic Analysis Division, US Department of Commerce, Washington, DC, 20230.

3. Output and employment effects of GLCM contract reductions and pass-throughs

Procurement and modification contract cancellations and reductions of US$57.7 million would result in an estimated reduction in output of US$114.6 million for these five states together. Since these states held 93 per cent of all GLCM contracts, this static estimate of the annual average impact provides a fair approximation of the more immediate effects of the Treaty's implementation on output. Table 7.4 depicts these impacts together with the effects on earnings and employment for each state.

The total employment impact of the procurement and modification contract reductions includes the direct, indirect and induced effect and totals 1,370 jobs, with 548 of those being made up by the direct employment losses of the primary and secondary contractors. The interpretation of these employment figures requires some caution, as the likely meaning of these figures is that regional employment growth would be slowed by this amount. Lacking a dynamic baseline forecast for each region over the three-year period, it is difficult to say exactly how these employment impacts would be reflected. These employment effects would probably be expressed as lower job growth and less overtime.

California is clearly the most affected state. Florida, whose principal GLCM contractor is McDonnell Douglas at Titusville, shows reductions in total output of nearly US$25 million resulting from procurement contract losses of US$13.3 million annually. Total employment losses amount to nearly 350 jobs, with about 150 in direct job losses. Michigan, whose major GLCM contractor is Williams International, shows total reductions in output of slightly more than US$7 million annually, and annual average losses of about 80 jobs.

Reductions in GLCM operation and maintenance contracts average US$55.5 million annually over the three-year implementation period, with nearly US$44.4 million occurring in these five states. The average effects on output, earnings and employment are shown in table 7.4 for each state. The total direct, indirect and induced effects on output for all five states amounts to US$88.4 million annually. Job losses from the O & M contract reductions average 424 annually. The major regional impacts from losses of O & M contracts would occur in California and Florida.

The Belgian aerospace and defence contracting firm SABCA S.A. has the European contract for maintaining all of the deployed GLCMs at Gosselies, north-west of Florennes in Belgium. Assuming that SABCA would win its historical share of O & M contracts, these losses would average US$11 million annually. Reportedly, 150 Belgian employees at the Gosselies European Missile Repair Facility are likely to affected by its closure, however, it is unclear whether these workers are directly employed by SABCA.[26]

---

[26] See Paul Montgomery: "Treaty leads sightseers to US base", in *New York Times*, 9 June 1988.

Table 7.4. *Annual average impact from contract reductions and pass-throughs for ground-launched Cruise missile programme: Top five states by contract shares, mid-1988 to mid-1991*

	Impact on output (US$ m/n)	Impact on earnings (US$ m/n)	Total employ- ment effect (numbers)	Direct employ- ment effect (numbers)
California				
Procurements	−71.8	−22.8	−810	−320
O & M contracts	−55.4	−17.6	−625	−247
Pass-throughs [1]	−136.1	−43.9	−1 492	−483
Florida				
Procurements	−24.8	−8.0	−347	−150
O & M contracts	−19.0	−6.2	−268	−116
Pass-throughs	−51.4	−16.9	−693	−230
Michigan				
Procurements	−7.3	−2.1	−81	−28
O & M contracts	−5.6	−1.6	−62	−22
Pass-throughs	−36.1	−10.5	−397	−134
Virginia				
Procurements	−4.7	−1.5	−64	−28
O & M contracts	−3.7	−1.2	−49	−21
Pass-throughs	−11.9	−4.3	−178	−84
Ohio				
Procurements	−6.0	−1.7	−70	−22
O & M contracts	−4.6	−1.3	−53	−17
Pass-throughs	−9.4	−2.8	−110	−32
Total	−448.0	−142.5	−5 299	−1 934

[1] Losses from pass-throughs of GLCM components and subassemblies to the SLCM programmes.

The largest losses, however, are attributable to the pass-through of airframe components, subassemblies and guidance and control systems from the GLCM programme to the SLCM programme. These pass-throughs, i.e. use of these GLCM components, would displace some of the revenues from SLCM contracts. While the top five states for SLCM contracts are the same as the GLCM, the individual shares differ, with California and Florida having most of the contracts but with slightly lower shares, and Michigan having a slightly larger share of SLCM contracts, principally for turbo-jets and engines. Overall these same five states account for 78 per cent of all the SLCM contracts.

The GLCM pass-throughs may reduce SLCM contracts by an average of over US$184 million annually, with about US$144 million in losses for these five states. These contract losses are distributed among industrial sectors differently from the O & M and production contract losses because the main industrial impact of the pass-through of components would occur in airframe production (92 per cent) and guidance and control instruments (8 per cent). Table 7.4 shows the major losses would occur in California, Florida and Michigan, with lesser losses in Virginia and Ohio.

When the economic impacts of these losses are taken together with the impacts from procurement and O & M contract reductions, the total impact on output averages nearly US$448 million annually, and job losses average nearly 5,300 annually. When the total state-by-state impacts are compared with each state's growth rates for employment and output, the economic impacts on the states' economies are negligible. However, there are minor impacts on manufacturing and employment growth rates.

For instance, California, with the largest contract losses, is estimated to experience an average annual reduction in output of US$263 million as a result of contract losses of nearly US$115 million per year. The manufacturing sectors that were directly affected by these losses exhibited lacklustre real growth in output between 1984 and 1987, and these contract losses would have slowed the anaemic growth rate further, from 0.27 to 0.16 per cent between 1987 and 1988.[27] Total direct, indirect and induced employment losses could have slowed total job growth in the state slightly from 2.66 to 2.64 per cent between 1987 and 1988. If it is assumed that all of the annual average direct employment losses would occurr in San Diego County, where the General Dynamics plant is located, the total direct employment effect would have eliminated the county's miniscule growth rate in manufacturing employment between 1987 and 1988.[28]

4. Economic impact of Pershing II O & M and modification contract losses

As a result of the elimination of the Pershing II missiles, United States contractors will probably lose an average of US$45 million annually in modification and operation and maintenance contracts over the three-year implementation period. Most of these losses will be concentrated in two states, Florida and Ohio, which are the locations for the two major contractors of the Pershing II: Martin Marietta in Orlando, Florida, and Loral Defense Systems Division in Akron, Ohio. Together these two contractors have historically accounted for nearly 93 per cent of all Pershing II contracts, with the prime contractor Martin Marietta accounting for 90 per cent of the contracts. However, the share of O & M and modification contracts differs, with Loral systems accounting for over one-third of these contracts, including the European repair contracts. Accordingly, two-thirds of these contract losses were distributed to Flordia and the rest to Ohio.

---

[27] Data on annual value of shipments by state are derived from the *Annual Survey of Manufacturers, Geographic Area Statistics, 1985 and 1987*, US Department of Commerce, Bureau of the Census, Industry Division. Data from 1984 through 1986 were used to derive the average annual growth rate for the selected industry groups in each state over the period and to project for 1987 and 1988. On balance, it is felt that the export-led recovery of 1988 probably makes these projections extremely conservative, and therefore probably overestimates the impact of these small demand changes on the growth rate for value of shipments. However, to date there are no official geographical industrial statistics available for these years.

[28] State and regional employment statistics are taken from *Employment and Earnings* (US Department of Labor, Bureau of Labor Statistics, Aug. 1988), table B-8, pp. 60-75.

Table 7.5.   *Average annual economic impact of Pershing II contract reductions: Top two states,*
       mid-1988 to mid-1991

	Impact on output (US$ m/n)	Impact on earnings (US$ m/n)	Total employ-ment effect (numbers)	Direct employ-ment effect (numbers)
Florida				
Modifications	−22.3	−7.3	−314	−135
O & M contracts	−28.6	−9.3	−402	−173
Total	−50.9	−16.6	−716	−308
Ohio				
Modifications	−16.3	−4.6	−188	−58
O & M contracts	−20.8	−5.9	−240	−75
Total	−37.1	−10.5	−428	−133

To model these losses, the DEIMS translator was used to distribute the demand shock proportionately among the industry groups which account for the major components of the Pershing II missile.[29] The proportions for both the modification and O & M contract terminations were distributed among five basic industry groups: machinery, except electrical (17.2 per cent); electrical and electronic equipment (41.5 per cent); motor vehicles (5.7 per cent); transportation equipment, except motor vehicles (29.5 per cent); and instruments and related products (6 per cent). Next, industry-by-industry RIMS II output, earnings and employment multipliers were applied to each industrial demand shock for each state's losses of modification and O & M contracts.

The resulting estimated impact on each state was comparable to those generated by the GLCM losses. As table 7.5 indicates, Florida has total direct, indirect and induced reductions in output of US$50.9 million annually, with US$22.3 million generated by losses of modification contracts and US$28.6 million generated by O & M losses. Earnings decline by an average of US$16.6 million annually. The total employment impact for Florida amounts to an average of 716 jobs annually, with 308 being direct job losses. Ohio shows an average total loss in output of US$37 million annually. Total earnings decline by an average of US$10.5 million annually. Ohio's total employment losses amount to 428 jobs annually, with 133 being direct job losses.

When these impacts are added to those generated by the GLCM impacts, Florida's state-wide losses expand considerably, but are still less than in California. Florida's total losses in output amount to an average of US$146 million per year, and its job losses amount to over 2,000 annually. However, these combined losses would probably have little overall impact on the state's growth of output and employment.

Clearly, these impacts are small, since they resulted from relatively minor cuts in two systems which were completed or nearly completed. However,

---

[29] Thomas et al., op. cit., p. IV and 113-115.

a disarmament treaty which might terminate weapon systems earlier in their product cycle could have potentially wide-ranging economic impacts. A similar assessment can be made about the effects of the INF Treaty on the nuclear warhead production complex.

5. *Economic impact of the termination of W-84 nuclear warhead production*

Termination of production of an estimated 155 to 191 W-84 nuclear warheads for the GLCMs would probably reduce some of the supply constraints within the nuclear warhead production complex. Since the beginning of the United States strategic nuclear weapons build-up in 1979, production, investment and employment within the complex have expanded, and overall spending on nuclear weapons activities has reached historically high levels.[30] Despite the higher levels of spending to support the build up, several supply bottlenecks have developed, especially at the Rocky Flats facility which fabricates the plutonium, beryllium and uranium structurals for the warheads, and at the final assembly facilities at Pantex, Texas. Cancellation of the remaining W-84 warhead orders would undoubtedly release manpower, production capacity and nuclear and non-nuclear resources and would thereby ease production schedules for other warheads.[31]

To model these impacts regionally, the contract reductions were distributed among the six facilities according to the proportion each constitutes of the operation and maintenance budget for the warhead production complex, excluding the materials production facilities and the national laboratories.[32] It was felt that the marginal impact of these reductions would only affect the operation and maintenance of the complex, and would not materially affect the capital investment and construction requirements for the complex. Next, the demand shock for each facility was sectorised according to proportions of the main industrial activities which characterise the production processes at each facility.[33] Finally, the industry-by-industry RIMS II multipliers for output,

---

[30] Cochran et al., Vol. II, op. cit., pp. 4, 14, 21, 29 and 40.

[31] This assessment was confirmed in telephone conversations with an official of the Office of Management and Budget, Paul Cassidy, 17 March 1989, and David Stevens, Acquisitions Branch, Office of the Secretary of Defense, on 17 March 1989.

[32] See detailed plant operation and maintenance budget lines for Atomic Energy Defense Activities, Weapons Activities, in *Department of Energy, FY 1984-1989 Congressional Budgets, Estimates for Laboratories and Plant*, by US Department of Energy, Comptroller, Budget Formation Branch.

[33] The sectorisation of the industrial proportions of main activities within each nuclear warhead production facility was based on information drawn from Cochran et al., Vol. III, op. cit., p. 78. Also see *United States Department of Energy Nuclear Weapons Complex Modernization Report*, Report to the Congress by the President of the United States, Dec. 1988, Washington, DC, and the Appendix on each facility. Additional detail on individual plants was derived from Battelle: *The social and economic impacts of changing missions at the Rocky Flats Plant* (Columbus, Ohio, Columbus Laboratories, June 1982), pp. 19-31; *Final Environmental Impact Statement for the Y-12 Plant* (Oak Ridge, Tennessee, Dec. 1982); *Draft Environmental Impact Statement for the Pantex Plant Site* (Amarillo, Texas, Dec. 1982), sections 2, 3 and 4.

earnings and employment were applied to the industrial demand changes affecting each facility.

This approach to modelling the demand reductions for the warhead complex is an approximation which depends on critical assumptions about the sectorisation of industrial activities at each facility. Moreover, the use of state-wide multipliers for these facilities introduces an additional distortion into these results. However, the acquisition of more localised multipliers was not possible. Perhaps the most important factor affecting the estimation of the economic impacts was the lack of information on the dollar value of the generic and long lead-time items which had probably already been produced for the cancelled warheads; this meant that these outlays could not be netted out from the demand shock. For these reasons the economic impacts may be overestimated. Nevertheless, this approach does provide important information about the industrial pattern of reductions in activity within the warhead production complex.

Table 7.6 shows the economic impacts which were calculated for the two demand shocks to reflect the range of possible cancellations of between 155 and 191 W-84 warheads. The demand shocks, after deducting one-third for fissile materials inventory charges, range between US$158.6 and US$181.3 million. The impacts are essentially very short-run effects which would occur over one or two years, depending on the production rates for the W-84.

The direct employment effects are best interpreted as a short-run impact on the growth in demand for labour within the complex, which will probably be expressed in fewer new hires and reduced overtime. Production reassignments to other warhead schedules will mean fewer stretch-outs for warhead production runs and speed-ups of production for some warheads. The indirect and induced effects on output, earnings and employment reflect the lowering of spending by the warhead production complex and its employees as a result of the W-84 contract cancellations.

The estimated impacts for Mound, Pinellas and Kansas City may be too high because some of the generic non-nuclear components were probably produced before the cancellations took effect. Over the long run, however, the reuse of some components will slightly reduce the production requirements for other systems. Thus, there will be some displacement effect in production at these facilities. At the Rocky Flats facility the bottlenecks in the fabrication of long lead-time structural nuclear components make it unlikely that a large number of components were produced prior to cancellation. At the Y-12 facilities, where other long lead-time nuclear components are fabricated, some structural components already produced for the W-84 might be re-machined for use in other warheads. As noted before, the most immediate impacts are likely to be felt at the final assembly process at Pantex with the freeing of assembly bays for other production schedules. Some of the high explosives produced at Pantex for use as charges in the warheads might have been produced prior to cancellation. Because these charges can be recycled for use in other warheads there might be some minor reduction in demand for these materials.

Table 7.6. *Average annual economic impact of terminating W-84 nuclear warhead production: Cancellations of 155 to 191 warheads, mid-1988 to mid-1991*

Facility	Impact on output (US$ m/n)			Impact on earnings (US$ m/n)			Total employment effect (numbers)			Direct employment effect (numbers)		
Kansas City Plant	−93	to	−106	−25	to	−28	−812	to	−928	−387	to	−443
Rocky Flats	−71	to	−81	−17	to	−19	−738	to	−844	−276	to	−316
Mound Laboratory	−35	to	−40	−9	to	−10	−383	to	−438	−125	to	−143
Pantex	−31	to	−36	−7	to	−8	−307	to	−351	−111	to	−126
Pinellas	−21	to	−24	−7	to	−8	−327	to	−374	−150	to	−172
Y-12 Plant	−74	to	−85	−21	to	−24	−1 140	to	−1 303	−364	to	−417
Total	−325	to	−372	−86	to	−97	−3 707	to	−4 238	−1 413	to	−1 617

Regionally, these indirect and induced impacts will have very negligible effects on output and employment in the states affected. The most tangible effects will be felt through reduced growth in the inter-industry purchases made to support production at the complex. Comparisons of these impacts with regional economic indicators show the same insignificant relationships as for the GLCM and Pershing II contract reductions.

The direct employment effects of the W-84 contract cancellations amount to between 5.4 and 6.1 per cent of the total contractor employment in the weapons production facilities.[34] Most of the direct employment effects would probably be realised through the reassignment of production workers within the complex, especially the skilled craftsmen such as machinists and metalworkers. However, other occupational groupings would also be affected. The next section evaluates these occupational effects from the INF Treaty for both the nuclear weapons complex and the aerospace sectors.

6. Occupational impact of INF contract reductions

While the weapons systems and warhead contract reductions resulted in little direct unemployment, it is clear that segments of the workforce within key industrial groups were particularly affected by the resulting shifts in workloads and by the changes in employment growth. Some measure of the occupational mix affected by these changes can be obtained from industry data on the nuclear weapons complex and from input-output occupational data for the transport industry group, which includes the aerospace sectors. The virtue of the input-output data is that the occupational effects of both the total and direct employment impacts can be evaluated.

Occupational data are available for the GOCO facilities within the whole nuclear weapons complex, including warhead and materials production and the National Laboratories. In 1987, 50,710 workers were directly involved in warhead and materials production (26,372 in warhead production). Including all other employees at the National Laboratories, construction workers employed within the complex, and security and support workers, total employment within the GOCO facilities stood at nearly 116,000 in 1987.

Table 7.7 gives a detailed breakdown for the major occupational groupings, based on a 1983 survey of GOCO employment. The largest single group is the craft and clerical workforce, followed by the technicians, managers and professionals, engineers and scientists. Clearly, the production workforce is not fully detailed in this occupational breakdown, with the critical craft workforce highly aggregated. Skilled machinists, such as millwrights, lathe operators, set-up men and tool- and die-makers are probably the craft workers who would be most affected by the production reassignments considered as well

---

[34] Data were derived from a computer printout entitled, *Contractor Employment Summary Report by Contractor Classification*, by the Office of Industrial Relations, US Department of Energy, Sep. 1987.

Table 7.7.   Major occupations in the nuclear weapons complex: Employment share by occupational group

Occupational group/subcategories	Per cent[1]	No. employed
Scientists	*9.3*	*10 780*
Mathematicians	15.3	1 649
Chemists	21.2	2 285
Geologists	1.3	140
Physicists	33.2	3 579
Metallurgists	3.8	410
Other physical science	9.2	992
Biological science	6.3	679
Health physics	6.5	701
Other life science	3.2	345
Engineers	*14.2*	*16 460*
Chemical	13.3	2 189
Civil	2.9	477
Electrical	23.9	3 934
Mechanical	24.8	4 082
Nuclear	10.1	1 662
Metallurgical	3.0	494
Other	22.0	3 621
Technicians	*20.5*	*23 763*
Draughtspeople	8.2	1 949
Electrical	22.2	5 275
Other engineering	18.5	4 396
Physical science	11.1	2 638
Life science	2.5	594
Health physics	6.8	1 616
Reactor operator	5.9	1 402
All other	24.8	5 893
Craft, clerical and other workers	*38.8*	*44 976*
Welders	2.2	989
Craft workers	26.9	12 098
Clerical	24.8	11 154
All other	46.1	20 734
Managers and other professionals	*17.2*	*19 938*
GOCO Total employment		115 917

[1] Percentages are taken from the 1983 survey reported in J. Baker and K. Olsen: *Occupational employment in nuclear related activities* (US DOD, June 1984), tables 3-2, 3-3, B-7, B-8, B-9.
Source. Office of Industrial Relations, US DOE for nuclear weapons contractor employment 1987.

as semi-skilled operatives in areas such as electrical assembly, mechanical repair and precision assembly.

More detailed data on plant-specific occupational employment shed some light on the likely effects on the warhead and materials production facilities. Occupational data from the Rocky Flats plant indicate a higher overall proportion of skilled craftsmen and operatives than for the complex as a whole and a far lower proportion of technicians. The proportion of scientific and engineering employment are about the same, while there are proportionately slightly fewer clerical, managerial and professional workers. Data from the Savannah River Plant, a nuclear materials production facility, show a similar pattern to Rocky Flats, indicating that the National Laboratories have a proportionately higher share of laboratory technicians, clerical workers, professionals and managers.[35] The composition of engineering employment at the plant level seems remarkably similar to the general pattern for the complex as a whole. From these data it is likely that occupations affected by INF-induced reassignments would be the skilled craftsmen, operatives, assemblers, and to a lesser degree, engineers and scientists.

However, this information does not describe the impact of changes in spending on occupational employment within the complex. Ideally, a dynamic input-output simulation of the changes in nuclear weapons spending would provide such data. While this information is not available for the nuclear weapons complex, table 7.8 shows the direct, indirect and induced employment and occupational effects of changes in spending (plus or minus US$100 million) on the transport equipment sectors (excluding motor vehicles), which includes the aerospace and other weapons-producing industries. These results were generated by the REMI input-output model, a dynamic input-output model joined to a regionalised econometric model.[36]

The simulation results provide a framework to investigate the occupational impact of the INF contract reductions, which are estimated to have resulted in an average loss of nearly US$137 million annually for the aerospace industry. Not surprisingly, the blue-collar occupations of craftsmen and operatives, which would be chiefly affected by the INF changes in spending, comprise 46.8 per cent of the direct employment affected by the simulated shock. The engineering professions, together with engineering technicians, comprise 11.9 per cent of the direct employment affected and managers and clerical workers together comprise 18.25 per cent. Clearly, there are also large induced effects for all of these occupational groups, but it is not surprising that the largest single induced effect is for other service and professional workers. The details of these occupational effects highlight some of the fields which are most sensitive to marked shifts in military spending. While the INF Treaty resulted in few direct lay-offs, there were reassignments and some dislocation in these occupations.

Taken together, all of these impacts induced by the INF Treaty resulted from very small reductions in contracts, including the cancellation of production contracts for less than 1 per cent of United States nuclear warheads. At the regional level, Florida's high-tech industrial corridor seems to have

---

[35] Battelle, op. cit., pp. 47-48. Data provided by the Office of Public Affairs, Savannah River Plant, Aiken, South Carolina.

[36] For documentation on the REMI input-output model see George Treyz and Ben Stevens: "The TFS regional modeling methodology", in *Regional Studies*, 1985, No. 19, pp. 547-562.

Table 7.8. **Impact on employment by occupation from a US$100 million demand shock: Transportation equipment industries, except motor vehicles**

Occupational group/subcategories	Total employment	Direct employment
Engineers	123	76
Aeronautical	39	34
Chemical	2	1
Civil	6	1
Electrical	24	12
Industrial	17	10
Mechanical	22	14
Metal and materials	2	1
Sales and engineers nec	11	3
Computer specialists	27	9
Computer programmers	15	5
Computer analysts	10	3
Computer specialists nec	2	1
Engineering and science technicians	64	28
Draughtspeople	22	9
Electrical technicians	15	7
Industrial engineering technicians	3	2
Mechanical engineering technicians	2	2
Technicians nec	22	8
Technical workers	32	13
Bio-physics scientists	10	2
Systems analysts	13	8
Research workers nec	4	1
Technicians and engineers nec	5	2
Craftworkers, except construction	428	182
Machinists	51	31
Repair and mechanics	151	51
Sheet metal workers	19	13
Tool and die makers	17	9
Craftworkers nec	190	78
Operatives, except transportation	574	226
Machine operatives	35	18
Co-operatives nec	539	208
Managers and administrators	349	55
Clerical and kindred workers	580	104
Construction craftsmen	210	92
Labourers and transport equipment operators	257	33
Other service and professional workers	802	53
Total	3 446	871

Note. nec = not elsewhere classified.

suffered the most concentrated economic impact because three major contractors affected by the INF Treaty are located there: McDonnell Douglas in Titusville; Martin Marietta in Orlando; and General Electric at the Pinellas plant. Central Florida may thus be the region most affected by this aspect of the INF Treaty.

One implication of this analysis is that an ambitious disarmament treaty which put an end to several warhead types and strategic systems not fully deployed, would have considerable regional economic and occupational effects which would merit serious consideration. However, such a treaty would likely involve far greater outlays for verification and monitoring and these might mitigate the economic losses from contract cancellations. In the INF Treaty, however, the stimulative effects of these outlays could only be evaluated for one aspect of the process, namely the portal monitoring system's development.

7. Impact of outlays for portal monitoring and Treaty verification

Outlays and activities for the verification of the INF Treaty will stimulate some modest economic activity. However, the regions benefiting from the principal verification investment are not those adversely affected by the Treaty. Perhaps the largest single technological investment associated with verification is the portal monitoring system, an array of imaging devices using X-ray technology to be installed outside the Votkinsk missile factory so as to determine that SS-20s are not being produced under the guise of SS-25s.[37] This portal monitoring system was managed and developed by Sandia National Laboratory in New Mexico at a total outlay of US$16.9 million in 1988 (US$16.29 million 1987 dollars).

Sandia National Laboratory was primarily involved in designing the system and administering the production contracts for its components and final assembly. Twenty technical and design people were engaged in the design and another 20 people administered the production contracts which were mostly let within New Mexico. The US$16.29 million outlay was estimated to generate US$28.5 million in additional output throughout New Mexico and nearly US$9 million in additional earnings. Total direct, indirect and induced employment was estimated at 422 jobs from this one-year injection of funds, with the direct employment for the contractors accounting for about 200 of the jobs over the year.[38]

---

[37] *Department of Defense Appropriations for 1989*, Hearings before a Subcommittee of the Committee on Appropriations, US House of Representatives, 100th Congress, Second Session, 1988, Part 7, p. 787.

[38] The expenditures for the portal monitoring system were distributed evenly to the machinery, except electrical equipment industry group, and the electrical and electronic equipment industry group. The 1987 RIMS II multipliers for these industry groups in New Mexico were as follows: for machinery, except electrical equipment, the output multiplier was 1.6774; the earnings multiplier was 0.5076; the total employment multiplier, which show the employment generated per million dollars, was 24.2 and the direct employment multiplier was 11.837; for electrical and electronic equipment, the output multiplier was 1.8238; the earnings multiplier was 0.593; the total employment multiplier was 27.5 and the direct employment multiplier was 12.719.

In addition to the portal monitoring system, other verification outlays will stimulate economic activity. However, these are not broken down in sufficient detail to evaluate their regional and industrial economic effects. Perhaps the most regionalised effects of the verification process involve on-site inspection costs.

Preparation costs for on-site inspection at the contractors' plants, which includes the shrouding of sensitive unregulated military production, will offset a small fraction of the INF contract losses. The total on-site preparation costs average US$12.8 million over the implementation period, with the majority going to Hercules Aerospace and General Dynamics. Martin Marietta did not report their reimbursable costs. At best, these activities will have a short-run stimulative effect, with most of the outlays in the first two years of the Treaty. These expenditures are hardly a serious means to mitigate the economic dislocations of the INF.

VI. The INF Treaty, disarmament and the prospects for conversion

The results of this analysis indicate that the INF-induced contract reductions for private firms will not be great enough to prompt an immediate consideration of converting from military to civilian production. Taken alone, the INF Treaty will cause only minor dislocations for the defence divisions of the major systems contractors and within the GOCO facilities of the nuclear weapons complex. As we have seen, the resulting regional economic dislocations were minor. Several factors explain why the economic impact of the Treaty was easily absorbed by the defence industry.

The most obvious reason is the extremely modest level of weapons cuts called for by INF which does not directly slow the rapid pace of strategic or conventional force modernisation. All three INF prime contractors have maintained a large and relatively constant share of military procurement since 1980. Both McDonnell Douglas and General Dynamics, the other GLCM prime contractor, have usually ranked first or second in prime contract awards. The Pershing II prime contractor, Martin Marietta, has usually claimed a smaller, eleventh or twelfth, but very stable share of the military prime contracts.[39]

Previous studies indicate that major United States defence firms tend to maintain their relative market shares throughout the cycles of expansion and contraction in military procurement spending.[40] Thus the three major INF contractors are likely to retain relatively constant shares of a slowly declining defence market. The loss of sales due to the INF Treaty will not occur in the

---

[39] The rankings of the three contractors are taken from *Defense Magazine*, Sep./Oct. Almanac, issues from 1982 through 1988.

[40] See Jacques S. Gansler: *The defense industry* (Cambridge, Massachusetts, MIT Press, 1982), p. 40.

general context of a major market shake-out or restructuring, and hence are easier for the firms to absorb without a significant decrease in their current capacity utilisation and employment levels.

More specifically, continued high demand for missiles and related weapons systems ensures that the divisions of these firms producing INF-regulated systems will face a relatively robust sales outlook in the near term. All are actively producing parallel missile systems, or other closely related missile or weapons systems.

Because of the production of these parallel and closely related weapons systems, production activity at McDonnell Douglas' Titusville facility which produced the GLCMs, is likely to remain robust. The conversion of this facility is therefore not an issue in the short term. In the longer term McDonnell Douglas has indicated that there was no civilian production at Titusville, so a future downturn in defence sales could not be offset by increased production of non-military products. It therefore seems likely that capacity utilisation and employment levels would fall rapidly without some site conversion planning.

The Convair Division of General Dynamics is continuing rapid production of the parallel SLCM, and is producing guidance systems for the air-launched Cruise missile. Convair's plant No. 19, where GLCMs were formerly produced, continues to produce fuel tanks for the Atlas and Centaur rockets, but the SLCM and ALCM production is taking place at the Kearney Mesa Plant at another location in San Diego. The Convair Division does have substantial contracts to produce civilian aircraft components in San Diego and could potentially redeploy some of its workforce and capital equipment into civilian aerospace work.

Martin Marietta's Defense Electronics and Tactical Systems Division produced the Pershing II. This division, located in Orlando and Ocala in Florida, is devoted to the development and production of missile systems, precision guided projectiles, air defence systems, and electronic and optical target acquisition systems.[41] However, this division is not engaged in the production of parallel missile systems or direct follow-ons to the Pershing II. However, the phase-out of Pershing II production had been planned for and the reduction in spare parts and O & M contracts were not enough to trigger any dislocations. Personnel were reassigned within the division which has active production lines for the Patriot anti-aircraft missile, the Copperhead laser-guided artillery shells and the Navy's guided missile drones. The INF contract cancellations have not required this division to contemplate conversion to civilian production. None the less, a long-term decline in defence orders would have a profound effect on Martin Marietta's military division and the surrounding region.

While the economic impact of the INF Treaty is not enough to force actual conversion, this analysis does reveal the existence of barriers to

---

[41] *Martin Marietta Corporation 1986 Annual Report*, Martin Marietta Corporation, p. 30.

conversion, as well as of some possibilities for conversion which might one day be appropriate. In particular, the structure and strategy of large defence firms make them, and their surrounding regional economies, especially vulnerable to major arms and military spending reductions.

Large-scale reductions in procurement and R & D budgets will fall heavily on the defence divisions of major aerospace contractors which are usually separate from their civilian-oriented divisions. Major declines in military demand, therefore, cannot be directly accommodated through shifting to civilian lines within the same corporate division. Prior studies have indicated that because of the peculiar nature of the military market, it is extremely hard to adapt the sales, management and the production practices of these defence divisions to the different requirements of civilian markets. Several key barriers to defence divisions entering civilian markets have been identified, including:

– the difficulty in utilising the specialised capital equipment in civilian production lines;
– the difficulty in applying the scientific and specialised technical skills of the workforce to civilian product development and production;
– sales and marketing techniques in the defence business which are unsuited to civilian markets;
– the practices associated with small production runs of high-quality products characteristic of military production which are not applicable to higher-volume, low-cost civilian production;
– because military products are produced for military standards and specifications they are difficult to apply to civilian uses.[42]

Because of these formidable barriers, major firms with large military divisions have historically responded to cuts in military spending through acquisitions of other civilian firms, rather than through internal diversification or conversion. Thus, without government incentives or conversion planning, cuts in military spending cause profound and wasteful reductions in capacity utilisation and employment levels in the defence divisions of major military contractors.

Examination of the INF Treaty's impact also underscores the particular pattern of occupational and regional effects that would follow from major military spending reductions. The direct occupational impact of the simulated reduction in aerospace demand indicate that major cuts would fall heavily on engineering, scientific and specialised craftsmen and machine operatives. Studies of the defence workforce have noted that many of the professional, scientific and technical workers employed in defence work have problems in orienting their training and expertise to civilian projects.[43] The unique skills and age distribution of the blue-collar aerospace workforce tend to limit their employment opportunities

---

[42] Gansler, op. cit., 1982, pp. 41-49. Also see Seymour Melman: *Profits without production* (New York, Knopf, 1983), pp. 256-264.

[43] Gansler, op. cit., 1982, pp. 50-54.

in civilian sectors.[44] Without a national retraining initiative, civilian labour markets would be hard pressed to absorb major lay-offs in aerospace divisions.

Regionally, defence aerospace production is highly concentrated, with large agglomerations in Florida, Missouri, Texas, California and Washington State. If major defence cuts did occur, subregions of these states would experience a dramatic increase in the demand for public services and assistance, just as their tax base was eroding. The absence of a positive conversion framework would be especially costly and wasteful for these regions.

The INF Treaty's impact on the nuclear weapons complex presents a different industrial, occupational and regional pattern than its impact on missile production. Nevertheless, many of the same lessons can be drawn. While the INF cuts in warhead production were extremely small, future disarmament treaties might result in sizeable regional effects for the contractors, workers and surrounding communities. With a comprehensive test ban treaty employment for all occupations within the nuclear weapons complex would be affected. Many workers within the nuclear weapons complex are already facing major dislocations because of the increasingly critical environmental and safety crisis, forcing the shutdown of several facilities in the complex.

Of course, such economic dislocations have occurred in the past, but the typical response by contractors and regions has been an ad hoc approach to conversion and diversification. Perhaps the most noteworthy example in the United States was when military procurement and R & D spending fell between 1970 and 1974 by over 40 per cent in real terms.[45] Major aerospace firms attempted to sustain overall corporate profits by acquiring firms with established civilian product lines, rather than using the facilities and labour of their defence divisions to produce civilian products. This caused major lay-offs of skilled professional and craft workers and defence-dependent regions such as Southern California, North Texas and Western Washington State took the brunt of this economic dislocation.

Aside from very modest efforts to aid communities through the Office of Economic Adjustment of the Department of Defense, the federal Government provided no planning or incentives to encourage the affected firms to convert structures, capital equipment or personnel to civilian production. Rather, the primary policy of the Government was to sustain the defence divisions of major firms and major military production lines with follow-on contracts. These allowed many major defence divisions to continue operations at a lower level of capacity utilisation. This "follow-on imperative" sustained most of the major weapons and aerospace production lines. In addition, there was the much publicised case of the government bail-out for Lockheed Aerospace in 1971 through a US$250 million guaranteed loan.[46]

---

[44] Ibid., p. 54. Also see Thomas Karier: "Wages in defense industries", unpublished manuscript, Eastern Washington University, 15 Jan. 1985, pp. 6-11.

[45] *National Defense Budget Estimates for FY 1988/1989*, op. cit., table 6-11, p. 96.

[46] See James Kurth: "Why we buy the weapons we do", in Thomas Ferguson and Joel Rodgers (eds.): *The political economy* (Armonk, New York, M. E. Sharp, 1984), pp. 317-320.

This policy of sustaining defence production lines was often justified as maintaining "surge capacity" for defence industry base. However, follow-on contracts may also have the effect of creating and maintaining political constituencies to support high defence spending.[47] Under such circumstances, Congressional representatives from defence-dependent regions, the defence firms themselves, and the affected professional groups and trade unions may see their only salvation in a revival in weapons spending. There are, however, signs that the conversion approach is beginning to get a more serious hearing among policy-makers in the United States Congress. Some combination of budget pressures and new, more substantial, strategic and conventional arms reduction agreements may allow major military spending reductions. These circumstances might advance conversion legislation to a Congressional vote.

The most comprehensive conversion Bill, H.R. 101, The Defense Economic Adjustment Act, addresses many of the key facets of the conversion problem. This Bill, authored by New York Congressman Ted Weiss, contains a set of provisions for the establishment of institutions and incentives to encourage the orderly and efficient transfer of capital, labour and raw materials to civilian uses.

Specifically, the Bill calls for the establishment of a Defense Economic Adjustment Council to co-ordinate conversion planning and provide procedures and support. It calls for a one-year prenotification of plans to reduce or terminate a defence contract or close a military base. It further calls for the establishment of Alternative Use Committees at all defence production facilities employing at least 100 people. The membership of these committees will be equally divided between labour, management and non-voting representatives of the community. Each committee is to develop a detailed plan to convert the facility and re-employ the workforce within two years of losing the military contract. The Bill provides for planning assistance, income support and retraining programmes for communities and workers once the conversion process is under way. Defence contractors are required to participate in the conversion planning process or face penalties, including the loss of eligibility for future contracts for a period of three years. Finally, in its original form the funding to implement these measures was to come from a 1.25 per cent levy on defence contractor revenues, with a federal contribution of 10 per cent from the savings of the cancelled or reduced contracts.[48]

If indeed the INF Treaty is a stepping stone toward more comprehensive disarmament agreements, then a central lesson of the United States experience is that the industrial regional economies could well suffer very severe dislocation. To ignore the economic effects of the INF Treaty because they are relatively small is to miss the important lesson that there are regional and industrial concentrations which make certain states and industries particularly vulnerable to substantial changes in military spending.

---

[47] Ibid. Also see Seymour Melman, op. cit., especially Chapters 8 and 14.

[48] "The Defense Economic Adjustment Act, H.R. 229", in *Congressional Record*, Vol. 131, No. 1, Washington DC, 3 Jan. 1985.

Chapter 8

The Soviet defence industry and conversion: The regional dimension

JULIAN COOPER

I. Introduction

The INF Treaty and the adoption by the Soviet Union of a policy of force reductions have transformed the issue of conversion of military production facilities to civilian purposes into an immediate practical concern. This chapter presents a preliminary examination of some of the issues, in particular the employment implications of the pursuit of a conversion policy in the USSR.

The Soviet Union has always maintained an extremely high level of secrecy in matters pertaining to armaments production. While some details of the military budget have now been published, at the time of writing there is no officially published information on the number of enterprises involved and the number of workers, managers and technical personnel employed in military production. This chapter is necessarily limited to the evidence available. It draws primarily on Soviet sources, in particular journals and newspapers, supplemented by some Western studies.

II. Conversion and the INF Treaty

In accordance with the INF Treaty, four Soviet enterprises have ceased the manufacture of intermediate and shorter range missiles and launchers. As discussed in another chapter, the Votkinsk machine-building works in the Udmurt Autonomous Republic, the principal manufacturer of solid-fuel missiles, has halted production of the RSD-10 (SS-20) and OTR-23 (SS-23) missiles and is using the freed capacity to increase and extend its already well-established civilian activities. One of the other enterprises named in the Treaty, the Volgograd "Barrikady" works, responsible for the launch units for the RSD-10, has for many years produced oil industry equipment and this activity is now being expanded. The civilian production and intentions of the Petropavlovsk heavy machine-building works in Kazakhstan (responsible for the OTR-23 launchers) are not known, but the fourth enterprise, the experimental factory of the Sverdlovsk "Mashinostroitel'nyi zavod im. M. I. Kalinina" association, is part of a works with extensive civilian production, including the manufacture of loading devices and light fittings.[1] Finally, it has been announced that the solid-fuel missile design bureau is to use released capacity to develop a new meteorological rocket which may be offered for export.[2]

Any conversion made possible by the treaty is unlikely to encounter major obstacles. At least three of the four enterprises concerned can build on well-established civilian activities and it is unlikely that those involved will suffer serious material hardship. It has been acknowledged that there may be problems of psychological adjustment – after all, the items covered by the Treaty are highly complex products in which considerable human knowledge and skill have been invested and, notwithstanding their potentially lethal character, objects of pride for those involved in their creation.[3] The INF Treaty put conversion on the policy agenda and drew attention to the need to go beyond the hitherto prevailing Soviet view of conversion in the conditions of the socialist planned economy.

III. Conversion and central planning

Until recently the generally accepted view had been that conversion should present no real difficulties for the Soviet Union. Social ownership of the means of production and central planning, it was maintained, made possible a planned, orderly transition from military to civilian production, facilitated by the absence of vested economic and social interests in the continuation of armaments development and manufacture. New interest in conversion was first signaled in a statement by deputy foreign minister Vladimir Petrovsky at the International Conference on the Relationship between Disarmament and Development in New York in August 1987. Petrovsky acknowledged that the process of conversion in socialist countries would not be trouble free, and called for the drafting by States of national conversion plans.[4] This prompted a series of discussion articles in the weekly journal *Novoe Vremya* and a substantial contribution in the monthly *International Affairs.*[5]

Contributors to the recent discussion acknowledge that the traditional position was oversimplified. In the words of E. Bugrov, a department head of the Institute of World Economy and International Relations of the USSR Academy of Sciences:

In socialist countries choice and implementation of conversion measures are linked with the role of such factors as public ownership of the means of production, management

---

[1] *Mashinostroitel'*, 1981, No. 1, p. 23; *Ekonomicheskaya Gazeta*, 1981, No. 26, p. 7.

[2] *Pravda*, 29 May 1988.

[3] Ibid., 27 Jan. 1988.

[4] USSR Mission to the United Nations, New York: *Press Release*, No. 110, 24 Aug. 1987, p. 7.

[5] See *Novoe Vremya*, 1987, No. 39, pp. 8-11; 1988. No. 1, pp. 24-27; No. 27, pp. 20-21; No. 30, pp. 21-22; A. Izyumov: "The other side of disarmament", in *International Affairs*, 1988, No. 5, pp. 82-88.

of the industrial process and the development of the social sphere on the basis of public national economic plans, together with the non-existence of social strata and groups which are keen supporters of the arms race. However, these social and economic conditions and levers do not provide an automatic smoothness and ease of the conversion process. Complex problems of structural renovation of industry, changes of investment policy, retraining and redistribution of personnel emerge and demand the application of exceptional efforts and resources for their resolution.[6]

Some authors have expanded on the difficulties of conversion in Soviet conditions. It has been acknowledged that some military production facilties are highly specialised and any conversion will require considerable time and effort.[7] The Soviet Union has a commitment to full employment and until now many regions have experienced labour shortages. However, it is recognised that employment problems may arise, in particular the need to provide appropriate retraining of workers and specialists. The question of the privileged conditions of work and pay of defence sector personnel has also been addressed. Izyumov, a leading conversion specialist of the Academy's Institute for the Study of the United States and Canada, rejects the view that such benefits predispose military enterprise personnel to oppose conversion proposals. Advantages in pay for workers in the military sector, he argues,

are primarily compensation for more difficult conditions of production there, as compared with the civilian sector (urgency of military contracts, stricter quality inspection, overtime work, unhealthy working conditions, limitations on travel abroad for security reasons, etc.). Such "compensational" additions to wages and salaries are widely practised all over the world ... In other words, the conditions for workers in the Soviet military industry are really not so privileged, and therefore the workers should not very much regret being in the civilian sphere, provided, of course, that civilian jobs would be offered to them in due time, while the cost of their retraining for new jobs will be borne by the State.[8]

In the recent discussion there has been recognition that conversion must be seen in the new conditions of economic reform. The economic management system now being introduced puts considerable emphasis on enterprises' financial viability. It is envisaged that enterprises will be obliged to make efficient use of all resources in order to earn the profits necessary to fund re-equipment and expansion and to create adequate incentive funds for their personnel, including the fund for social development and housing. As Izyumov points out, unlimited employment at civilian enterprises will no longer be possible and personnel will not be hired unless properly trained. This could create problems for demobilised servicemen and the redeployment of workers with specialised military sector skills.[9] There are differing views on the implications for the remuneration of defence sector personnel. In the opinion of S. I. Shukin, secretary of the central committee of the trade union for defence

---

[6] E. B. Bugrov: "Disarmament, conversion, development", *ENF Papers Seventeen ... into Ploughshares*, Winter/Spring 1988, p. 6. See also A. Izyumov, op. cit., p. 86.

[7] P. Litavrin: *Novoe Vremya*, 1988, No. 27, p. 21.

[8] A. Izyumov: *International Affairs*, 1988, No. 5, p. 87.

[9] Ibid., pp. 86-87.

industry workers, the new economic conditions could mean even higher pay for those switching to civilian work, presumably because the linkage between pay and performance will be stronger under the new reformed system than it is at present in the defence industry.[10] This presupposes that the military enterprises concerned are successful in switching to genuinely profitable civilian work. Izyumov points out that defence industry enterprises switching to civilian production may lose not only their superior pay and bonuses, but also their priority in obtaining labour, material and financial resources. In circumstances of economic reform, enterprises converting to civilian work will be forced to abandon the "results at any price" approach characteristic of some types of military production. In order to adapt successfully they will have to adopt new management methods and attitudes. However, he believes that many leaders of military institutes and enterprises would even now be prepared to lose their privileges in return for the greater economic independence becoming typical of the civilian sphere, and also the possibilities of open public acknowledgement of their talents. Conversion plans must nevertheless take account of the fact that some managers now engaged in high priority military production will not take kindly to being transfered to "ordinary" civilian work.[11] This problem of the need for a psychological reorientation on the part of some defence industry personnel has been acknowledged by other writers.[12]

Discussion of conversion problems initially remained at a high level of generality. This is hardly surprising in view of the lack of factual information on the defence industry available to Soviet specialists and publishable in open sources. From the spring of 1988 the need to rationalise the secrecy provisions of the defence sector began to be raised as a policy issue.[13] Izyumov, for example, stressed that, "a necessary condition for analysis of questions of conversion is an extension of *glasnost* in the sphere of military affairs". It is not a question of revealing genuine military secrets, he added, but of providing basic information on military-economic matters of a kind generally available for other countries.[14]

In the early months of 1989 there was evidence of a distinct improvement in the provision of information. A decision was taken to identify enterprises and institutes of the defence sector by their real names, ending the use of secret post office box numbers.[15] As the implementation of conversion gets under way, journalists are being allowed access to hitherto secret facilities, including establishments of the nuclear weapons industry.

---

[10] *Trud*, 1 Mar. 1988.

[11] *Novoe Vremya*, 1988, No. 30, p. 21.

[12] See, in particular, the letter of an engineer, S. Sukharev, to the paper *Literaturnaya Gazeta*, 1988, No. 18, p. 14.

[13] The issue was first raised publicly by the newspaper *Vechernaya Moskva* (see 21 Apr. 1988 (A. Prilutskii: "O 'yashchikakh', sekretakh polishinelya i vedomstvennykh interesakh") and 14 June 1988 (letters in response to Prilutskii); also *Pravda*, 6 Aug. 1988 (A. Pokrovskii, "A chto v 'yaschike'?")).

[14] *Novoe Vremya*, 1988, No. 30, p. 22.

[15] *Izvestiya*, 21 May 1989.

IV. The Soviet defence industry

Before turning to some employment aspects of conversion, it is necessary to consider briefly the basic features of the Soviet defence industry. The military sector is a component part of the planned economy. It consists of enterprises specialised in the manufacture of end-product weapons systems and support equipment, and factories supplying assemblies, components and materials. Apparently there are more than 150 major end-product weapons enterprises and shipyards plus a further 150 enterprises producing combat-support equipment such as radar and communications systems and trucks. Some of these enterprises are very large, employing in excess of 20,000 workers. These end-product enterprises are supported by thousands of suppliers. Prior to the government reorganisation of July 1989, the core defence industry was administered by nine industrial ministries; afterwards reduced to seven. There are no official data on the number of enterprises subordinate to these ministries and the number of employees, but some idea of the likely orders of magnitude is provided by the scale of the civilian engineering industry. As of January 1989 the civilian component of the engineering industry was administered by seven ministries having a total of some 2,250 enterprises (an average of 320 per ministry), employing almost 5.5 million personnel (an average of 785,000 per ministry).[16] Some of the defence industry ministries are likely to be very large in terms of enterprises and employment, in particular those for the aviation and electronics industries: a plausible assumption would be that total defence sector employment is comparable to that of the civilian engineering industry, and possibly even larger, i.e. in the range 5.5-6.5 million personnel.[17]

Before July 1989 the nine predominantly defence industry ministries were as follows:

(1) *Ministry of Medium Machine-building* (MSM): nuclear bombs and devices, high-energy lasers, uranium mining and processing for both military and civilian purposes.

(2) *Ministry of General Machine-building* (MOM): ballistic missiles and space launchers, space vehicles.

(3) *Ministry of the Defence Industry* (MOP): ground forces equipment (tanks and other armoured vehicles, artillery systems, short-range missiles, small arms, optical equipment), solid-propellant missiles.

(4) *Ministry of Machine-building* (MM): conventional munitions, fuses, solid-propellants.

---

[16] Number of enterprises: 1986 data, calculated from *Planovoe Khozyaistvo*, 1987, No. 5, p. 122. Personnel employed from Goskomstat, *Statisticheskii Press-Byulleten'*, 1989, No. 2, pp. 19-29.

[17] Total employment in the engineering industry is 16.5 million (*Trud v SSSR* (Moscow), "Finansy i Statistika", 1988, p. 49). As this total includes those employed at a large number of small metal-working and repair factories it provides little help in determining the scale of employment in the defence sector. The total number of industrial production personnel is approximately 38 million.

(5) *Ministry of the Aviation Industry* (MAP): military and civilian fixed-wing aircraft and helicopters, aerodynamic missiles and spacecraft.

(6) *Ministry of the Shipbuilding Industry* (MSP): naval and civilian ships, naval weapons, acoustic and radar systems.

(7) *Ministry of the Radio Industry* (MRP): radar and communications systems, computers, guidance and control systems.

(8) *Ministry of the Communications Equipment Industry* (MPSS): communications equipment, facsimile equipment, electronic consumer goods.

(9) *Ministry of the Electronics Industry* (MEP): electronic components, micro-computers.

In July 1989 the Ministry of Medium Machine-building took over the civilian nuclear power industry and was renamed the Ministry of Nuclear Power and Industry. At the same time the Ministry of Machine-building was amalgamated with the Ministry of the Defence Industry and the communications industry ministry was merged with the radio industry.

In addition to the enterprises of these ministries, some military products and many inputs are supplied by enterprises of civilian ministries.[18] The defence industry also has its own network of research and development organisations and draws on the research facilities of the academies of sciences and the higher educational system.

The defence industry has many characteristics in common with the rest of Soviet industry, but also a number of special features. Its planning and management procedures are similar to those in the civilian economy, but more highly centralised. The military customer exerts pressure for compliance with contractual obligations and has its own quality acceptance personnel at the enterprise to ensure that technical specifications are met. The defence industry has first priority access to resources in terms of both quantity and quality and this priority is secured through the operation of the planning and supply systems. While defence enterprises are expected to make efficient use of resources, it is likely that they operate in less constrained financial circumstances than their civilian counterparts, with easier access to central investment funds. An extremely strict secrecy regime is enforced within the military sector placing real constraints on the freedom of personnel to travel, publish, meet foreigners and gain open public recognition. On the other hand, as noted above, defence sector workers have higher wages and salaries and access to more substantial bonuses, although the military-civilian differentials appear to have narrowed over the years in line with the general pay levelling characteristic of the Brezhnev

---

[18] At the time of writing it has been revealed that ministerial mergers are proposed. Details have not been released, but it appears likely that the Ministry of Machine-building will merge with the Ministry of the Defence Industry, and the Communications Equipment Industry with the Ministry of the Radio Industry. The number of civilian engineering ministries is to be reduced to four (*Pravda*, 11 June 1989; *Trud*, 14 June 1989).

period. Finally, enterprises of the defence industry are usually able to offer superior housing and welfare conditions for their employees; a very important consideration in their ability to attract and retain skilled workers and qualified managerial and technical personnel. One of the advantages of the defence sector, helping to account for the relatively high quality of its production, may be precisely the stability of its labour force. Civilian engineering enterprises, especially in labour-scarce regions, often experience high rates of labour turnover and may be forced to employ workers of inadequate skills and experience.

V. The regional distribution of defence industry employment

In the absence of suitable employment data it is necessary to adopt an alternative approach to the analysis of the employment implications of conversion. The only possibility open to the researcher is the use of the distribution of defence sector enterprises on the assumption that this provides a reasonable approximation to the distribution of employment. Such data are not published, but it is possible to assemble sample evidence on a scale considered adequate to provide a satisfactory approximation to the actual regional distribution of the Soviet defence industry. The author has assembled information on 100 end-product weapons-producing enterprises and a total sample of 510 enterprises believed to be affiliated to eight of the nine defence industry ministries as of the end of 1988. (The nuclear weapons producing Ministry of Medium Machine-building has been excluded for lack of appropriate evidence.) [19] The end-product weapons enterprises are listed in full in J. Cooper: *The Soviet defence industry and conversion: A regional perspective* (Geneva, ILO, 1988; mimeographed World Employment Programme Research Working Paper; restricted). Of the total sample, 86 have been positively identified as belonging to the aviation and missile industries, 64 as belonging to the Ministry of the Defence Industry and Ministry of Machine-building (predominantly ground forces equipment and conventional munitions), and 85 to the Ministry of Shipbuilding. A further 175 enterprises have been identified as being subordinate to the radio, communications equipment and electronics ministries, leaving 100 enterprises of unknown ministerial affiliation but strongly suspected defence sector allegiance.[20]

---

[19] The information has been assembled over many years from a wide range of sources, in particular Soviet newspapers and industrial-technical journals. In some cases ministerial affiliation is directly indicated in the Soviet source; in other cases it can be identified indirectly, sometimes from knowledge of the civilian production of the enterprise concerned. For the sample of end-product weapons enterprises, information from Soviet sources has been supplemented by United States government publications, in particular *Soviet military power* (various editions) Department of Defense, Washington, DC, and *The Soviet weapons industry: An overview*, Central Intelligence Agency, Washington, DC.

[20] It is possible that this group of 100 enterprises of unknown ministerial affiliation includes some belonging to the nuclear weapons industry.

For some purposes the Soviet Union is divided into official economic regions.[21] From the known locations of the sample of defence industry enterprises it has proved possible to allocate them all by economic region. The results are presented in tables 8.1 to 8.5.

Table 8.1 shows the regional distributions of both the 100 end-product weapons enterprises and the total sample of 510 enterprises affiliated to defence industry ministries. It emerges that the Soviet defence industry is concentrated to a marked extent in the RSFSR and that this bias is especially notable in relation to actual weapons production: 88 per cent of the weapons enterprises are located in the major Soviet republic, as opposed to 73 per cent of the total sample. There appear to be very few weapons producing enterprises in republics other than RSFSR and the Ukraine (only 4 per cent of the sample), but a much higher proportion of other defence-related enterprises (13.4 per cent of the total sample).

Within the RSFSR the weapons-producing enterprises are heavily concentrated in the Urals (20 per cent), the Central economic region around Moscow (17 per cent), the Volga region (13 per cent), and in and around Leningrad (10 per cent). Taking the total sample, the Central region is predominant with more than one-fifth of the enterprises, while the Urals is more weakly represented (11 per cent).

In some regions a high proportion of the identified defence sector enterprises are concerned with end-product weapons. In table 8.1 this is shown by an index of "relative weapons intensity": the regions are ranked according to this index in table 8.2. Not surprisingly in view of its historic role, Tula emerges as the leading region, followed by the Chelyabinsk region and the Far East, the latter because of its prominent role in shipbuilding. Also highly ranked are some regions of Siberia, the Kirov, Kuibyshev and Perm' regions, and the Tatar and Udmurt Autonomous Republics (the latter, in the Urals, including the major centre of Izhevsk and the Votkinsk missile plant).

The various branches of the defence industry have their own characteristic location patterns. This dimension is shown in table 8.3. It can be seen that the aerospace industry is heavily concentrated in the Central region, but also strongly represented in the Volga and Urals regions. The predominance of the Central region would be even more marked if account had been taken of the location of the leading design bureaux and their prototype factories, many of which are located in, or near, Moscow. The Urals region is the principal centre of the ground forces equipment and conventional munitions industries, followed by the Central, North-Western, Volga and West-Siberian regions. Not surprisingly, the shipbuilding industry has its own specific location pattern, with major centres in the Leningrad region, the Southern Ukraine and the Far East. The electronics-related industries also have their own distinct regional distribution. The RSFSR's contribution is only 60 per cent, with the Moscow

---

[21] For the current system of economic regions, see A. N. Lavrishchev: *Ekonomicheskaya geografiya SSSR*, 5th ed., Moscow, "Ekonomika", 1986, pp. 375-379.

Table 8.1. **Regional distribution of enterprises of the Soviet defence industry**

Region	100 end-product weapons enterprises		510 defence industry enterprises		RWI[1] (A)/(B)
	No. and % (A)		No.	% (B)	
Russian Soviet Federated Socialist Republic (RSFSR)	**88**		**372**	**72.9**	**121**
Central Economic Region	*16*		*104*	*20.4*	*78*
Moscow region		5	59	11.6	43
Tula region		4	6	1.2	333
Vladimir region		4	18	3.5	114
Other regions		3	21	4.1	73
North-Western E.R.	*10*		*45*	*8.8*	*114*
Leningrad region		10	34	6.7	149
Northern E.R.	*1*		*4*	*0.8*	*125*
Volgo-Vyatka E.R.	*7*		*32*	*6.3*	*111*
Gor'kii region		4	21	4.1	98
Kirov region		2	4	0.8	250
Mari ASSR		1	3	0.6	167
Central Chernozem E.R.	*2*		*13*	*2.5*	*80*
Voronezh region		2	9	1.8	111
North Caucasus E.R.	*2*		*23*	*4.5*	*44*
Rostov region		2	13	2.5	80
Volga E.R.	*13*		*43*	*8.4*	*155*
Saratov region		1	6	1.2	83
Kuibyshev region		4	8	1.6	250
Ul'yanovsk region		1	5	1.0	100
Tatar ASSR		5	13	2.5	200
Urals E.R.	*20*		*54*	*10.6*	*189*
Perm' region		4	8	1.6	250
Udmurt ASSR		3	8	1.6	188
Sverdlovsk		3	15	2.9	103
Chelyabinsk region		6	11	2.3	273
West-Siberian E.R.	*7*		*31*	*6.1*	*115*
Novosibirsk region		2	9	1.8	111
Omsk region		2	9	1.8	111
Altai region		2	4	0.8	250
East-Siberian E.R.	*4*		*11*	*2.2*	*182*
Krasnoyarsk region		2	5	1.0	200
Buryat ASSR		1	2	0.4	250
Far Eastern E.R.	*6*		*12*	*2.3*	*261*
Ukraine	**8**		**70**	**13.7**	**58**
Donetsk-Dnieper E.R.	*4*		*20*	*3.9*	*103*
Dnepropetrovsk region		1	5	1.0	100
Khar'kov region		2	9	1.8	111
Other regions		1	6	1.1	91

Table 8.1. *(continued)*

Region	100 end-product weapons enterprises		510 defence industry enterprises		RWI[1] (A)/(B)
	No. and % (A)		No.	% (B)	
South-Western E.R.	2		*31*	*6.1*	*33*
Kiev region		2	12	2.4	87
Other regions		–	19	3.7	–
Southern E.R.	*2*		*19*	*3.7*	*54*
Byelorussian E.R.	**0**		**17**	**3.3**	**0**
Baltic E.R.	**1**		**19**	**3.7**	**27**
Transcaucasian E.R.	**1**		**14**	**2.8**	**36**
Kazakh E.R.	**1**		**5**	**1.0**	**100**
Central Asian E.R.	**1**		**8**	**1.6**	**63**
Moldavia	**0**		**5**	**1.0**	**0**
All USSR	100		510	100.0	

[1] RWI – Relative weapons intensity index, i.e. measure of degree to which defence industry enterprises in a region are engaged in end-product weapons production.

Table 8.2. *Ranking of regions by relative weapons intensity*

	RWI			RWI			RWI
1. Tula r.	333		9. Tatar ASSR	200		15. Voronezh r.	111
2. Chelyabinsk r.	273		Krasnoyarsk r.	200		Novosibirsk r.	111
3. Far Eastern E.R.	261		11. Udmurt ASSR	188		Omsk r.	111
4. Altai r.	250		12. Mari ASSR	166		Khar'kov r.	111
Buryat ASSR	250		13. Leningrad r.	149		19. Sverdlovsk r.	103
Kirov r.	250		14. Vladimir r.	114		20. Ul'yanovsk r.	100
Kuibyshev r.	250					Dnepropetrovsk r.	100
Perm' r.	250					Kazakh E.R.	100

Source. From table 8.1.

region predominant, but in this case the Ukraine is strongly represented. Some republics making an extremely modest contribution to traditional weapons technologies are actively involved in the production of radio, communications and electronic equipment, including Byelorussia, the Baltic republics, Moldavia, Georgia, Armenia and Uzbekistan.

Another approach to the analysis of the distribution of the defence industry is presented in table 8.4. Again, data limitations dictate the indicator chosen. In the absence of any regional data on the distribution of the industrial

Table 8.3. *Regional distribution of Soviet defence industry enterprises by branch of industry (per cent total[1])*

Region	Aerospace[2]	G.F.Eq.[3]	Ship-building[4]	E.R.C.[5]	All defence industry
RSFSR	**86.0**	**87.5**	**69.4**	**60.6**	**72.9**
Central E.R.	*27.9*	*18.7*	*8.2*	*19.4*	*20.4*
Moscow r.	22.1	9.4	1.2	12.0	11.6
Tula r.	–	6.2	1.2	0.6	1.2
Vladimir r.	2.3	3.1	4.7	4.0	3.5
Other regions	3.5	–	1.1	2.8	4.1
North-Western E.R.	*3.5*	*9.4*	*20.0*	*8.5*	*8.8*
Leningrad	3.5	9.4	20.0	2.9	6.7
Northern E.R.	–	–	*3.5*	–	*0.8*
Volgo-Vyatka E.R.	*8.1*	*7.8*	*8.2*	*4.6*	*6.3*
Gor'kii r.	5.8	4.7	7.0	2.9	4.1
Kirov r.	2.3	1.6	1.2	–	0.8
Mari ASSR	–	1.6	–	1.1	0.6
Central Chzem. E.R.	*3.5*	*1.6*	*1.2*	*2.3*	*2.5*
Voronezh r.	3.5	–	1.2	2.3	1.8
North-Caucasus E.R.	*4.7*	*1.6*	*4.7*	*4.0*	*4.5*
Rostov r.	4.7	1.6	3.5	1.7	2.5
Volga E.R.	*12.8*	*9.4*	*8.2*	*6.9*	*8.4*
Saratov r.	2.3	–	1.2	1.1	1.2
Kuibyshev r.	5.8	1.6	–	0.6	1.6
Ul'yanovsk r.	1.2	1.6	–	0.6	1.0
Tatar ASSR	3.5	3.1	1.2	2.3	2.5
Urals E.R.	*12.8*	*28.1*	*2.4*	*6.3*	*10.6*
Perm' r.	2.3	4.7	1.2	0.6	1.6
Udmurt ASSR	2.3	3.1	–	1.7	1.6
Sverdlovsk r.	3.5	7.8	1.2	1.1	2.9
Chelyabinsk r.	2.3	4.7	–	0.6	2.2
West-Siberian E.R.	*4.7*	*9.4*	*1.2*	*6.3*	*6.1*
Novosibirsk r.	1.2	3.1	–	2.3	1.8
Omsk r.	2.3	1.6	–	1.7	1.8
Altai r.	–	3.1	–	1.1	0.8
Other r.	0.2	1.6	1.2	1.2	1.7
East-Siberian E.R.	*5.8*	*1.5*	*1.2*	*1.7*	*2.2*
Krasnoyarsk r.	2.3	1.5	–	1.1	1.0
Far Eastern E.R.	*2.3*	–	*10.6*	*0.6*	*2.3*
Ukraine	**10.5**	**7.8**	**20.0**	**15.4**	**13.7**
Donetsk-Dnr. E.R.	*8.1*	*4.7*	–	*4.0*	*3.9*
Dnepropetrovsk r.	2.3	–	–	1.1	1.0
Khar'kov r.	4.7	3.1	–	1.1	1.8
South-Western E.R.	*2.3*	*1.6*	*4.7*	*10.3*	*6.1*
Kiev r.	2.3	1.6	3.5	2.9	2.3
Southern E.R.	–	*1.6*	*15.3*	*1.1*	*3.7*

Table 8.3. (continued)

Region	Aerospace[2]	G.F.Eq.[3]	Ship-building[4]	E.R.C.[5]	All defence industry
Byelorussian E.R.	–	1.6	1.2	7.4	3.3
Baltic E.R.	–	–	5.9	7.4	3.7
Transcaucasian E.R.	2.3	–	3.5	4.0	2.8
Kazakh E.R.	–	1.6	–	0.6	1.0
Central Asian E.R.	1.2	1.5	–	2.3	1.6
Moldavia	–	–	–	2.3	1.0
Number of enterprises	*86*	*64*	*85*	*175*	*510*

[1] Total includes 100 enterprises of unidentified affiliation.   [2] Aerospace – aviation, missile and space industries (MAP, MOM).
[3] G.F.Eq. – ground forces equipment (MOP, MM).   [4] Shipbuilding – shipbuilding industry (MSP).   [5] E.R.C. – electronics, radio and communications equipment industries (MEP, MRP, MPSS)

labour force (not to speak of engineering industry personnel), we are obliged to relate the number of defence sector enterprises to total population. In this case the concentration of end-product weapons enterprises and also of the total sample are measured by the number of enterprises per 10 million popoulation. The regional rankings are shown in table 8.5. This shows the clear predominance in end-product weapons production of the Central regions of Vladimir and Tula, the Urals regions of the Udmurt ASSR and Chelyabinsk, and Leningrad. There is also a close correlation between the ranking by this indicator and by the relative weapons intensity index shown in table 8.2 (six of the regions appear in the top ten in both cases; 14 of the top 15). Taking the total sample of 510 defence sector enterprises, the top ranking is modifed: the Vladimir region again occupies first place, but the Gor'kii, Moscow, Omsk, Ul'yanovsk and Voronezh regions are now strongly represented.

This analysis focuses attention on a number of leading regional centres of the Soviet defence industry; centres which would inevitably become prominent in the event of the implementation of a national conversion policy. These regions include Vladimir, Tula and Chelyabinsk, the Udmurt and Tatar Autonomous Republics, Perm', Kuibyshev, Kirov, and, if shipbuilding were included, Leningrad, the Far East and the Southern region of the Ukraine. The Moscow region should probably be added to this list in so far as it is a major research, design and development centre. Conversion of broader scope involving combat-support and auxiliary production would also have consequences for the Gor'kii, Ul'yanovsk, Voronezh, Omsk, Novosibirsk and Sverdlovsk regions, plus the Khar'kov and Kiev regions of the Ukraine. This broad regional approach abstracts from important local concentrations which could present difficult conversion problems: a notable example is the vast Severodvinsk submarine-building yard in the remote Northern economic region.

Table 8.4. Number of defence industry enterprises per 10 million population by economic region

Region	Population (1 Jan. 1987) (thousands)	EPW[1] (per 10 million population)	All D.I.[2] (per 10 million population)
RSFSR[3]	**144 454**	**6.1**	**25.8**
Central E.R.	*29 964*	*5.3*	*34.7*
Moscow r.	15 396	3.2	38.3
Tula r.	1 863	21.5	20.9
Vladimir r.	1 638	24.4	109.9
Other r.	11 067	2.7	19.0
North-Western E.R.	*8 200*	*12.2*	*54.9*
Leningrad r.	6 603	15.1	51.5
Northern E.R.	*6 069*	*1.6*	*6.6*
Volgo-Vyatka E.R.	*8 396*	*8.3*	*38.1*
Gor'kii r.	3 688	10.8	56.9
Kirov r.	1 675	11.9	23.9
Mari ASSR	739	13.5	40.6
Other r.	2 294	3.9	17.4
Central Chernozem E.R.	*7 661*	*2.6*	*17.0*
Voronezh r.	2 459	8.1	39.6
N. Caucasus E.R.	*16 473*	*1.2*	*14.0*
Rostov r.	4 290	4.7	30.3
Volga E.R.	*16 212*	*8.0*	*26.5*
Saratov r.	2 646	3.8	22.7
Kuibyshev r.	3 264	12.3	24.5
Ul'yanovsk r.	1 354	7.4	36.9
Tatar ASSR	3 568	14.0	36.4
Urals E.R.	*20 116*	*9.9*	*26.8*
Perm' r.	3 071	13.0	26.1
Udmurt ASSR	1 587	18.9	50.4
Sverdlovsk r.	4 703	6.4	31.9
Chelyabinsk r.	3 583	16.7	30.7
Other r.	7 172	5.6	16.7
W. Siberian E.R.	*14 607*	*4.8*	*20.5*
Novosibirsk r.	2 770	7.2	32.5
Omsk r.	2 088	9.6	43.1
Altai r.	2 777	7.2	14.4
Other r.	6 972	1.4	11.5
E. Siberian E.R.	*8 984*	*4.5*	*12.2*
Krasnoyarsk r.	3 520	5.7	14.2
Buryat ASSR	1 030	9.7	19.4
Other r.	4 434	2.3	9.0
Far Eastern E.R.	*7 772*	*7.7*	*15.4*
Ukraine	**51 201**	**1.6**	**13.7**
Donetsk-Dnieper E.R.	*21 679*	*1.8*	*9.2*
Dnepropetrovsk r.	3 857	2.6	13.0
Khar'kov r.	3 163	6.3	28.5
Other r.	14 659	0.7	4.1

Table 8.4. *(continued)*

Region	Population (1 Jan. 1987) (thousands)	EPW[1] (per 10 million population)	All D.I.[2] (per 10 million population)
S. Western E.R.	*21 962*	*0.9*	*14.1*
Kiev r.	4 446	4.5	27.0
Other r.	17 516	–	10.8
Southern E.R.	*7 560*	*2.6*	*25.1*
Byelorussian E.R.	**10 078**	–	**16.9**
Baltic E.R.	**8 701**	**1.1**	**21.8**
Transcaucasian E.R.	**15 489**	**0.6**	**9.0**
Kazakh E.R.	**16 244**	**0.6**	**3.1**
Central Asian E.R.	**31 337**	**0.3**	**2.6**
Moldavia	**4 185**	–	**11.9**
Total USSR	281 689	3.6	18.1

[1] End-product weapon enterprises per 10 million population.   [2] All defence industry enterprises per 10 million population.
[3] Excluding Kaliningrad region, included in Baltic E.R.
Source. Population by region – *Narodnoe Khozyaistvo SSSR za 70 let*, M., 1987, pp. 377 and 389-394. Number of enterprises – table 8.1.

Table 8.5. *Ranking of economic regions by number of defence industry enterprises per 10 million population*

A. *End-product weapons enterprises*

1. Vladimir r.	24.4
2. Tula r.	21.5
3. Udmurt ASSR	18.9
4. Chelyabinsk r.	16.7
5. Leningrad r.	15.1
6. Tatar ASSR	14.0
7. Mari ASSR	13.5
8. Perm' r.	13.0
9. Kuibyshev r.	12.3
10. Kirov r.	11.9
11. Gor'kii r.	10.8
12. Buryat ASSR	9.7
13. Omsk r.	9.6
14. Voronezh r.	8.1
15. Far Eastern E.R.	7.7
16. Ul'yanovsk r.	7.4
17. Altai r.	7.2
Novosibirsk r.	7.2
19. Sverdlovsk r.	6.4
20. Khar'kov r.	6.3

B. *All defence industry enterprises*

1. Vladimir r.	109.9
2. Gor'kii r.	56.9
3. Leningrad r.	51.5
4. Udmurt ASSR	50.4
5. Omsk r.	43.1
6. Mari ASSR	40.6
7. Moscow r.	34.7
8. Ul'yanovsk r.	36.9
9. Voronezh r.	36.6
10. Tatar ASSR	36.4
11. Novosibirsk r.	32.5
12. Tula r.	32.2
13. Sverdlovsk r.	31.9
14. Chelyabinsk r.	30.7
15. Rostov r.	30.3
16. Khar'kov r.	28.5
17. Kiev r.	27.0
18. Perm' r.	26.1
19. Ukraine – Southern E.R.	25.0
20. Kuibyshev r.	24.5

Source. From table 8.4.

VI. The regions, labour and the engineering industry

Pursuit of a conversion policy could give rise to employment problems arising from the release of labour from defence industry enterprises, some of which may be closed down, wholly or in part. In these circumstances the labour market situation of different regions could be of considerable importance.[22] From this point of view the Soviet position is relatively fortunate: the main concentrations of defence sector enterprises tend to be in regions of relative labour scarcity. The Urals, Siberia and Far East are all labour-scarce regions. The labour-plentiful regions of Central Asia and Kazakhstan are also those with the smallest defence industry presence. Other areas of relative labour scarcity include the North-Western (Leningrad) and Volgo-Vyatka regions. The labour market situation is less constrained in the Central and Volga regions, while in the Ukraine and Byelorussia labour is relatively plentiful. The relative availability of labour, in particular female labour, has been an important factor in the location of electronics-related industries outside the RSFSR.

Another consideration is the role of the engineering industry in the various economic regions.[23] Those regions with well-developed civilian machine-building industries may be better placed with regard to conversion than those without. As expected, the regions with a strong defence sector presence tend to be those with strong civilian engineering industries. But there are also important regional differences in the character of the engineering industries of the various regions and they could be of potential importance for a conversion policy.

Machine-building is the largest industry of the Central region, accounting for more than one-third of the total labour force. The most highly developed branches are those requiring skilled labour: machine tools, electrical engineering, instrument-making, and the production of specialised industrial equipment, including textile machinery. The bias towards machine-building is even stronger in the North-Western region and, again, the emphasis is on branches requiring highly skilled labour. In the city of Leningrad almost two-thirds of the labour force are employed in the engineering industry. Machine-building does not play a large role in the Northern Region and tends to be focused on local requirements, notably equipment for forestry and the paper and pulp industries. The Volgo-Vyatka region is distinguished by an unusually high share of engineering in industrial output, more than half, and focuses on branches of a relatively labour- and skill-intensive nature, not requiring large metal inputs (machine tools, diesel engines, trucks, electrical equipment). A similar pattern is found in the Volga region, where skill-intensive, low metal-intensity branches predominate.

---

[22] This section draws on A. N. Lavrishchev, op. cit., pp. 246-348, and A. T. Khrushchev: *Geografiya promyshlennosti SSSR* (Moscow), "Mysl'", 1986, pp. 49-57.

[23] This section draws on the works cited in footnote 24 and also S. I. Mozokhin and E. N. Tatarintseva: *Territorial'naya organizatsiya mashinostroitel'nogo proizvodstva* (Moscow), "Mashinostroenie", 1984; and A. P. Gerko and A. I. Kazakov: *Problemy formirovaniya mashinostroitel'nykh kompleksov* (Moscow), "Nauka", 1981.

The Urals region has its own distinctive engineering industry biased towards heavy, metal-intensive products, often requiring skilled labour. There is also metal-intensive machine-building in the West Siberian region, with the more skilled branches concentrated in the Novosibirsk and Omsk regions. Here, as in East Siberia, there is a bias towards branches of low labour intensity. In the Far East, also a labour-scarce region, machine-building accounts for about one-fifth of total industrial output and is biased towards shipbuilding and repairs. In both Siberia and the Far East branches of the engineering industry catering for local needs are relatively underdeveloped, offering ready alternatives in the event of the pursuit of a conversion policy.

The machine-building of the Ukraine also has its own characteristic features, tending to be focused on labour- and metal-intensive products, including rail transport and metallurgical equipment, and also electrical and electronic products, the production of the latter being well developed in the labour plentiful South-Western region. The engineering of the Southern Ukraine is rather narrowly focused on shipbuilding and agricultural machine-building. Labour-intensive branches predominate in Byelorussia, but in the labour-scarce Baltic republics there is a bias towards high-precision products. The machine-building of other regions tends to be labour-intensive, often focused on meeting specific local requirements. As discussed below, any conversion policy would have to take account of the specific local circumstances in terms of both labour and the character of the civilian engineering industry.

VII. The civilian role of the defence industry

One important aspect of the Soviet defence industry relevant to potential conversion is its present-day civilian role. This question has been discussed by the present author elsewhere; here we present revised and updated quantitative data and review some issues directly related to the problem of conversion.[24] The available evidence suggests that a large proportion of Soviet defence industry enterprises are engaged in some form of civilian production, sometimes on a substantial scale. The total volume of civilian production is not known, but taking account of the full range of products from civilian aircraft and ships to electronic goods and consumer items it is possible that as much as one-third of the total output of the nine defence sector ministries is of a civilian nature. Thus many employees of the defence sector are already engaged in civilian work and within each of the ministries there exist organisations and administrative arrangements specifically concerned with non-military activities.

The defence industry's share of total Soviet output of a range of civilian products is shown in tables 8.6 and 8.7. Unfortunately, the range of products

---

[24] See J. Cooper: "The civilian production of the Soviet defence industry", in R. Amann and J. Cooper: *Technical progress and Soviet economic development* (Oxford, Basil Blackwell, 1986), pp. 31-50.

Table 8.6. The share of total Soviet output of civilian products from enterprises of the defence industry (percentage of total output in physical unit terms, unless otherwise specified)

Product	1965	1970	1975	1980	1985	1988
Crude steel[1] (MOP, MOM, MSP)	(10)	(9)	(8)	(8)	(8)	9
Inc. electric-arc steel[1]	55	53	53	50	49	n.a.
Metal-cutting machine tools (MAP, MOP, MM, MOM, MSP, MRP)	n.a.	(14)	(14)	(14)	(13)	(20)*
Inc. NC machines	n.a.	(42)	(36)	(30)	(26)	(18)
Tractors (MOP, MOM)	13	13	(14)	(15)	(15)	13*
Irrigators (MSP)[2]	–	–	n.a.	9	12	17*
Rail freight wagons (MOP)	n.a.	(33)	(30)	(27)	n.a.	n.a.
Tramcars (MOM)	72	55	65	60	n.a.	n.a.
Passenger cars (MOP)	–	11	10	10	(12)	10
Motorcycles and scooters (MOP)	73	69	68	(64)	(63)	56
Bicycles (MM)	44	37	(39)	(42)	(40)	57
Refrigerators (MOM, MAP, MOP, MM, MRP, MSP)	48	48	(48)	(48)	n.a.	98[x]
Washing machines (MAP, MM, MOP, MOM, MOM, MSP)	(41)	(38)	(32)	(27)	(27)	69[x]
Vacuum-cleaners (MAP, MOP, MOM, MRP)	49	(42)	(46)	(43)	n.a.	78[x]
Television sets (MPSS, MRP, MOM, MEP)	100	100	100	100	100	100
Radios (MPSS, MRP, MEP, MAP, MSP, MOM)	100	100	100	100	100	100
Tape-recorders (MPSS, MRP, MEP, MAP, MM, MOM, MOP, MSP)	(95)	(95)	(95)	(95)	(95)	98
Video-recorders (MEP)	–	–	100	100	100	100
Personal computers (MRP, MEP, MPSS)	–	–	–	–	(90)	98
Inc. home computers (MRP, MEP)	–	–	–	–	100	100
Clocks and watches (MM, MAP, MEP, MRP)	12	12	(11)	(14)	(19)	22
Cameras (MOP, MAP)	100	100	100	100	100	100
Furniture (value terms)	n.a.	n.a.	n.a.	2	2	3
All consumer durables and household goods (value terms)[3]	n.a.	n.a.	n.a.	n.a.	n.a.	23[x]

(..) = estimate; * = 1987; n.a. = not available; – = not produced.

[x] Includes output for whole of 1988 from enterprises transferred to the defence industry during the year from the former Ministry of Machine-building for the Light and Food Industries.

[1] Proportion shown is that produced outside the Ministry of Ferrous Metallurgy; somewhat overstates the share of the defence industry as there is some limited production by civilian machine-building ministries, notably the Ministry of Heavy and Transport Machine-building. [2] Share of total deliveries to agriculture. [3] Total non-food consumer goods less output of light industry.

Sources. 1965-85: J. M. Cooper: "The scale of output of civilian products by enterprises of the Soviet defence industry", in CREES Discussion Paper, University of Birmingham, 1988. (Note: some of the 1985 estimates probably require revision in the light of evidence available since the paper was written). 1988: Calculated by the author from a range of Soviet sources, in particular Vestnik Statistiki, 1989, No. 5, pp. 70-73, and Goskomstat: Statisticheskii Press-Byulleten', 1989, No. 2.

Table 8.7.   *Output of civilian products by enterprises of the defence sector*

Product	1965	1970	1975	1980	1985	1988
Steel (m.t.)	(9.5)	(10.0)	(11.4)	(12.4)	(11.7)	14
Metal-cutting machine tools (t.u.)	n.a.	(28.3)	(32.3)	(30.2)	(23.7)	(32)*
Inc. NC mc.t. (t.u.)	n.a.	(0.7)	(2.0)	(2.7)	(4.6)	(4.0)
Tractors (t.u.)	44	61	(77)	(83)	(87)	76*
Irrigators (t.u.)	–	–	n.a.	1.8	2.9	3.5*
Rail freight wagons (t.u.)	n.a.	(19.2)	(23.1)	(18.9)	(15.4)	n.a.
Tramcars (u.)	890	430	688	601	n.a.	n.a.
Passenger cars (t.u.)	–	36	115	136	(160)	130
Motorcycles (t.u.)	516	571	696	(694)	(718)	601
Bicycles (t.u.)	1487	1423	(1677)	(1965)	(2125)	3176
Refrigerators (t.u.)	808	1995	(2689)	(2863)	n.a.	6228
Washing machines (t.u.)	(1405)	(1988)	(1056)	(1046)	(1393)	4239
Vacuum-cleaners (t.u.)	390	(635)	(1342)	(1395)	n.a.	3722
Television sets (t.u.)	3655	6682	6960	7528	9371	9628
Radios (t.u.)	5160	7815	8376	8478	8849	8026
Tape-recorders (t.u.)	(430)	(1130)	(2400)	(2900)	(4250)	5406
Video-recorders (t.u.)	–	–	–	n.a.	6.8	72.9
Personal computers (t.u.)	–	–	–	–	(7.9)	50
Clocks and watches (m.u.)	3.8	4.8	(6.0)	(9.6)	(12.6)	16
Cameras (t.u.)	1053	2045	3031	4255	2085	2415

Abbreviations. m.t. = million tons; t.u. = thousand units; m.u. = million units.
Notes and sources. As for table 8.6

covered is dictated by the availability of appropriate statistical data. Among the excluded products are civilian aircraft and ships, radio and communications equipment, computers (other than personal models), medical equipment, chemicals, power equipment, many types of industrial machinery, lasers and a wide range of consumer goods. It will be seen that the defence industry makes an important contribution to the manufacture of a wide range of products, including tractors, rail freight wagons, machine tools (especially the more complex models), motor cycles, and electrical and electronic consumer durables. Given the defence sector's importance in electronic-related technologies, it is likely that the civilian share of the defence industry output has grown since 1965.

   Early in 1988 the decision was taken to disband the civilian Ministry of Machine-building for the Light and Food Industries and transfer its 260 enterprises to eight other engineering ministries. Since the beginning of March, when the decision took effect, it has become apparent that most of the enterprises have been taken over by ministries of the defence industry, at a stroke enhancing appreciably the sector's civilian role. The disbanded ministry was responsible for a diverse range of equipment for consumer activities, including the textile and footwear industries, food processing, and the retail trade sector, and also many consumer goods including such items as refrigerators and washing machines. This measure, in line with the current policy of increasing the defence industry's contribution to the modernisation of the Soviet economy, has involved the creation of new administrative arrangements within the defence industry.[25] Within the Military-Industrial Commission of the USSR Council of Ministers (the principal government oversight agency for the defence industry), a new department has been organised for co-ordinating the activities of the transferred enterprises, and each of the ministries concerned has also created an appropriate management body.[26] The thinking behind this development is clear: it is hoped that the involvement of the skills, experience and resources of the defence industry will permit a rapid advancement of a seriously lagging sector of industry vital to the improvement of living standards. But one can also envisage that the organisational arrangements and experience accumulated could be of considerable value in the implementation of a conversion policy.

Some of the civilian production of the defence industry has been undertaken for many years with long-standing traditions and experience. This applies in particular to major enterprises of the Ministry of the Defence Industry and also, in so far as they were based on established artillery works, some of the enterprises of the missile industry. Examples of the former include the Leningrad "Kirovskii Zavod" association, Izhevsk "Izhmash", Perm' imeni Lenina and Volgograd "Barrikady" works; of the latter, the Votkinsk machine-building works, covered by the INF agreement. In some cases military sector enterprises were founded on what were originally civilian factories: examples include the Saratov aviation works (originally built in the early 1930s as a combine harvester factory), the missile building Dnepropetrovsk "Yuzhnii mashinostroitel'nyi zavod" (planned in the immediate post-war years as a motor vehicle works) and another missile plant, the Krasnoyarsk "Krasmash" (a factory for the production of extractive industry equipment). Conversion of some of these facilities could be regarded as re-conversion, although in the cases cited the civilian experience is so distant as to have little meaning today.[27] There may be some cases, however, where the previous civilian role could have direct relevance to conversion.

---

[25] The current policy with regard to the defence sector is discussed in J. Cooper: "Technology transfer between military and civilian ministries", in United States Congress, Joint Economic Committee: *Gorbachev's economic plans* (Washington, DC, USGPO, 1987), Vol. 1, pp. 388-404.

[26] *Izvestiya*, 2 Mar. 1988.

[27] Two of the three enterprises do in fact have well-developed civilian production, but of a different nature from their original profiles: the Dnepropetrovsk works builds the small "YuMZ" tractor; "Krasmash" is the leading Soviet producer of refrigerators, making the popular "Biryuza" model.

There is little doubt that the quality of civilian products manufactured within the defence sector generally compares favourably with the quality of similar items produced by enterprises of civilian industrial ministries.[28] This does not mean, as many Soviet television owners are only too well aware, that the products are invariably of high quality. But in so far as they are not made at all by enterprises of civilian ministries, the example of television sets provides supports for the general point (and if they were it is likely that their quality would be even worse). The defence sector also has experience of exporting civilian products to Western markets: examples include tractors, optical equipment and refrigerators. This ability of the defence industry to produce at a relatively high and consistent quality is 45of great potential importance for any conversion strategy.

VIII. Conversion and Soviet economic policy

One of the central goals of the Gorbachev leadership is the modernisation of the Soviet economy with the aim of achieving significant improvements in both living standards and the country's international competitiveness. This is now the context in which the question of conversion must be considered.

First priority in the modernisation programme has been granted to the civilian engineering industry. It is recognised that its technological level is inadequate to meet the economy's needs for production equipment and consumer goods. The Soviet share of world machinery and equipment exports declined from 3.2 per cent in 1970 to a mere 2.1 per cent in 1985: a substantial increase in exports of machine-building products is essential, and urgent, if the heavy dependence on primary product exports is to be diminished. During the current 1986-90 five-year plan, investment allocations to the civilian engineering industry are being increased by 180 per cent and strenuous efforts are being made to improve product design and quality. However, this modernisation drive is being hampered by a number of factors such as the inadequate system of economic incentives which leads to a certain "irresponsiveness" of the economy to innovation. Furthermore, there are the inadequate, and inappropriate, skills and experience of personnel of all kinds, from shopfloor workers to engineers and managers, in particular the skills required to generate genuinely original modern designs and to secure volume production at a consistent high quality. This problem of expertise is being exacerbated by the simulataneous adoption of new management methods in accordance with the provisions of the economic reform; a reform essential if the first mentioned set of problems is to be overcome.

In principle, these circumstances should be favourable for the implementation of a defence industry conversion policy. Many defence sector

---

[28] See J. Cooper, 1986, op. cit., pp. 44-45.

enterprises must possess precisely the skills and experience now so urgently needed by the civilian engineering industry. One can imagine that in some cases it may be more expeditious to organise the production of modern items from scratch using converted military capacity than attempt to modernise already established, but extremely backward, civilian enterprises. Some defence sector facilities may be well placed to contribute to the expansion of machinery exports: indeed, any conversion strategy could well incorporate a deliberate export expansion programme. Such a strategy could also involve the organisation of joint ventures with Western firms and this approach could assist in tackling what Soviet specialists recognise could be a difficult transitional problem – the need to reorient military producers to the economic criteria of the market. This latter problem is not, however, unique to the defence industry: it is one facing Soviet industry as a whole as the economic reform gathers pace.

Another aspect of the economic reform has relevance to the conversion question, namely the new incentives for enterprises to shed surplus labour and the acceptance of the inevitability of redundancies. Now, in line with trends in other economically advanced countries, the size of the industrial labour force is beginning to decline. Lay-offs and retraining for new jobs are becoming standard features of Soviet economic life. During the 18 months from January 1987 approximately 1.5 million industrial shop-floor and white-collar workers were released from their jobs and found alternative work. Many were retrained for alternative employment at the same enterprise, the training being carried out at the enterprise's expense with the workers concerned receiving their average wages during the periods of study.[29] This development is relevant to the conversion question in at least two respects. First, experience is being gained of regular procedures for securing displaced personnel alternative employment and retraining. Second, there is the psychological readjustment now under way; the acceptance that job security in Soviet conditions does not necessarily mean that workers will hold the same job for life. On the negative side, however, as noted above, these new economic conditions could in some cases make more difficult the absorption of labour released through conversion.

Returning, finally, to the regional dimension, the problem remains of deciding which civilian products are to be made by which enterprises. Every time the specific nature of the capacity concerned, the existing production technology and skills will have to be considered. But in the conditions of the Soviet economy, with its pronounced regional variations, account will also have to be taken of the particular circumstances of the region in which each enterprise is located. Relevant factors will include the labour market situation, including rates of pay,[30] the availability of materials, transport facilities and costs, and local needs for certain types of machinery and equipment. Soviet planners and economists have already accumulated experience of tackling this type of

---

[29] *Trud*, 6 July 1988.

[30] Workers in Siberia, the Far East, parts of the Urals and elsewhere receive pay supplements to compensate for the difficult conditions of life and to attract labour. Location decisions must take account of the higher labour costs in comparision with other regions.

location problem. One recent study, using mathematical-economic techniques, investigates which categories of civilian machinery and equipment are suited to the economic conditions of each of the country's economic regions.[31] Studies of this type provide a foundation for the analysis essential for the elaboration of a national conversion plan; they will be more meaningful after the major reform of the price system to be implemented before the next five-year plan. Whereas in the past it may have been possible to devise a conversion plan for the Soviet defence industry with limited account of economic rationality, this will no longer be possible in the new circumstances of economic reform.

---

[31] See S. I. Mozokhin and E. N. Tatarintseva, op. cit.

Chapter 9

Conversion from military to civilian production: The Votkinsk plant

G. K. KHROMOV

The Soviet Union-United States Treaty on the Elimination of Intermediate-Range and Shorter-Range Nuclear Forces signed in Washington at the end of 1987, which entered into force on 1 June 1988, following the exchange of instruments of ratification in Moscow, was the first practical step along the road of disarmament.

Publications on defence industry conversion before 1988 were mostly non-specific and theoretical while the conclusions drawn were frequently divorced from reality. Only later has it proved possible to tackle these problems on the basis of real facts.

A specific analysis of measures involved in the implementation of the Treaty will make it possible both to determine the volume of the discontinued military production, i.e. to generate the data base for assessing the problems involved in conversion, and to identify some appropriate areas for further disarmament.

The elimination of intermediate-range and shorter-range missiles involves 3 to 4 per cent of nuclear arms currently existing. According to some estimates, the average annual expenditures for building the United States and Soviet missile forces now being eliminated represent only about 0.25 to 0.3 per cent of their military expenditures. Nevertheless, discontinuing the production of intermediate and shorter-range missiles, and the use of the production capacities thus released for non-military production, the end of maintenance expenses for that missile force and the potential use of the released military equipment in the national economy – all these factors are very significant in their own right.

Under the Treaty the following types of missile are subject to elimination:

- on the Soviet side – the OTR-22 (SS-12), the OTR-23 (SS-23), the RSD-10 (SS-20), the R-12 (SS-4) and the R-14 (SS-5);
- on the United States side – the Pershing-IA, the Pershing-II and the BG M-109G.

However, when the treaty was signed (December 1987) only the following missiles were in production:

- on the Soviet side – the SS-20 and the SS-23;
- on the United States side – the Pershing-II and BG M-109G.

Table 9.1. *Missile production at the Votkinsk plant*

Missile designation	Starting year of missile production	Closing year of missile production	Number of missiles available in 1988 (e.g. to be eliminated)	Number of missiles fired during testing (including testing missile modifications, production quality proof testing, and combat training)	Total number of missiles manufactured
SS-23	1978	1987	239	211*	450
SS-20	1974	1987	654	126	780

* Including missiles supplied to Warsaw Pact countries.

Thus, any estimate of the volume of the discontinued military production should take into account those missiles alone.

The total number of the missiles manufactured at the Votkinsk plant is shown in table 9.1.

If the first two years of production are disregarded, when test missiles were basically manufactured (up to 25-30 items of each type), then the average annual output of missiles over the period of production can be estimated as:
- SS-23 missiles – 53 per annum,
- SS-20 missiles – 63 per annum.

In addition, a certain number of training missiles was produced. The Treaty mentions 121 SS-23 training missiles and 34 SS-20 training missiles. These were as a rule substantially simpler than regular missiles in their equipment, and were sometimes manufactured from substandard parts, unsuitable for use in operational missiles. If the training missiles are added, the total annual output of missiles covered by the Treaty, produced at the Votkinsk plant, amounts to:
- SS-23 missiles – 60 per annum,
- SS-20 missiles – 65 per annum.

Therefore, the production capacities made available by virtue of the Treaty consist of production space, equipment and production personnel involved in manufacturing these missiles.

While it has ceased to produce the SS-20 and SS-23 missiles, the Votkinsk plant continues to manufacture other military products, e.g. SS-25 intercontinental ballistic missiles which have a certain similarity to the SS-20 missiles. Thus, the released capacities can to a certain extent be used to improve the production processes of other military equipment and to ease up working conditions.

The production of high-technology, complex solid-propellant ballistic missiles, such as the SS-20, Pershing-II and SS-23, requires the involvement of a network of specialised subcontractor plants. Their number may reach several dozens. The following may be listed as belonging to this category:
(i)   plants producing nuclear charges with the necessary automatic control devices. As a rule such items are delivered directly to army units where

they are mounted on the missiles. They are disregarded in this examination of the missiles production process;

(ii) plants producing solid-fuel missile engine cases;

(iii) plants producing various types of instruments and equipment, such as gyro-instruments, on-board computers, chemical power sources, sensors, etc., for controls systems, as well as plants producing complete controls systems;

(iv) missile assembly plants or groups of plants making launch containers and manufacturing various sections and mechanical parts included in the overall missile assembly. Normally such plants (groups of plants or associations), which are principal missile producers – or prime contractors – also manufacture all the parts and accessories required for the production of the missile itself and for its maintenance by army units.

The group of plants located in Votkinsk belongs to the fourth category. It consists of the Votkinsk engineering plant, which is in charge of the final missile assembly and where continuous verification is established under the Treaty, and of the Votkinsk plant in charge of other operations. In this study the group of plants will be considered as a whole, as the Votkinsk plant.

Like every Soviet military plant specialising in engineering, the Votkinsk plant is not a purely military facility. Throughout its history (with the exception of the Great Patriotic War period) it has manufactured substantial amounts of non-military products alongside military ones. As a rule, non-military production is closely intertwined with military production in such establishments, many plant shops furnishing items which are part of both non-military and military products.

Among non-military products manufactured in recent years have been:

– milling and numerically controlled (NC) manufacturing-unit machines;

– small-size washing machines;

– prams and pushchairs;

– components for products manufactured at other plants.

In 1987-88, i.e. when the production of intermediate- and shorter-range missiles was stopped, Soviet defence industry enterprises were assigned to manufacture production equipment for the light and food industries, and equipment for trade and public catering establishments. In accordance with these assignments, the Votkinsk plant started to manufacture packing and bottling machines of four types, to bottle and pack milk and baby-food products, as well as milk-cooling and pasteurising equipment.

The civilian production items were assigned to the plant by the Ministry of the Defence Industry, which has administrative control over it. The established procedure is for the Ministry to issue a list of items to be manufactured by the plant and to include it in the state procurement order. The list of items then becomes part of the production plan assigned by the State to the enterprise.

The plan of production incorporating the list of the military and of the new civilian items has been drawn up by the Ministry of the Defence Industry in collaboration with the state planning bodies and with the enterprise management. At the discussion stage of the state procurement order and of its volume (prior to the official approval), the trade union organisation and other workers' bodies (the Council of the "Working Collective", i.e. of all the personnel) at the plant participated in the setting up of the production targets. Workers' representatives were also involved in the process of decision-making, when the various measures destined to guarantee the fulfilment of the assigned targets were being discussed.

The inclusion of the civilian production items in the state order (along with military items) means that the plant becomes entitled to priority deliveries of materials and of component parts even for the civilian items, which in this case would be supplied mainly from the central funds. The possibility to obtain supplies from central funds should facilitate substantially the task of production restructuring in the plant and should make the conversion process easier.

The criteria for the choice of civilian products to be manufactured included:

- the plant's capabilities, based on the equipment available or to be acquired, production space and the skills of the workforce (production capacities on the civilian side were increased by 72 units of machine tools formerly used for military production at the Votkinsk plant);
- the availability of materials and components (to be facilitated by the supplies from central funds);
- maximisation of profit: it should be noted that the criterion of maximum profitability of individual production items is not predominant in the process of plan drafting. The primary consideration is to fulfil the tasks assigned to the enterprise by the state plan. After these tasks have been fulfilled, however, the profitability criterion becomes determinant for the enterprise management concerning any production above plan targets;
- long-term needs for such products;
- finally, when opting for a type of product, the problem of re-employing workers after the end of military production is also to be taken into account.

Currently, the enterprises face a relatively easy task when choosing the products to manufacture, because of the severe shortage of consumer goods and of technologically up-to-date equipment on the Soviet market.

The question of the replacement of military products at the Votkinsk plant by non-military products can be approached by comparing the types of operations to be performed and their share in the aggregate labour input for manufacturing an SS-23 missile and a VM-501 NC manufacturing unit (table 9.2).

An examination of the data in table 9.2 reveals that the basic operations in manufacturing the two seemingly different products are comparable. The example cited shows a similarity not only in basic operations, but also in total labour inputs. In other words, one VM-501 NC manufacturing unit can be

Table 9.2.   Labour inputs per unit produced (in rate-hours)

Operations	Items produced:	
	SS-23 missile	VM-501 numerically controlled manufacturing unit
Casting	123	146
Forging and pressing operations	161	58
Machining operations	1 714	1 530
Welding operations	198	66
Fitting and assembly operations	1 919	1 636
Heat-resistant coating operations	510	–
Painting and galvanic coating operations	422	262
Electric wiring operations	397	631
Quality control operations	955	503
Miscellaneous operations	421	301
Total labour inputs	6 820	5 133

manufactured instead of one SS-23 missile. Given the design similarities of ballistic intermediate-range and shorter-range solid-fuel missiles manufactured during the same period of time, it can be said that the production of the SS-20 type missile was characterised by approximately the same structure of basic operations.

The same pattern of operations in manufacturing military and non-military products makes it possible to expect the same ratio of male and female production personnel. (The share of women working at the Votkinsk plant amounts to about 50 per cent of the total workforce.)

While rockets for weather research, of course, will be the most "convenient" non-military product for the Votkinsk plant, actual conversion to non-military production is naturally more complicated than would seem from table 9.2 because:

– of the unique nature of individual operations. For example, the assembly of a missile and subsequent testing are carried out at a separate special-purpose production site, in view of the danger involved in operations with complete missile engines and pyrotechnic devices;

– specific operations are inherent to missile manufacturing only, although such operations are not basic, e.g. the application of thermal coating;

– of the need to change and adjust technological processes and technological equipment: in the same operations such processes and equipment may differ for every type of product as a result of the differences in materials and the shape of parts;

– workers need to master of new techniques. Although the similarity of basic operations for non-military and military products makes it possible to speak, in general terms, about the acquisition by workers of new skills and of new techniques, rather than of a change in their profession, the conversion can be, nevertheless, relatively long for some of those concerned.

At the Votkinsk plant some 5 per cent of the total number of skilled workers had to be converted from military to civilian production and had to adjust to a really different type of work. About 150 workers had to be retrained for completely new tasks. They acquired their new skills on-the-job, in the plant. During their retraining period, which could have lasted for up to six months, they were paid the average wage. The cost of the retraining operation has been put at 0.5 million roubles.

As for the wages of the blue-collar workers who were transferred to the civilian side of production without retraining, they were not affected, because, at the Votkinsk plant, workers of the same skill category are paid equal wages whether they produce military or civilian products. In the case of engineers and technicians, the decision was taken that their occupational status would not change when individual shops and production lines were converted to civilian output. In accordance with a special measure of the Government, their salaries would not change either.

Apart from the relatively limited retraining programme mentioned above, the post-INF Treaty partial conversion at the Votkinsk plant has not resulted in any employment problems or employment loss. The 1989 plan targets for the plant's civilian production have been set so high that not only were sufficient jobs created for the redeployed workers, but additional labour was said to be required. To meet the plan targets, the output of workers engaged in civilian production in "double-purpose" workshops (with both civilian and military production) was increased. A rise in labour productivity should also help to fulfil the plan.

In 1989 the value of the non-military production at the Votkinsk plant, including both civilian equipment and consumer goods, has been planned to grow by 33 per cent as compared with 1987, when intermediate-range and shorter-range missiles were still produced there. Labour inputs for civilian products are to increase by 14-15 per cent. The growth rate of civilian production at the Votkinsk plant could have been even higher if the conversion of its military production had been planned in advance. The discontinuation of the production of intermediate-range and shorter-range missiles came, to some extent, as a surprise for the plant. No advance conversion plans had been prepared. Yet the relatively small increase in non-military production necessitated the conversion and retooling of tens of thousands of square metres of released production-related space in the course of 1988. Special efforts were also required to organise extra deliveries of raw materials, supplies and components needed for civilian production.

However, the total amount of work related to the restructuring of the plant and the establishment of new production processes for civilian output did not much exceed the amount of work required during previous restructuring operations destined to alter the production structure. But this time the conversion, decided as a result of the Treaty, was not planned in advance.

Table 9.3. Output plan of selected civilian products at the Votkinsk plant, 1989

Product designation	Quantity (sets)
VM-501 NC manufacturing unit	160
VM-131 NC milling machine	250
VM-127M general-purpose milling machine	600
"Feya" washing machine	420 000
Prams and pushchairs	300 000
Packing and bottling machines with the capacity of up to 12,000 bottles per hour	289
Cooling and pasteurising production lines with the capacity of up to 25 tons of milk per hour	75

Labour inputs grew more slowly than the costs of civilian production, because the plant drastically increased the production of the non-military goods it had previously manufactured, mainly through additional technological improvements. Only later did the plant begin the production of new equipment for agro-industrial complexes. There are plans to introduce other civilian products, particularly car parts for the Izhevsk Automobile Works located nearby.

The output plan for 1989 includes the civilian items set out in table 9.3, in addition to which the plant manufactures a significant amount of products in co-operation with other engineering facilities, including equipment for drilling rigs, as well as cast blanks. As for packing and bottling machines and cooling and pasteurising equipment, the Votkinsk plant intends to produce them in such quantities that they will meet the needs of the whole country, all the more so that a well-developed railway network connects Votkinsk with the major Soviet cities. Certain types of products including machine tools are expected to be exported.

The social issue is central to conversion. Currently, social development funds are accumulated by way of deductions from the plant's profits. Under the Law on the State Enterprise, adopted recently, enterprises are responsible, in the social field, not only for the implementation of the principles of fair remuneration according to the work performed and of social justice, but also for the creation of a working environment favourable to the growth of labour productivity, and – more directly – for the social welfare and the improvement of social and working conditions of their personnel, as well as for the development of modern services benefiting their workforce. Enterprises are entitled to deduct and to keep a certain proportion of their profits as funds for social activities. The social activities fund, deducted from profits, and the wage fund, represent a major share of enterprises' operating funds, which they use in their current transactions as autonomous cost-accounting units. In accordance with the present rules, the funds deducted from profits for social activities are distributed between:

- the production, science and technology development fund,
- the social development fund, and
- the material incentives fund.

The last two funds have a direct and important impact on the workers' personal and social income. The bulk of the social development fund is used to finance housing construction and the building and maintenance of child-care facilities, as well as the development of other communal services. The fund is also used for loans to co-operative and individual housing schemes, and for the financing of vacations and stays in spas and health resorts.

It is consequently very important for the workers to ensure that after conversion the plant does not suffer a drop in its profits (or at least that no cuts are made in the funds allocated to meet the plant's social needs). However, this presents difficulties in the case of defence industry conversion, because the cost of the end-product compared with the plant's labour input (roubles against rate-hours) for military products is, as a rule, several times higher than for civilian products and, as a result, the gross profit is much higher. For example, for a Votkinsk-type plant this factor can be 3.5 or even 4.

A major reason for this is that the Votkinsk plant as a prime contractor, or principal missile builder, is supplied by subcontractors with major missile components, the cost of which is included in the cost of the missiles manufactured at the plant. Due to the strict requirements regarding missile accuracy, combat readiness and immunity from destructive effects, certain components such as controls systems, are very expensive. For instance, the cost of the controls system of a Pershing-II intermediate-range missile accounts for nearly 30 per cent of its total cost and exceeds US$1 million . Equipped missile engine cases can be no less expensive, because of the use of very powerful solid propellants and of highly sophisticated construction and thermoprotective materials.

Therefore, the cost of the supplied components makes up a high proportion of the total cost of the missiles manufactured by the prime contractor. For example, the cost of the component systems and elements included in the SS-23 missile accounts for 60 per cent of the missile's total cost. With larger-size missiles this proportion may reach 70-80 per cent or more.

In contrast to missiles, all the non-military products are characterised by a substantially lower cost of components supplied by other plants in relation to the total cost of the end-product manufactured by the plant. Thus, for instance, the cost of components accounts for as little as 40 per cent of the total cost of a numerically controlled manufacturing unit, with an even smaller proportion in the case of the other less sophisticated products such as prams and pushchairs.

Given the current situation, the problems resulting from a fall in profits due to defence industry conversion could have the following solutions:

- switching production to more sophisticated items with a higher content of high-quality (high-cost) components supplied from outside;
- fixing or charging higher prices for products.

A fundamentally different solution to the problem might be a fresh economic approach towards the assessment of the plant's performance, with the focus shifted from the cost of supplied components to labour productivity and quality. The latter approach is likely to be taken under the economic restructuring now proceeding in the Soviet Union.

For the time being, however, to offset the costs caused by the discontinuation of production of intermediate- and shorter-range missiles and by the conversion to civilian output, the Government has decided to allocate funds to the Votkinsk plant for the years 1988-90, to make up for the drop in profits from which the plant's social development funds are financed.

As mentioned earlier, the output of the discontinued missiles corresponded to a relatively small part of the labour inputs into the entire range of the plant's products. In other words, Votkinsk is only undergoing a partial conversion, or the first stage of conversion. Most of the workforce released is now employed in the manufacture of new products. The transfer from INF-banned missile manufacturing has been facilitated by the fact that prior to the conversion the plant has experienced shortages of labour leading to constant overtime work.

Finally, the compliance with the Treaty requires a certain number of the plant's blue- and white-collar personnel to assist in the Treaty implementation activities, e.g. for experts to attend verification operations; for appropriate personnel to escort United States inspection teams at the continuously monitored site and to escort United States nationals en route; for car drivers and other employees to organise transport, etc. These activities should employ a total of about 80 persons. Under the Treaty, the Votkinsk engineering plant has been designated as a continuously monitored site. Personnel will also be required for eliminating Soviet and United States missiles at the designated sites (operations to be conducted with the participation of Votkinsk engineers and workers), and for manufacturing special equipment to verify compliance with Treaty provisions. Annual costs of all these activities and operations (to be conducted over a period of several years) are estimated to reach 3 to 4 million roubles. They will be financed directly from the state budget.

The conclusions which may be drawn from this study are that concrete measures to convert military to civilian production have become an urgent task today. If planned in advance, disarmament programmes would allow the preparation of effective conversion plans. The more complete these programmes would be and the greater range of armaments they would cover, the higher the efficiency of planned conversion and the better the results. Limitations to some types of armaments only and insignificant numerical reductions in selected types of arms could nullify the effectiveness of conversion, particularly if their qualitative parameters were left undefined. Conversion to civilian production under way at the Votkinsk plant will not affect the employees' social conditions. Lessons from the Votkinsk plant experience may be used for the process of restructuring now proceeding in the Soviet Union.

Chapter 10

Employment implications of defence cutbacks in China

C. Z. LIN

This chapter offers a preliminary assessment of the employment implications of cutbacks in Chinese defence spending. Given the sensitivity of matters related to defence in China, it is not surprising that the quantitative data necessary for a proper treatment of this issue are scarce or altogether unavailable. At the same time, it is surprising that this issue to the best knowledge of the author has never been studied in the West. This means that secondary sources and guess-estimates of the employment implications of Chinese defence cutbacks are similarly unavailable.[1] Nevertheless, rough and broad figures exist for certain items of information which permit an indirect and preliminary quantification of the scale of certain aspects of the subject-matter. Aside from the direct impact of demobilisation on employment, the scaling down and reorientation of military-related industrial activities (for which some data are available) also allow an assessment of some of the indirect impacts. Finally, our knowledge of Chinese economic institutional arrangements, systemic characteristics and policies also provide a framework for evaluating the overall implications of defence cutbacks for the economy more generally.

I. The context of defence cutbacks in China

The end of the Maoist era in 1976, and the reascendancy of Deng Xiaoping in particular, resulted in a fundamental reappraisal by the Chinese leadership of the country's economic situation and of international security trends.

On domestic issues, the Party leadership repudiated the so-called "ultra-leftist" economic strategy and institutions pursued since 1958 and their underlying ideological premises. It reintroduced with a vengeance the Four Modernisations Programme (modernisation of agriculture, industry, science

---

[1] Nor have there been any Chinese studies published on the subject so far as the author is aware (an impression confirmed by recent discussions with some leading Chinese governmental and academic economists).

and technology, and national defence in descending order of priority).[2] The relaunching of the Four Modernisations in the late 1970s was accompanied by a recognition of the inadequacy of previous patterns of economic performance which had been characterised by extensive growth, slow technological progress and deteriorating economic efficiency.[3] To enhance economic efficiency and redress slow consumption growth, the decisive 3rd Plenum of the 11th Central Committee of the Communist Party of China (CPC) in December 1978 introduced fundamental changes in the development strategy and market-oriented systemic reforms.

Both these measures had important implications for defence spending as well as for reforming military strategies, objectives, organisation and personnel. The new development strategy, in contrast to the previous obsession with maximising the growth rate of producer goods output, stressed structural balances and consumption in investment and production planning. This entailed not only an attempt to reduce the accumulation (investment) rate, but also sectoral reallocations of resources away from the producer and the defence-related goods sector to consumer goods. In the process, many defence industries were forced to reorient their production towards meeting civilian needs. At the same time, market-oriented systemic reforms were introduced to promote greater economic efficiency. The defence sector consequently faced increasingly severe budgetary restrictions and was required to rationalise its operations and structure. Like every other sector and unit in the Chinese economy, it had to promote revenue-gathering and profit-oriented market activities to meet shortfalls in budgetary allocations.

The low priority attached to defence modernisation was in part compelled by a desire to promote a peaceful international environment within which China could concentrate on economic development and participate in the international division of labour (i.e. the "Open-Door Policy" announced in 1979) necessary to raising its technological levels and productivity. But it was largely a reflection of changes in China's assessment of international security trends.

Since the 1960s China's defence strategy had been guided by Mao Zedong's aphorism that there was "great disorder under the heavens" and that the contention between the two superpowers would lead inevitably to a nuclear war sooner rather than later.[4] Accordingly, China's defence strategy was to prepare for "an early war, a large-scale major war, a nuclear war". In line with

---

[2] The Four Modernisations Programme was first proposed in 1964 by Zhou Enlai but was postponed due to the Cultural Revolution in 1966-7. In 1974 Zhou relaunched the Four Modernisations Programme, but it was again pre-empted by intra-party disputes caused by the so-called Gang of Four.

[3] Extensive growth refers to growth derived primarily from growth in factor inputs rather than from growth in factor productivities or "intensive growth".

[4] Mao's view was that war would break out between the two superpowers as a result of their conflict of interests in the West European theatre, and that Soviet tensions with China (e.g. the border conflict with China in the Ussuri and Amur Rivers in 1969) were a camouflage – "feint in the East, strike in the West", as Mao put it.

this policy, China undertook a major programme of expanding and locating new industrial and ordnance production capacity in the remote and backward south-west region of the country where greater protection from aerial and nuclear strikes was afforded: the so-called Third Capital Construction Front.[5]

This strategy held valid well into the 1980s despite the full rapprochement with the West and the commencement of improvement in relations with the Soviet Union. In June 1985, however, at an extended meeting of the Central Military Commission, Deng Xiaoping announced a major shift in Chinese strategic perceptions. Deng announced that

The danger of war still exists. Because of the two superpowers' arms race, the factors of war will continue to grow. However ... the growth of the forces for peace in the world will outpace the growth of the forces for war ... It is possible large-scale world war will not break out for a relatively long time."[6]

This effectively meant that in the Chinese perception, war was no longer imminent or inevitable. With this re-evaluation of international security trends, Deng announced that China would reduce its military force by 1 million men (or by an estimated 20 to 25 per cent).[7]

II. The scope and scale of defence cutbacks

The demobilisation of 1 million men was only part of a larger and wide-ranging programme of cutbacks in Chinese defence spending. In line with the subordination of defence to economic development, the cutbacks also entailed major organisational streamlining, the promotion of better skilled and more professional staff, enhancing cost-effectiveness and a major reorientation of the army's resources to serve civilian needs. These elements, together with the reduction in the size of the country's standing army, had the dual and inter-related objectives of reforming (modernising) the military as well as reducing its burden on the economy simultaneously.[8] One initial consequence was a reduction in the *absolute* levels of defence expenditures. Subsequently, the *relative* share of defence expenditures as a percentage of both total budgetary expenditures and GDP has either been reduced or kept constant.

---

[5] The First Front (line of defence) comprised the coastal provinces facing Taiwan, China and the East China Sea, where it was believed that any seaborne invasion by enemy forces would probably be directed; the Second Front was the inland provinces immediately adjacent to the coastal provinces which would serve as a line of defence to draw enemy forces into Chinese territory where a guerrilla-type "people's war" could be mounted.

[6] Cf. Deng's speech in FBIS China, 12 June 1985, pp. K1-2.

[7] For descriptions and analyses of changes in Chinese military policy, see Ellis Joffe: "People's war under modern conditions: A doctrine for modern war", and Paul H. B. Godwin: "Changing concepts of doctrine, strategy and operation in the People's Liberation Army", both in *China Quarterly* (London), Dec. 1977, No. 112, pp. 555-571 and pp. 573-590.

[8] See Robert G. Sutter: "The military modernisation of the PLA and the PRC's International Security Policy", and Jammong Rolph: "The long road to modernisation", both in Richard H. Yang (ed.): *SCPS Yearbook on PLA affairs, 1987* (Kaohsiung, Taiwan, China, Sun Yat-sen Centre for Policy Studies, 1988), pp. 15-26 and 51-70.

Table 10.1.   *Defence expenditures (in billion Rmb, current prices)*

Year	Total budgetary expenditure	Of which national defence	Per cent
1978	111.10	16.784	15.1
1979	127.39	22.266	17.5
1980	121.27	19.384	16.0
1981	111.50	16.797	15.1
1982	115.33	17.635	15.3
1983	129.25	17.713	13.7
1984	154.64	18.076	11.7
1985	184.48	19.153	10.3
1986	233.08	20.075	8.6
1987	242.69	20.977	8.6

Source. State Statistical Bureau: *China Statistical Yearbook 1988* (Beijing, China Statistical Information of Consultancy Service Centre, 1988), pp. 665, 674 and 676.

One Chinese source states that from 1949 to 1985 military expenditures accounted for an average of 23.48 per cent of total state budgetary expenditures while another Chinese source gives a different figure (for 1950-85) of 16.6 per cent.[9] The figure of 23.48 per cent was argued to be excessive, because "international experience" suggested 12 to 20 per cent as the "appropriate" range. In light of China's economic underdevelopment, the authors proposed that military expenditures should range between 8 to 10 per cent, and that China should display patience in army building until further economic progress can allow the figure to be raised to 12 per cent.[10]

The attempt to achieve a more "appropriate" and lower ratio of defence spending actually began in 1980 (see table 10.1). There was a sizeable increase in defence spending in 1979, occasioned by the border conflict with Viet Nam earlier in the year, when defence expenditures accounted for 17.5 per cent of total budgetary expenditures. For the next two years, defence spending fell both in absolute terms and as a percentage of budgetary expenditures. There was a slight acceleration in the annual percentage increase in defence spending in 1985, 1986 and 1987. This was apparently caused by the substantial short-run, once-and-for-all costs associated with the demobilisation of a million men.[11] Nevertheless, the ratio of defence spending has fallen considerably. With major

---

[9] Wang Pufeng, Wang Zengquan, Li Yunlong and Chen Fang: "Economic construction and army building in the New Period", in *Jiefangjun Bao (Liberation Daily)*, Shanghai, 31 Jan. 1989; and Liu Dizhing: " 'Third Line' relocation, renovation stepped up", in *China Daily* (Beijing), 20 Oct. 1988.

[10] Wang Pufeng et al., op. cit.

[11] *Jiefangjun Bao*, 31 Mar. 1987.

economic growth following the introduction of economic policy changes and systemic reforms, the economy grew by an average of about 10 per cent (in GDP terms) in 1980-87. The rate of increase in absolute levels of defence spending since 1982 was significantly lower than the growth in budgetary expenditures and in GDP, such that by 1987 defence expenditures (20.98 billion Rmb Yuan or about US$5,600 million) was only 8.6 per cent of the former and about 2.5 per cent of GDP when calculated according to official statistics. The CIA estimates that actual Chinese defence spending is about twice the official figure when calculated according to Western formulae, but admits that even so it still represented less than 5 per cent of GDP to maintain the world's largest standing army. Since the figures given in table 10.1 are in current prices, this means that Chinese defence spending in real terms has fallen dramatically.[12]

Given the paucity of reliable data, it is impossible to determine exactly how cutbacks in defence spending have been achieved. According to Yu Qiuli (then head of the PLA's General Political Department), total investment in military projects was cut by 170 million Yuan in 1987, on top of drastic cuts in 1986 compared with 1985.[13] Since the decision by the Central Military Commission in 1981 to subordinate defence to economic construction, the PLA has already reduced defence-related capital construction investments by 44 per cent or 2 billion Yuan, with most of the money saved used to build barracks and improve living conditions for personnel.[14]

The various elements comprising Chinese cutbacks in defence expenditures have various direct and indirect impacts on the economy. A priori, one of the most important of these impacts would be on employment: the demobilisation of 1 million men, as well as the scaling down of military-related industrial activities, came at a time when unemployment has, for the first time since the mid-1950s, re-emerged in serious proportions.

III. Demobilisation and force reduction

The decision announced in June 1985 to demobilise 1 million men was perhaps the most important in Chinese history but it was not the first (excluding the post-Korean war demobilisation in the early 1950s). In the early 1970s a highly controversial demobilisation, estimated to have numbered in the hundreds of thousands, occurred under the alleged auspices of the now discredited Lin Biao. In 1975, upon his political rehabilitation, Deng Xiaoping had already criticised the "swelling" of the Chinese army and stressed the need

---

[12] Other estimates are given in Yung-chuan Wang: "PRC's military expenditure and arms transfer 1975-86", in Richard H. Yang, op. cit., pp. 169-182; and Ed Parris: "China's defence expenditure", in JEC (US Congress): *China's economy looks towards the year 2000* (Washington, DC, US Government Printing Office), 1986, Vol. 2, pp. 148-168.

[13] Xinhua News Agency, 31 Mar. 1987, in FBIS-CHI, 3 Apr. 1987, pp. K/9-10.

[14] Report in *Pravda*, trans. in FBIS-Sov-88-180, 16 Sep. 1988.

to reduce the size of the country's standing army in line with economic and budgetary realities.[15]

A second major demobilisation occurred in the early 1980s, following Deng Xiaoping's reascendancy to power. The exact size of this demobilisation is unknown, but Western sources estimate the size of the Chinese armed forces in 1981-82 and in 1984-85 at 4.75 million and 4.0 million, respectively:[16] this suggests a demobilisation of about 750,000 men over a five-year period.[17]

The demobilisation in the early 1980s coincided with, and must have contributed significantly to, serious unemployment which at that time was officially acknowledged and publicised widely by the Chinese authorities. It has been estimated that urban unemployment at that time amounted to over "10 million" annually.[18] Other estimates of urban unemployment range between 12 and 16 million.[19] Official figures only give the rate and number of people in the urban areas "awaiting jobs" (see table 10.2). This category refers to unemployed people who have registered with state employment agencies; in such cases, the State guarantees job placement but the jobseeker has little or no choice in the type of employment. The number of people "awaiting jobs" represents therefore only a subset of the actual total unemployed. For the latter total, we have to include those who have decided not to register with state employment agencies (because they are seeking specific types of employment) or are ineligible for registration.[20] Thus, another Chinese source acknowledged that "real" unemployment totals and rate "may be higher" than that given by the "rate of people awaiting jobs".[21] The scale of the employment (unemployment) problem is indicated by official statistics showing that nearly 50 million people were given work between 1981 and 1987,[22] while another set of official figures show that

---

[15] See *Selected works of Deng Xiaoping* (Beijing, Foreign Language Press, 1984), p. 11. There is no evidence that action was taken to demobilise at this time, presumably because Deng fell into disgrace shortly afterwards and did not return to power until late 1977.

[16] See *Military balance 1981-82, 1984-85* (London, International Institute of Strategic Studies). Other estimates of the Chinese armed forces in 1981 range from between 4.75 million to 5.0 million to 5.6 million men; see June T. Dreyer: "The PLA: Demobilisation and its effects", in *Issues and Studies* (Taipei, Taiwan, China, Institute of International Relations), Feb. 1988, pp. 88-89. The fact is that there are no reliable Western estimates of the size of the Chinese armed forces.

[17] Yang Shangkin, Secretary-General of the Central Military Commission, acknowledged in 1985 that "minor cuts" in the size of the army had been made in previous years (see Dreyer, op. cit., pp. 102-103).

[18] *Beijing Review*, 24-30 Oct. 1988, Vol. 31, No. 43, p. 25.

[19] Field interviews by the author in China in the summer of 1982 at the Chinese Academy of Social Sciences, State Planning Commission, and various central and local (provincial and municipal) government economic departments.

[20] Only people registered as resident in a particular town or city are eligible to register with the state employment bureau in that town or city. Many rural migrants to the cities are illegal or extra-legal, and as such cannot avail themselves of any of the services (e.g. food coupons, housing, etc.) provided by state agencies without proof of residency registration for the particular locale.

[21] "China sees some unemployment", in *Renmin Ribao (People's Daily)* (Beijing), 29 July 1988.

[22] Ibid.

Table 10.2. *Labour force and employment rate*

	1978	1979	1980	1981	1982	1983	1984	1985	1986	1987
Persons awaiting jobs (mn)	5.30	–	5.41	4.40	3.80	2.71	2.36	2.39	2.64	2.77
Job waiting rate	5.3	–	4.9	3.8	3.2	2.3	1.9	1.8	2.0	2.0
Total employed labour force (mn)	401.52	410.24	423.61	437.25	452.95	464.36	481.97	498.73	512.82	527.83
National labour force (mn)	–	–	–	–	566.83	583.37	601.57	621.14	640.66	656.67
Employment rate (%)	–	–	–	–	79.9	79.6	80.1	80.3	80.0	80.5

Source. State Statistical Bureau: *China Statistical Yearbook 1988* (Beijing, China Statistical Information and Consultancy Service Centre, 1988), pp. 145, 123 and 125.

the employed force grew by about 90 million over the same period (see table 10.2). According to the former set of statistics, the urban unemployment rate was 5.3 per cent in 1978, fell to 4.9 per cent in 1980 and to 2.8 per cent in 1985. Since then, the rate has been around 2 per cent.[23] Yet another indirect indicator of the scale of unemployment in China is the employment rate given in official statistics (see table 10.2) which shows that about 20 per cent of the country's total labour force is unemployed.[24]

The unemployment problem is also exacerbated by the phenomenon of serious overstaffing (overmanning) or disguised unemployment in the Chinese economy. According to a survey of Shanghai's industries, 78 to 98 per cent of state enterprises were overstaffed, with redundant labour amounting to between 14 and 25 per cent of the total workforce. Calculations by state labour departments estimate that there were about 20 million redundant workers and staff in state enterprises nationally.[25] In addition, various Chinese reports have suggested that there would be as many as 100 million surplus labourers in agriculture attendant upon comprehensive mechanisation of the sector.

Unemployment in the early 1980s resulted from two principal sources: first, the Government's reversal of earlier rustication policies and its allowing the return to cities of youths sent to the countryside during the Cultural Revolution period; second, the systemic reforms designed to enhance economic efficiency entailed a reduction in overmanning and surplus labour in state enterprises. The second factor would have posed particularly serious obstacles to the absorption of demobilised soldiers into the civilian economy.

The decision in June 1985 to demobilise 1 million men, or about one-quarter of the country's standing army, therefore came at a particularly difficult stage in the Chinese economy. The year 1985 was the final one of the Sixth Five-Year Plan (1981-85). The demobilisation of 1 million men was to be phased-in over 1985-87, which overlapped with the first two years of the Seventh Five-Year Plan (1986-90) when it had been estimated that over 6 million youths in the urban areas needed to be found employment each year, and when reforms and reorganisation of state enterprises would shed over 10 million redundant workers who needed to be found alternative employment.[26] This is perhaps one reason why the original timetable of implementing the demobilisation over two years had to be prolonged over three years instead. Thus, it was only in April 1987 that Xu Xin, Deputy Chief of Staff of the People's Liberation Army (PLA), was able to announce that the demobilisation of 1 million men had "basically"

---

[23] *Beijing Review*, Vol. 31, No. 43. Note that this rate differs from the "rate of people awaiting jobs" given in table 10.2, which is taken from the official statistical yearbook.

[24] This rate, obviously, cannot be taken to mean that there is a 20 per cent unemployment rate in the country: on the one hand, the total employment figure excludes those, say, in the armed forces, and on the other hand, not all unemployed are seeking employment.

[25] *Renmin Ribao*, 29 July 1988.

[26] See *China Quarterly*, Documentation No. 103, Sep. 1985, p. 562.

been completed.[27] Some Western analysts question whether the demobilisation of 1 million men had in fact been completed even by mid-1988.[28]

The actual nature of demobilisation may have alleviated the adverse consequences of such a large-scale demobilisation on the economy. Some Western analysts have speculated that the demobilisation of 1 million men was achieved largely through transferring various non-combatant units of the PLA to civilian control.[29] For example, there was an organisational transfer of the military's 500,000 strong Railway Corps, as well as of its Capital Construction Corps, to civilian administration. Apparently, other PLA units engaged in internal security duties were also transferred more or less *en bloc* to civilian control through the creation of the People's Armed Police Force, thus removing the PLA from normal internal security responsibility. Chinese sources have also reported, as mentioned earlier, that 2,000 civilian defence departments had been transferred to civilian control. It is not clear, however, whether these organisational transfers were counted by the Chinese authorities as part of the demobilisation of 1 million men or were supplemental to it. On the one hand, since 1985 there have been frequent and extensive reports in the Chinese press of the resettling and re-employment of hundreds of thousands of newly demobilised soldiers which clearly suggest an actual demobilisation rather than just organisational changes in control; on the other hand, the PLA annually demobilises nearly a million men as part of its routine turnover, and this may account for the numbers, although it should be pointed out here that the press reports usually refer to demobilisation in the context of the June 1985 decision to demobilise a million men.

To facilitate the return to civilian employment, the PLA and local government authorities provide specialised (re)training for demobilised personnel. In 1985, 85 per cent of army cadres transferred to civilian work were given specialist training and successfully resettled.[30] By the end of 1986, 410,000 personnel had been demobilised, a considerable number of whom were either retired or transferred to civilian jobs. It was reported in early 1987 that the authorities had retrained and provided jobs for 1.2 million demobilised soldiers and resettled 21,000 retired officers in 1986. For officers, the State had also built over 31,000 apartments and set up 900 sanatoria. Of those demobilised, 250,000 took up "leading" (i.e. cadre) posts at the rural grass-roots (village, township, county) level; another 260,000 were employed in rural factories and 110,000 were working as individual farm and non-farm labourers. According to the report, a total of 2 million demobilised soldiers had been retrained and resettled in civilian work since 1979.[31]

---

[27] BBC SWB, FE/8537/C1/1.

[28] Ibid.

[29] See Dreyer, op. cit.

[30] BBC SWB FE/8385; *China Quarterly*, Documentation No. 107, Sep. 1987, p. 581.

[31] BBC SWB FE/8496/BII/5, 19 Jan. 1987. These numbers presumably include those routinely demobilised or retired.

While the precise number of personnel actually demobilised is unknown, there can be no doubt that the scale of demobilisation and the constricted time period over which it was implemented would have serious repercussions on an economy already confronting servere unemployment problems. However, the peculiarities of the Chinese economic system is such that the absorption of a million men into civilian employment is relatively more readily implemented than in a market economy. Despite major progress in economic liberalisation attendant upon market-oriented reforms since 1978, the Chinese economic system is still in many respects a centrally planned system of the Soviet type. In the absence of labour markets, it is the State's responsibility to guarantee employment through reliance on direct, administrative methods of labour planning and allocation. This principle applies also to demobilised personnel. Consequently, the reintegration of demobilised servicemen in China has been achieved relatively smoothly through quasi-compulsory directives to local governments, and through them eventually to various state production and administrative units, to provide jobs for demobilised personnel.

IV. The reorientation of defence-related industries

There is another important feature of the Chinese economic system which determines the overall impact of defence cutbacks and demobilisation on the economy in general and on employment in particular.

The PLA, like its counterpart in the Soviet Union and other socialist countries, is not only a consumer of goods and services but is also a major producer. The military in most Western market economies engages in R & D but procures most of its required hardware and services from the civilian (private) sector through purchasing orders and contracts. In Soviet-type centrally planned economies, however, the preponderant share of ordnance and other requirements are produced by enterprises directly under military control.

In China the potential gains resulting from defence cutbacks are proportionate to the size and scope of military-controlled or defence-related productive capacity and resources available for conversion to civilian production. The size and scope of military-controlled industries in China is in fact immense.

In China the PLA engages in a very wide range of productive activities, from agriculture to machine building, which are normally not the competence of the military in Western economies. In part, this aspect of the PLA's activities followed from the wholesale replication of Soviet economic and military institutional arrangements during the 1950s. But it is in large part a result of distinctive and indigenous Chinese policies that the range, volume and importance of such activities in China are arguably much greater than in other socialist countries.

From the late 1950s onwards, the Chinese sought to depart from the Stalinist development strategy by pursuing an indigenous one in which self-reliance was stressed. The problems confronted by the Chinese in replicating highly centralised Soviet-type command planning led them, amongst other things (e.g. decentralisation of economic planning and management), to promote regional and sectoral self-sufficiency as a means of reducing the central planners' task in integrating and balancing inter-sectoral and inter-regional flows of goods and services. During the Cultural Revolution in particular, the Chinese sought to set up a "cellular" economic system in which each and every productive unit was to be as self-contained and self-sufficient as possible under the slogan "small yet comprehensive, large yet comprehensive". This meant that each unit tried to be as highly integrated vertically and horizontally as possible in its production process. Thus, Chinese industrial enterprises often produced their own inputs in addition to their normal range of output, leading to extremely low levels of functional specialisation in the Chinese economic structure. The Chinese military had to adopt such a policy with even greater force. A cardinal principle in Chinese military strategy was that each military region and unit should be self-contained and self-sufficient in order that its fighting ability would not be impaired by the destruction of other parts of the economic or military structure.

The extent to which this principle was pursued in China is unprecedented in the world and truly astounding.[32] Although this basic principle derived from the experience with fighting a successful guerrilla war in the pre-1949 period and had already been applied during the 1950s, it was only in the mid-1960s that it was acted upon in remarkable proportions. Immediately following the Gulf of Tonkin incident, which preceded a major escalation of United States involvement in the Viet Nam war in 1964, the Chinese Government launched a major programme of building and relocating a vast number of military-related industries in the so-called Third Capital Construction Front. The Third Front programme was intended to develop a large, comprehensive self-contained and self-sufficient industrial and economic system which could survive a nuclear strike and prosecute a major war by relying entirely on its own resources and food and ordnance production. For this purpose, industries and plants were deliberately sited in the most remote and inaccessible locations, often dug into mountainside and underground facilities so as to be able to withstand a nuclear strike.

The scale of the Third Front programme was so vast, and its importance in the economy generally so great, that an evaluation of the impacts of defence cutbacks on the Chinese economy, and on employment in particular, can only begin with an appreciation of the scale, scope and nature of the programme itself.

The scale of the Third Front was immense. Its geographic coverage encompassed one major municipality and eight provinces or autonomous regions: Chongqing municipality, the western regions of Henan, Hubei and

---

[32] This section is based on a major study which the author has engaged in for the past seven years. The findings of this research will be published as a monograph co-authored by a Chinese specialist.

Table 10.3. Distribution of investment: Third Front areas, by Plan period (percentages)

	1st FYP	2nd FYP	1963-65	3rd FYP	4th FYP	5th FYP
National total	100.0	100.0	100.0	100.0	100.0	100.0
Third Front areas						
Henan	3.7	5.2	4.2	4.0	4.2	4.1
Hubei	3.6	4.3	3.1	5.6	5.9	6.5
Hunan	1.6	3.4	3.2	3.7	3.7	2.9
Sichuan	4.5	5.8	7.5	13.6	7.7	5.4
Guizhou	0.6	1.8	3.3	4.2	2.8	1.7
Yunnan	1.7	2.8	3.4	4.2	2.6	2.4
Shaanxi	4.0	2.9	2.5	4.1	4.9	3.2
Gansu	3.7	4.0	4.3	4.5	3.1	2.1
Sub-total	23.4	32.0	31.5	43.9	34.9	28.3

Source. Taken or calculated from *SMCFAI* (1987), p. 51.

Hunan provinces and all of Guizhou, Yunnan, Sichuan, Shaanxi and Gansu. The area covered amounted to nearly one-quarter of the country's territory. The foci of the programme, however, centred on two main key areas: *(a)* Sichuan province (in turn centred on the city of Chongqing and the Panzhihua integrated iron and steel works), Guizhou, Yunnan and part of Gansu which comprised the principal raw materials, intermediate product and defence industry infrastructure; and *(b)* the southern parts of Gansu and Shaanxi, and the western parts of Henan, Hubei and Hunan, which were developed as bases for weapons manufacture and assembly, machine building and other major manufacturing industries. Unconfirmed reports also indicate the siting of nuclear material processing and weapons manufacturing plants within the Third Front area.

The scale and overwhelming importance of the Third Front can be seen from the vast amount, both in absolute and in percentage terms, of national resources that was poured into the region. In the period immediately prior to the Third Plan period (1966-70), the Third Front area accounted for 31.5 per cent of total national (capital construction) investment (see table 10.3). The figure shot up dramatically to 43.9 per cent during the Third Plan, dropped to 34.9 per cent during the Fourth Plan (1971-75) before returning to normal levels in the Fifth Plan period (1976-80). Sichuan's share of investment alone was greater than the combined total of Beijing, Tianjin and Shanghai (5.4 per cent of total investment) and was only marginally less than the combined total (14.3 per cent) of the six provinces of Liaoning, Jilin, Heilonjiang, Zhejiang and Jiangsu which constituted China's industrial base.[33] Annual time series show

---

[33] Calculated from figures given in *Statistical material on China's fixed asset investments (1950-85)* (Beijing, China Statistical Press, 1987), p. 51.

even more clearly the scale of the Third Front programme. Investment in the Third Front areas shot up from 27.1 per cent (of national total) in 1964 to 43.0 per cent in 1965 and to nearly 45 per cent in 1966. Except for Hunan, Hubei and Henan, all other provinces (or autonomous regions) within the Third Front witnessed major increases in their investment shares, with those for Sichuan and Guizhou doubling within one year. After declines in 1967 and 1968 due to the disruption of the Cultural Revolution (when investment nationally fell sharply), the Third Front's share of investment reached a peak of nearly 50 per cent in 1970 and stayed high at around 40 per cent or over in 1971-72.

It is presently impossible to calculate precisely the total investment in the Third Front programme.[34] A significant amount of investment was allocated to or undertaken by the military for which statistics are neither available nor included in the civil capital construction data. Various Chinese sources have stated that investments totalling 200 billion Yuan (US$52,000 million at current exchange rates) had gone to the Third Front since the mid-1960s.[35] The value of capital construction from 1964 to 1983 totalled 700 thousand million Yuan for the whole country.[36] Over 1,000 key industrial enterprises and a large number of ordnance bases were built. Third Front industries in the early 1980s accounted for 25 per cent of the nation's total industrial output, 75 per cent of nuclear industrial output capacity, 60 per cent of aeronautics, 50 per cent of space technology, 60 per cent of electronics and 50 per cent of armaments output.[37]

The overwhelming importance of the Third Front investment programme can also be seen from the share of new large and medium-sized projects located within the region. Prior to the Third Plan period, the region's share of such projects ranged between 20 and 25 per cent of the national total. But after 1965, during the Third and Fourth Plan periods, the region's share rose to 44 per cent and stayed high (at 35 per cent) even during the Fifth Plan (1976-80) when the scale of the Third Front programme was being reduced.

---

[34] The figures given in tables 10.3 and 10.4 do not give an accurate account of the actual amount of investments in the Third Front programme: they are provincial investment totals which include expenditures (e.g. agriculture, etc.) that were not associated with the Third Front. Moreover, our investment totals for Hunan, Hubei and Henan overstate the amount going to the Third Front since only parts of these provinces were included in the programme. They do, however, indicate the trends and scale of Third Front investments: if we assume that the Third Front provinces' share of national investment during the Third and Fourth Plan period had remained similar to the average of the First and Second Plan periods, then the difference between the actual and the expected averages can be imputed to the Third Front. This would mean that 61 and 26 per cent of total investments during the Third and Fourth Plan periods, respectively, were associated with the Third Front. Against these figures must be added investments undertaken by central government ministries which were regional or supra-provincial in character, such as railways, which would not be captured in the provincial investment data.

[35] *Renmin Ribao* (overseas edition), 7 Nov. 1987, p. 1.

[36] State Statistical Bureau: *Statistical Yearbook of China, 1984* (Hong Kong, Economic Information and Agency, 1984), p. 301.

[37] Liu Dizhong, op. cit.

Nearly 30,000 enterprises were constructed in the Third Front region,[38] including 2,200 large- and medium-sized enterprises, accounting for about 28 per cent of the national total; by the mid-1980s the region's newly created fixed assets exceeded 140 billion Yuan.[39] This massive investment created an industrial system comprising producer goods, nuclear industry, metallurgy, aerospace and aeronautics, electronics, chemical industry and machine building. In the early 1980s the region accounted for 50 per cent of the nation's productive capacity in military-related industries. Workers and staff within the region amounted to about 16 million, or about a third of the national total. It also enjoyed a higher ratio of scientists, technicians and skilled workers than anywhere else in the country.

Defence cutbacks in China since the early 1980s have inevitably involved a restructuring of Third Front industries. A decision was taken around 1979 to reorient the majority of Third Front enterprises to serve civilian needs as part of the overall policy of subordinating defence to economic construction. A special State Council office was established in Chongqing (capital of Sichuan province) in the early 1980s to administer this restructuring. About 150 million Yuan (or US$40 million) was allocated by the Government in 1988, or 40 per cent more than in 1987, to reorient Third Front enterprises' production for exports of civilian products. The State had also allocated 2 billion Yuan to relocate about 100 Third Front factories to nearby small- or medium-sized cities, with the first phase of relocation to be completed within two years. Under the restructuring policy, a third of all ordnance factories was to shift completely to civilian production while the remainder was to produce both military and civilian goods.[40]

With defence subordinated to economic construction, a significant proportion of military facilities have been reoriented towards civilian needs. In the past few years, aside from switching over 10,000 lines of defence industry technologies and production to civilian use, 59 airfields, over 300 special railway lines, 30 special telecommunications lines, 29 docks and over 100 warehouses controlled by the military for its exclusive use were opened up to serve local economic development.[41] All army hospitals have also been opened up to

---

[38] Investment in the Third Front programme took two forms. One was new capital construction, technical renovation and expansion and the creation of new productive capacity; the other was the literal dismantling of equipment and complete plants in the developed coastal region and their relocation in the Third Front region under the so-called policy of *yi fen wei er* ("one becomes two", or cloning). The latter form of "investment" was particularly used in the machine building industry where investments in the Third Front alone amounted to a third of total investment in the industry during the entire post-1949 period. Two hundred and forty new machine building plants and R & D facilities were constructed in the Third Front region, which, by 1985, accounted for about a third of all machine building plants in the country. The overwhelming share of new and more technologically advanced plants in the machine building sector constructed since 1986 was in the Third Front region.

[39] *Renmin Ribao* (overseas edition), 7 Nov. 1987, p. 1.

[40] Liu Dizhong, op. cit.

[41] Interview with Zhu Yunqian (Deputy Director of the PLA general political department) in *Jiefangjun Bao*, 19 Aug. 1987.

civilians, treating 43.24 million patients in 1985-87. The army has also initiated over 2,000 farms and runs over 1,600 small mines and factories (with an output value of 700 million Yuan and tax and profit contributions of 130 million Yuan to the State) for purely commercial purposes.[42] In the province of Guangdong alone, the army has established over 1,000 PLA-related economic entities, producing nearly 4,000 lines of products. The PLA trading organ in Guangdong, the Jia He United Development Company, already runs hotels and produces electronic components, building materials, vehicle parts, agricultural produce, etc. Even the Shenyang Aircraft Factory, makers of one of China's most advanced jet fighter aircraft (the F-8), has now converted part of its assembly lines into producing sewing machines and rubbish compactors; other ordnance factories are now producing fertilisers and refrigerators, while factories previously making military uniforms are now turning out teddy bears and T-shirts for the domestic and export markets.

The share of civilian consumer goods production in military factories doubled between 1978 and 1983 to one-fifth of total output and is reported to have reached 50 per cent in 1987, and is expected to increase to 70 per cent by 1990.[43] To reorient military production to serve the civilian economy, major organisational changes in military administration were introduced in the mid-1980s. The Ministries of Ordnance Industries, of Nuclear Industry, of Aeronautics Industry and of Astronautics were removed from military jurisdiction and placed under the State Council. The entire capacity of these industries is now able to serve civilian needs. In addition, the State Machine Building Industry Commission was established to integrate military production units into the civilian sector. Research units and enterprises in the military were reclassified into three groups: those exclusively serving military needs; those producing both military and civilian products; and finally, those producing entirely for civilian use. Since May 1988 preferential tax and credit policies have been introduced for military industries converted to civilian production.[44] With these changes, total industrial output of military industries serving civilian needs amounted to over 5 billion Yuan in 1987.[45]

In addition to subordinating defence to economic construction, the restructuring of Third Front enterprises to serve civilian production was also compelled by the military's need to find alternative sources of funding for its own modernisation programme in the face of reduced budgetary provisions from the central Government. According to Zhao Nanqi, a senior PLA official, defence appropriations through the state budget meet only 70 per cent of the army's total expenditure. Consequently, the army has had to rely on commercial

---

[42] *The Economist*, 14 May 1988, p. 91.

[43] Zhang Aiping: "Strengthen the modernisation of the army – In commemoration of the 60th anniversary of the founding of the PLA", in *Renmin Ribao*, 24 July 1987. However, according to *China Daily*, 31 July 1990, the share had reached 65 per cent.

[44] BBC SWB FE/0274.

[45] *China Daily*, 2 Nov. 1988, p. 1.

sales from its own industries to meet the remaining 30 per cent shortfall.[46] Given an official defence appropriation of about 21 billion Yuan in 1987, this suggests that total military expenditures amounted to 30 billion Yuan, and that 7 billion Yuan was earned through sales of military industrial output for civilian as well as military purposes. This is a major factor behind the Chinese military's drive to earn foreign exchange through arms exports. Between 1982 and 1986 Chinese arms sales overseas made it the world's sixth largest supplier. These sales have been estimated by the United States Government's Arms Control and Disarmament Agency to have reached 1,040 million Yuan in 1986, and are estimated to have doubled in 1987 with cumulative sales in 1980-87 of US$11,000 million. In 1987-88 China was widely believed to have become the world's fourth largest arms exporter.[47] Chinese sources have also estimated that the country can easily earn over US$1,000 million in arms sales annually, with the figure doubled after further reorganisation and streamlining in the management apparatus.[48]

---

[46] *Ming Bao* (Hong Kong), 24 Apr. 1988.

[47] *Far Eastern Economic Review* (Hong Kong), 2 June 1988, p. 22.

[48] Hao Si, op. cit.

Chapter 11

Employment impact of industrial conversion: A comparative analysis

LIBA PAUKERT and PETER RICHARDS

While the present study has focused mainly on the regional and local aspects of defence expenditure cuts and their employment consequences, this approach has to be complemented by analysing conversion problems at the national, macro-economic level, in order to set the regional analysis in a global perspective. The macro-economic approach, and the micro-economic approach focusing on enterprise and regional problems and responses, are complementary facets of the same investigation. Macro-economic analysis in terms of aggregate demand and total numbers of workers and in terms of specifying a prescriptive use of released government funds (a "counterfactual") has been the most often used conceptual approach to defence conversion so far. Although such an approach is essential, and although to discuss conversion without specifying a counterfactual leaves part of the analysis hanging in the air, it has its limitations in terms of predicting behaviour of the actors involved and pinpointing where the problems may be most acute. As the defence industry is characterised by a high degree of regional concentration, this study has mainly addressed the regional and local aspects of defence expenditure cuts, while a macro-economic approach can set the problems in the proper framework.

Cuts in defence expenditure necessarily have immediate effects on employment and, as has been stressed, these effects will be regionally concentrated. Their extent depends on the size of the cuts, and on the general labour market and economic situation, including the extent and use of active labour market policies. The issue of conversion is that of making the best use of all the resources released by such cuts, particularly the previously employed labour force, at the least social cost. A wide range of response has to be kept in mind. The phenomenon of finding an "alternative (yet profitable) use" of the machinery and skills of an armaments factory is, of course, the least disruptive form of conversion. It is probably also, at least in IMECs and without the benefit of considerable government subsidy, the least common. Examples abound, of the most disruptive path involving scrapping, labour dislocation and skill wastage, either because no diversification was attempted or because it failed.

The issues discussed in this chapter, which compares and summarises the different national, regional and enterprise experiences presented earlier, can be grouped under four main headings: (1) defence expenditure and defence-related employment: the extent of the conversion problem; (2) defence production and experiences of defence cuts in a regional and local perspective; (3) reactions and attitudes of the main decision-makers, i.e. governments, company managers and trade unions, to defence conversion problems; and (4) conclusions.

This chapter, like the rest of the study, concentrates on the employment consequences of defence expenditures in the industrial sector, and apart from China, reviews experience and problems in the industrialised countries, where disarmament can be expected. In this context some points raised in Chapter 1 deserve repetition. There is considerable current interest in disarmament partly because it is a very welcome by-product of demilitarisation and liberalism. But the extent of the changes which appears to be taking place cannot be specified. As a result very many economic parameters may change, most obviously in the formerly centrally planned economy countries but perhaps elsewhere also. The nature of the conversion problem may turn out to be different from what is expected.

I. Defence expenditure and defence-related employment: The extent of the conversion problem

The shares of military expenditure in GDP for many industrialised countries and for China, which provide one global measure of the overall military effort in different countries, are shown in table 11.1. The GDP shares of military expenditure are situated between roughly 1 and 9 per cent in the industrialised market economies and in the two leading planned economy countries for which official data, approximately comparable in coverage, could be obtained. There are considerable country differences: in the small, neutral countries, such as Austria, Finland or Switzerland, the GDP share of defence expenditure amounts only to 1 or 2 per cent, and in Japan a 1 per cent limit on military spending has long been maintained (although 1 per cent of a fast rising total gives a large absolute amount). In the countries belonging to the major alliances, NATO and the Warsaw Pact, the military burden is considerably higher, and also relatively uneven. Weapons procurement, maintenance and research and development is, of course, only a part of the total amount. But, on the other hand, the size of the defence-related sectors of industry is also sensitive to the amount of defence-related production exported to third countries; this can sometimes equal 25 to 50 per cent of domestic procurement.

In the United States the share of military expenditure in GDP amounted to 6 per cent in 1988, after a second consecutive year of decline, following the peak of military build-up in 1986, when it had reached 6.7 per cent. However, these shares remained below those of the 1960s or early 1970s, during the Viet Nam build-up, although in real terms the absolute level of military expenditure was equal or higher in the 1980s.

**Table 11.1. Military expenditure as a percentage of gross domestic product
in selected countries, 1960-88**

Country	1960	1970	1975	1980	1985	1986	1987	1988
Austria	1.2	1.1	1.2	1.2	1.3	1.3	1.2	1.1
Belgium	3.6	2.9	3.0	3.3	3.0	3.0	2.9	2.8
Finland	1.7	1.4	1.5	1.9	1.9	2.0	1.9	1.9
France	6.4	4.2	3.9	4.0	4.0	3.9	4.0	3.8
Germany, Federal Republic of	4.0	3.3	3.6	3.3	3.2	3.1	3.1	3.0
Greece	4.9	4.8	6.5	5.7	7.0	6.1	6.2	6.6
Ireland	1.4	1.3	1.9	1.9	1.6	1.7	1.5	1.5
Italy	3.3	2.7	2.7	2.1	2.3	2.2	2.4	2.3
Netherlands	4.1	3.5	3.2	2.9	3.1	3.1	3.1	3.0
Norway	3.2	3.5	3.2	2.9	3.1	3.1	3.4	3.2
Portugal	4.2	7.0	5.3	3.5	3.2	3.2	3.1	3.1
Spain	2.2	1.6	1.7	2.3	2.4	2.2	2.4	2.1
Sweden	4.0	3.6	3.4	2.9	2.5	2.5	2.5	2.5
Switzerland	2.5	2.2	2.0	1.9	2.0	1.8	1.6	1.7
Turkey	5.1	4.3	6.1	4.3	4.5	4.8	4.3	4.1
United Kingdom	6.5	4.8	5.0	4.7	5.1	4.9	4.7	4.4
Yugoslavia	7.2	5.0	5.7	4.9	3.9	3.9	2.4	2.0
United States	8.9	7.9	6.0	5.4	6.6	6.7	6.4	6.0
Japan	1.1	0.8	0.9	0.9	1.0	1.0	1.0	1.0
USSR	..	..	..	..	..	..	..	8.6 (1989 plan)[1]
China	..	..	..	..	..	..	2.5	..

.. Figures not available.
[1] Military expenditure as a percentage of GNP.
Sources. *SIPRI Yearbook*, 1989 and 1988 (Stockholm); C. Z. Lin (1989); *Pravda*, 11 June 1989.

The Soviet share of military expenditure in GNP shown as 8.6 per cent
was calculated on the basis of the Soviet defence budget for 1989, announced
by Mr. Gorbachev, as totalling 77,300 million roubles,[1] expressed as a
percentage of the planned level of GNP for the same year. The Soviet figure may
not be strictly comparable with those shown for the market economy countries
because of the effects of subsidies on in the price structure generally. No
comparable Soviet data are available for earlier years. Between 1989 and 1991,
however, Soviet domestic arms procurements are to be cut by 19.5 per cent.
Together with the reduction of the armed forces by 500,000 men and the cuts
following the INF Treaty ratification, this should enable the country to decrease
the defence budget by 40 per cent, between 1989 and 1991.[2]

---

[1] *Pravda*, 11 June 1989.
[2] Ibid.

In China defence expenditure represented 2.5 per cent of GDP in 1987, calculated on the basis of official statistics. This rate tends to be undervalued in comparison with the IMECs, partly because of some military "self-financing" (e.g. retaining profits from arms exports and some commercial operations). But even if it were double, as suggested by some Western sources, it would still appear as a relatively moderate expenditure for maintaining the world's second largest standing army. China's armed forces represent a remarkably low percentage of the active population (less than 1 per cent of the labour force). After the reorientation of economic policy in China in 1978, the share of defence in total budgetary expenditure fell from 17.5 per cent in 1979 to 8.6 per cent in 1987. More recently, however, military expenditure has been increased – by 15 per cent in 1990.

Table 11.2 provides information on defence-related manufacturing employment in the countries for which reasonable estimates can be built up. The data are not strictly comparable between countries (see the remarks at the end of Chapter 2) and furthermore differ from that chapter's survey. The table shows that this employment is rarely a significant share of total manufacturing employment (although perhaps the Italian figure should be treated with caution). However, if, which is not entirely legitimate, all defence-related employment is shown only as a share of ISIC category 38 (the production of fabricated metal products, machinery and equipment) then the percentage figure often rises quite high. Of course, comprehensive data of this kind go beyond employment in what might be called durable goods manufacturing (for example, they include paper, boots and shoes). However, it is necessary to make the point that defence-related employment can be a major proportion of certain industrial subsectors (93 per cent of the output of United States shipping was produced for the military in 1985). As such, some workers are very much at risk in disarmament and furthermore they are frequently workers with expensively gained skills.

Some of the data in table 11.2 were provided by governments in response to an ILO questionnaire.[3] The Government of Belgium gave estimates for defence-related employment in manufacturing, rising from 15,700 in 1977 to 18,460 in 1980. These would appear to be the results of a study carried out in the early 1980s, based on a questionnaire presented to enterprises. As such, there is reason to believe that indirect and thus total employment would have been underestimated. Given that the frequent relation of direct to indirect employment is 4 to 3 (see Filip-Kohn et al. for the Federal Republic of Germany[4] and the annual *Statement of Defence Estimates* in the United Kingdom) this would give a figure of 32,300 for 1980. Given a real fall in military expenditure of some 15 per cent from 1980 to 1986, and an annual

---

[3] Sent to all ILO member States in October 1984.

[4] R. Filip-Kohn et al.: *Macro-economic effects of disarmament policies on sectoral production and employment in the Federal Republic of Germany, with special emphasis on development policy issues* (Berlin, May 1980). This exercise yielded shares of manufacturing employment somewhat lower than those given in table 11.2.

Table 11.2. Manufacturing employment

	Year	Defence-related '000	% of total manufacturing employment	% of ISIC category 38 employment
United States[1]	1985	1 812	9.4	21.2
United Kingdom[2]	1986-87	410	7.6 (5.9)[1]	18.2 (13.1)[1]
France[2]	1981	400	7.8 (5.2)[1] (7.9)[3]	17.6 (11.7)[1] (18.0)[3]
Federal Republic of Germany[2]	1984[2]	230	2.9 (2.4)[1]	6.2 (5.2)[1]
Italy[2]	1984	86	2.0 (2.7)[4]	5.9[5] (7.7)[4; 5]
Belgium[2]	1986	23	3.1	8.8

[1] Not including exports. [2] Including exports. [3] 1987 estimate, see text. [4] Alternative estimate, see text. [5] Share of EUROSTAT category NACE 3, which is similar to ISIC 38.

Sources. United States: US Department of Labor, *Monthly Labor Review*, Aug. 1987; United Kingdom: HMSO, Statement on the Defence Estimates 1989 (employment dependent on equipment expenditure and exports); Federal Republic of Germany: C. Wellmann, *Abrüstung und Beschäftigung – ein Zielkonflikt*, Campus Verlag, Frankfurt, 1989; France: Ministère de la Défense, *Dossier d'information*, No. 77, May 1985. Italy and Belgium, see text.

growth rate of labour productivity in all manufacturing of some 3 per cent, this would justify a 23,000 figure for 1986.

The reply of the Government of Italy to the ILO questionnaire mentioned 80,000 defence-related manufacturing jobs. No source or explanation was given. However, the figure is close to that estimated by Battistelli in 1979, of 75,250. This was based on replies from 300 larger enterprises and an estimate of employment in subcontractors. Possibly these data are an underestimate and a better figure might be 112,400, i.e. the 64,250 workers identified in the larger enterprises multiplied by 7/4.

The French data are fairly old. They also include exports, at approximately one-third of output. Between 1981 and 1987 these fell in volume by some 33.5 per cent. However, given time lags it seems unlikely that employment fell in parallel. Domestic military expenditure rose in real terms by 10-13 per cent. Trend productivity growth would probably have cancelled this out. Thus the size of the defence-related manufacturing labour force in 1987 depends on what happened in the export sector. If it were cut in line with volume then the adjusted percentage figures for France (an estimate of 350,000) would be 7.9 for all manufacturing, and as much as 18 per cent for ISIC category 38; if not cut in line with exports the percentages would be higher. For the Federal Republic of Germany it can be noted that the data do not include employment associated with the many foreign troops stationed on its territory. Neither, of course, do the data for any other country cited. However, the numbers estimated are fairly large, 104,000 in manufacturing, which would raise the shares given in table 11.2 by 1.3 percentage points and 2.8 points respectively.

Any remotely comparable data for the USSR are speculative. The reply of the USSR Government to the ILO questionnaire indicated that 55 per cent of workers in the military branches of industry were producing defence materials, as were 550,000 workers in civilian industry. Chapter 8 ventured a total number of workers in defence industries at 6 million, i.e. 3.85 million producing military goods altogether. This is respectively 25.1 per cent of all ISIC category 38 employment and perhaps 12.0 per cent of all manufacturing employment. However, it has been reported that the Ministry of Defence Industry alone (see Chapter 8 for the ministerial structure in the USSR) employs 4 million workers. That the numbers may be expected to be fairly high is also suggested by data given on the occupational breakdown of defence workers. Of these, 77.4 per cent were manual workers, 14 per cent professionals, 7 per cent administrators and only a small share, 1.4 per cent, were clerical. The high share of manual workers (compared with 44 per cent in the United States) suggests relatively low productivity levels and hence, labour-intensive methods of work.

Apart from quantitative factors such as the level of defence expenditure and the size of defence-related employment, the extent of the conversion problem is influenced by qualitative factors. Very important among them in determining the ease with which whole enterprises or divisions of enterprises can move from one sector to another are the specific characteristics of the defence industry and civilian industry. In terms of stylised facts, the defence industry is oriented towards marginal strategic advances, while cost considerations have tended to be secondary for their managements although perhaps less so for their limited number of customers. Defence industry companies may be state owned or to some extent state supported, particularly with respect to having R & D costs underwritten. They have tended to operate on a cost-plus basis and key suppliers have often enjoyed considerable protection from foreign competition, although this trend is being reversed in West European countries now. Start-up costs in certain areas of shipbuilding, aerospace, etc., are prohibitive for new entrants. However, this picture should not be overstressed, many subcontractors need to be highly efficient and new enterprises do enter the market. Furthermore, many conglomerate enterprises work for both markets, although the two activities may be separately managed.

Civilian industry, on the other hand, is in principle geared more towards competitive, cost-effective and mass production techniques. With the progress of technology, the divergence between the technological level of defence and civilian products is believed to have been widening, as maximum performance equipment and supplies tended to be acquired for defence production, with little regard to cost. At the same time a stylised fact is that, in civilian industry, cost considerations have been paramount and technological advance has consisted to some extent of "spin-offs" from the defence industry. While the cost of technology derived from defence "spin-offs" is, no doubt, lower for civilian enterprises than the cost of specifically targeted R & D, the technological level of civilian output may have suffered from the competition of military R & D and from the concentration of large amounts of resources in the military technology field.

This issue is, however, extremely complex and has been marked by changing, or even contradictory trends. In electronics, for example, military

R & D represented the vanguard of progress in the 1950s and 1960s, but since then it has gradually lost its role of technology pioneer. Technological advances made in the civilian sector in a number of countries, including Japan, have been taken over for military use more than the other way round. The pattern of technology transfer between military and civilian production has changed, while the relationship between defence and civilian technology has become closer.[5]

For defence conversion, the differences in management objectives and methods in military and civilian industries which, if not an obstacle to production for civil markets certainly predispose enterprises to cling to military markets as long as possible, might be aggravated by the existence of high-tech, high-cost production capacities. There is no doubt that some equipment will certainly be made redundant and finding products particularly suited to installed capacity may be impossible. Certainly past experience in the United States has often been unfavourable.[6]

However, in the market-economy countries the gap between management methods in military and civilian industries may be starting to close, under the influence of the increased exposure of the defence industry to market pressures. This has been the case particularly in Western Europe, as a result, among others, of the Action Plan, prepared by the IEPG (Independent European Programme Group) in 1988, which aimed at creating a more open European market in armaments. An important protagonist of the IEPG Action Plan has been the Government of the United Kingdom, which started to apply the "value for money" principle in defence procurement at home several years earlier. However, even if a European defence market is created, it will differ in a number of basic aspects from the Single European Market for civilian goods. It is doubtful whether the defence industry will ever entirely lose its special status and specific characteristics.

A further important factor differentiating the defence industry from the civilian industry concerns the workforce, particularly its qualification profile and occupational structure. The composition of the workforce in the defence industry is skewed towards highly skilled groups, both in manual and non-manual occupations, and especially towards the technical and scientific occupations. Highly qualified scientific and technical workers are overrepresented, in comparison with non-military industries, while minority groups, and women, are underrepresented and crowded into the service worker category.

This occupational pattern is quite typical of the defence industry and can be observed in all countries for which there is information, as well as in all defence industry branches, such as aerospace, vehicle manufacturing, small

---

[5] W. Walker and P. Gummett: "Britain and the European armaments market", in *International Affairs* (London, RIIA), 1989, Vol. 65, No. 3, Summer.

[6] See R. W. DeGrasse: "Corporate diversification and conversion experience", in J. E. Lynch (ed.) *Economic adjustment and conversion of defence industries* (Boulder, Colorado, Westview Press, 1987).

arms production, electronics, etc. The country chapters in this volume provide valuable information on the occupational breakdown of the defence workforce at the national and regional level, and in leading defence industry companies. A comparative analysis of the occupational profile of the defence industry workforce in different countries is not possible, however, because of wide differences in classification and coverage. But there is total convergence in the country chapters concerning the above-average proportion of highly qualified professional and craft workers in the defence industry.

The occupational bias goes hand in hand with a similar bias attached to the educational background of defence workers. Employment in the defence industry is characterised by an above-average proportion of workers with higher degrees, particularly in science and technology, while the share of workers with only compulsory education is markedly low.

In all countries, including the European socialist countries, the defence workforce in the key and leading enterprises is paid above-average wages and salaries, not only the scientists, engineers and other professionals, but also the production workers. Of course, to some extent this is a feature of leading firms in the engineering industry, whatever they produce, although the existence of assured product markets may frequently reinforce such a trend.

A high average level of qualification is a factor which should make the transfer of defence workers to civilian jobs easier, since – other things being equal – there are more vacancies for qualified technicians and engineers than for unskilled employees. On the other hand, the often narrow specialisation of defence workers might create problems and make the transition to civilian jobs or the retraining of workers more difficult than in the case of the non-military sunset industries, for example. The differential in earnings between military and non-military industries would probably add to the difficulty of getting an equivalent job as well as reinforcing the tendency to extend the period of job search.

While the employment issue is crucial to the conversion process, and satisfactory conversion depends on solving the associated employment problems, conversion might be helped by analysing recent experience in the field of industrial change, including in defence. Changes in defence production are taking place constantly. The country chapters refer to many examples of defence cuts, particularly including the post-INF Treaty experiences in the United States and in the Soviet Union, and the defence cutbacks in China following the reorientation of economic policy in 1978. The former experiences are, however, negligible in terms of employment while the latter is not likely to be generally applicable. But other countries experienced defence cuts, namely the United Kingdom in the 1970s when unemployment began to grow (but demand picked up again in the mid-1980s and between 1985 and 1988 the United Kingdom defence industry was remarkably successful on export markets). In Italy defence production expanded rapidly in the 1970s as a result of rising foreign demand and started to decrease in the first half of the 1980s when demand, particularly in Third World countries, declined as a result of growing foreign debt problems and competition from other, including Third World, producers. A similar pattern of up and down fluctuations could be observed also in Belgium. However, the option of seeking third country markets may be one past experience which will not be available in future.

Moreover, there have been inter-regional shifts and even inter-country shifts in defence production. The relocation of armaments industries in the United States from the Great Lakes area to the East Coast, down to Florida, and to the West Coast and particularly in California, offers interesting study materials. Italy started to manufacture and to export sophisticated military equipment produced by its rapidly growing electronics and aerospace industries, the growth of which was largely prompted by rising export demand. Spain has increased its aircraft production. At the same time, in the more established arms-producing countries, aerospace and electronics industries went through a long series of difficulties leading to reorganisations and restructurings, in order to remain competitive. Mergers and takeovers have been frequent, as described in the chapters devoted to Greater London and to the Munich area. Also, in France there has been long series of reorganisations and takeovers in the aerospace industry particularly, largely orchestrated by the Government which played an important role, as, indeed, governments have elsewhere.

Technological changes in the engineering sector and the transition from obsolete to sophisticated production items, also represent experiences which are relevant to defence industry conversion. The engineering sector in Europe has been undergoing considerable restructuring; there has been a marked tendency towards the transnationalisation of the industry. Engineering companies have been acquiring foreign components, in order to strengthen their position on foreign markets. The transnationalisation trend has concerned the whole engineering industry, including the defence industry. (Siemens and GEC have taken over Plessey; and Daimler-Benz has acquired a holding in the French company Matra, etc.) Useful lessons could also be drawn from the recent crisis and restructuring experiences in the sunset industries, such as steel or shipbuilding.

Much of this transformation and change has been forced by foreign competition. That competition can be fought by classic means of making new investment, raising productivity and lowering costs, or indeed it can sometimes be avoided at least partially by enlisting state support by one of a range of arguments. Competition is likely to lead to a phenomenon of gradual fighting back in which the workforce is reduced, working conditions are worsened and indebtedness increased to finally unsustainable levels. The disarmament scenario may well be different in that the phase of recognising the enterprise's weakness and attempting to remedy it may be missing. Some enterprises in relevant sectors, of course, have been successful in winning new markets, although it should be noted that success is likely none the less to be associated with a reduced labour force. To the extent that the defence industry has been spared much of the competitive pressures of the 1980s, its task in converting to alternative, profitable forms of production using the same labour force will be the more difficult. Labour displacement is inevitable in a market-driven adjustment and conversion process.

The 1980s have seen very considerable shake-outs of the manufacturing labour force in the industrialised market economies. Few jobs have been secure, and the policy of most governments has been not to preserve job security but to increase flexibility through labour market policies, aiming in principle at producing the multi-skilled worker and stressing the role of wages as an incentive. In fact, the situation has been more prosaic. Government support for threatened enterprises has been arbitrary and often wasteful. Most displaced manufacturing workers have managed to find new jobs within a period of months, generally in a different occupation or industry. Better educated workers generally find jobs more quickly, less educated workers may take longer than average to find new jobs and are more likely to have to accept lower wages. Geographical mobility can help, but few workers are willing to move and many who do so will return. Older workers are least willing to move and least likely to be re-employed. A sizeable proportion of displaced workers is likely to be unemployed for an extended period as was found even in, for example, the Swedish steel industry. On average, displaced workers must expect an income loss, although a few may even gain.[7]

II. Defence production and experience of defence cuts at the regional and local level

An important advantage of the regional and local approach is that it allows a close and detailed investigation of defence industry problems in the area where most of the workers are resident and where usually they would prefer to remain. In each region, the defence industry is dominated by a relatively small number of armaments-producing firms. If these firms are willing to co-operate in the studies required, or if enough information can be collected on them from various sources, and if detailed surveys can be made of their production, production prospects, and of their workforce, of its structure, qualification profile, etc., the results can provide very useful elements for decision-making on defence conversion and for possible concrete decisions to be taken by the authorities in the regions concerned. Moreover, the regional and local approach allows direct consultations with enterprise management and with trade union representatives on their attitudes and policies with respect to defence production cuts and to industrial conversion.

A regional approach does not, of course, substitute for appropriate macro-economic policy action. However, a regional approach, with active manpower policies, assisted job search, etc., supported by the local authorities is a necessary complement to national policies of demand expansion or compensation for defence cuts. Demand switches to other items of general government expenditure or to increased private consumption will quite possibly

---

[7] See E. Sussex: *Workers and trade unions in a period of structural change* (Geneva, ILO, 1989; mimeographed World Employment Programme Working Paper; restricted) and the sources listed therein.

benefit other regions, and, quite possibly, benefit regions which are anyway expanding. Some defence-dependent regions have relatively low unemployment rates, others are among the unemployment black spots.

The country studies provide a largely converging picture on the regional concentration of defence production. In all countries for which we have information, the regional distribution of the defence industry is uneven. The defence industry is concentrated in particular areas for reasons combining strategic, historical and economic considerations. These areas depend on defence contracting to varying degrees which can be illustrated by the following readily available statistics.

In the United Kingdom 64 per cent of defence industry employment is located in three regions out of the total of 11, namely in the South-East (40 per cent), in the South-West (12 per cent) and in the North-East (also 12 per cent). However, the South-East and the South-West regions, where about one manufacturing worker in ten works directly or indirectly for defence, are more dependent on defence contracting than the North-West, where only about one in 20 manufacturing workers does. The most defence industry-dependent part of the United Kingdom, however, is Northern Ireland, where one in eight manufacturing employees works for defence but which only accounts for 2 per cent of the United Kingdom's defence industry workforce.[8] Northern Ireland has the United Kingdom's highest unemployment rate.

In Italy the defence industry workforce associated with domestic military expenditure represents a relatively small share of manufacturing employment, as indicated in table 11.2. Even the purely hypothetical suppression of the entire armaments industry would raise the existing two-digit unemployment rate by less than half a percentage point. But in Italy the regional contribution of the defence industry is very unequal and some Italian regions are highly defence dependent. About 80 per cent of defence industry employment is concentrated in five regions out of the total of 20 (Piemonte, Liguria, Lombardia, Lazio and Campania), while nine regions have no defence industry at all. In Liguria one manufacturing job in ten is defence related. In Campania and Lazio the ratio is less important but still substantial.[9]

In France, in some departments such as Hautes-Pyrénées, Var or Finistère, one manufacturing job in five depends on defence production.[10] Similarly in the United States, over 50 per cent of defence contracts are concentrated in six states (California, Texas, New York, Massachusetts, Florida and Missouri, in that order).[11] In the USSR five of the 20 major economic regions have 54 per cent of defence industry enterprises.[12]

---

[8] *Statement of Defence Estimates 1989* (London, HMSO), Vol. 2, *Defence Statistics.*

[9] Data made available by the Government of Italy in reply to the ILO Questionnaire of 1984.

[10] Data made available by the Government of France in reply to the ILO Questionnaire of 1984.

[11] US Department of Commerce, Bureau of the Census: *Statistical Abstract of the United States 1988* (Washington, DC).

[12] See Chapter 8.

These few examples illustrate the scope of the conversion problem on the regional level, and underline the importance of the regional and local approach to defence conversion. They show that armaments production can account for quite a high share of employment – up to 20 per cent – in certain regions. Some localities may be almost entirely dependent on it. Any cuts in defence spending would affect these regions, and even more the localities concerned, very considerably. For compensatory measures to be taken in order to preserve jobs and attract new investment, local conditions would have to be studied in detail, with reference not only to the local labour market, but also to housing, transport and other infrastructure, and even local customs and traditions.

The country chapters also largely concur on the qualitative pattern of the regional concentration of the defence industry. In a number of countries the capital city and its surroundings have generally had an above-average share of defence industry. This is partly because the distance from, and communications with, the administrative and political centres which make decisions on military output and procurement are shorter and easier, and partly because the supply of qualified scientific and technical personnel and of skilled workers has tended to be better. The high level of industrialisation of its surrounding region usually guarantees an adequate supply of skilled labour. However, more recently, rising land values are driving defence-related enterprises away from capital cities. Defence industry facilities also tend to be located in and around large ports, some of which have a long history as naval bases. Naval yards have often attracted other military industries, which later diversified into the production of armaments not directly related to naval supplies. Defence industries can also be located in other strategically convenient regions, particularly if they offer additional advantages, such as a cheap supply of energy (e.g. hydroelectric power) or transport facilities, etc. Finally, historical (traditions, opinions and past attitudes of the population) as well as party political considerations are frequently present in the choice of the location of defence production.

While the regional concentration of defence production has many common features in different countries, what differs is the economic environment in the regions where the defence industries are implanted.

Certain highly industrialised regions may produce a substantial proportion of the national defence output, but in relative terms the share of defence production may be only moderate. In such regions the defence industry workforce would probably find alternative employment more easily, in the case of defence cuts, than in the regions where the defence industry represents a substantial share of industrial activity. The degree of dependence on defence contracting in manufacturing in some regions has increased in the past decade or two, not because defence expenditure has increased much, but because de-industrialisation, observed in most industrialised countries, in terms of a fall in the manufacturing workforce, has reduced the size of the other industries in the region. To that extent released workers would have to shift to other industrial sectors. Many civilian industries have been cut down or relocated and the defence industries were in a sense "left behind". This type of situation is illustrated particularly by Greater London, where the engineering industry as a whole has lost labour at a considerably faster rate than the defence industry. The relocation of production facilities has been the major reason for London's industrial decline since the 1960s, caused by the increasing opportunity cost of real estate, difficulties of transport, obsolete production facilities, etc. The defence industry has been slower to move, because until recently it has been largely protected from market pressures. This situation has changed and defence production is becoming more cost-effective. But even if defence manufacturing is relocated out of London, like the rest of the engineering industry, military R & D activities would mostly remain there. This relocation pattern would have to be taken into consideration for the preparation of defence conversion plans.

In the Rome area there has been a fast growth of employment in the 1970s and 1980s, due both to a remarkable expansion of the service sector, and also to the growth of the – admittedly much less important – manufacturing sector. In the 1980s manufacturing labour started to decline, as in most other industrialised countries and regions. The leading defence industry firms in the area, however, mostly kept their arms-producing workforce, while their production continued to grow, at least in the early part of the decade. Later on, the expansion of the regional arms industry and the role of "leader of industrial development" ascribed to it by some authors,[13] became threatened by the decline in arms exports. Italian arms exports had expanded rapidly between 1975 and 1982, but in 1983 the trend was reversed because of falling demand in Third World countries, faced with serious debt problems, and also because of rising foreign, largely Third World, competition. The embargo on arms exports to both sides in the Gulf War which the Italian Government imposed in 1986, further contributed to the decline.[14] Confronted by these developments, managers of defence industries have been changing their attitudes to converting to non-military production. As pointed out by a Rome publication dealing with disarmament issues, "perhaps for the first time ever, it has become profitable for the Italian military industry to study the possibilities of diversification into the civilian sphere".[15] However, in the present economic and particularly industrial environment in the Rome area, the task might not be an easy one.

The Munich area has been among the fastest growing regions in the Federal Republic of Germany. Manufacturing production has increased at a higher rate than the national average and the capital goods sector has expanded particularly rapidly. Total manufacturing employment declined between 1980 and 1987, as in the rest of the country – and like most IMECs – but in the Munich region there was no employment decline in the industries with a high share of arms production, particularly aerospace, or in the booming motorcar industry. The implantation of the arms industry in a region with a high rate of

[13] Fabrizio Battistelli: *Armi: Nuovo Modello di Sviluppo* (Turin, Einaudi, 1982).

[14] Stockholm International Peace Research Institute: *World Armaments and Disarmament: SIPRI Yearbook, 1989* (Oxford, Oxford University Press, 1989). *Financial Times*, 12 Sep. 1989.

[15] *IDOC Internazionale* (Rome), Vol. 19, No. 5/88.

growth and industrial development, in the post-war decades, has had advantages and disadvantages. Among the disadvantages was that the defence industry further added to the "overheating" of the regional economy, to the rise in the cost of production factors, to the increase in the demand for land, especially industrial land, which is now becoming scarce, to overcrowding, transport congestion, etc. The advantages of a highly industrialised, high-growth region, however, have been many, such as the easy contact with subcontractors and easy access to supplies of the required level of technology, the availability of qualified trained labour, etc. A different kind of advantage in having the arms industry situated in a densely industrialised region is that the region's dependence on defence contracting is more limited. In the Munich area demand for highly qualified technical labour continues to be high in the civilian sector. Engineers, technicians and other skilled worker categories would find jobs in non-military industries relatively easily.

The State of Michigan, analysed in Chapter 6, cannot be easily compared with the small regions of Europe just referred to. It has, however, some common features with, e.g. the Greater London area, namely the overall de-industrialisation trend. In Michigan the manufacturing labour force has declined at a faster rate than the national average over the past decade, and the share of the state's manufacturing output in the national total has decreased. Government support was not forthcoming to maintain the defence industries. On the contrary, defence manufacturing largely moved to other states which were more successful in obtaining federal defence funds. Michigan is no longer the "arsenal of democracy". The rather difficult economic environment in which defence cuts were made in Michigan provided a good ground for the analysis of the impact of conversion on the local level, particularly with reference to labour adjustment problems. The examination of the occupational structure of the defence workforce against the background of available job vacancies and their trends, the evaluation of the practices of defence contracting firms concerning methods of layoff and termination benefits, and the survey of the social benefits available to displaced workers, illustrate important aspects of practical solutions to defence conversion problems at the enterprise and local level.

The economic environment in the Soviet Union and other Eastern European countries has differed in many respects from that of the market economy countries. Enterprises have had no experience of being forced to adjust through competition. Furthermore, there has beoven an excess demand for civilian products resulting from a combination of monetary expansion and price controls. It was conventional wisdom to observe that existing resources reallocated to civilian production would help to satisfy consumer or intermediate demand, if prices were stable. In addition, the general framework and the mechanisms of the central planning system were thought, in principle, to make the conversion of the defence industry a manageable task, although perhaps an expensive one in terms of re-investment. However, at least two things are happening: industrial policy in most of Eastern Europe is shifting away from that of a "command economy". Second, the monetary overhang of high personal savings may be eliminated precisely by allowing prices to rise. If so, there will not be an automatic demand for any level and quality of goods produced. None the less such countries as Czechoslovakia and Hungary are taking disarmament extremely seriously and are talking of "disarmament and defence".

In the Soviet Union the current process of economic restructuring should provide precedents for the mechanisms of switching from military to civilian production, in particular setting a framework for solving issues concerning the redeployment, relocation and retraining of workers. However, recent discussions on conversion in the Soviet Union have highlighted a number of problems. The switch to new production within an existing enterprise and the setting up of new production lines obviously requires new investment and supplies of materials and components. Given the absence of wholesale markets such provisions have to be planned well in advance. The conversion process might thus require considerable time. Furthermore, under the new economic conditions, where enterprises must be self-financing, management might well be more reluctant than before to take on extra workers. This is a problem which seems not really addressed and indeed so far most displaced workers have been re-employed inside their enterprises. In addition, defence workers receive higher wages and trying to match these will aggravate the problem of reinsertion into the civilian sector. In the partial conversion which followed the signing of the INF Treaty, the level of earnings of relocated defence workers and technicians has, however, been maintained, in the technicians' case by a special decision of the Government.

In the Soviet Union the post-INF Treaty partial conversion did not result in frictional unemployment – on the contrary, some enterprises concerned hired more workers – nor, because of special state intervention, did it result in cuts in money wages and salaries for the workers with new work assignments. The main problem was that in switching to civilian production the enterprises had difficulties in selecting and starting to manufacture civilian items that were sufficiently technologically advanced and made of sufficiently sophisticated materials and components to maintain the former profit level. They also had difficulties in using their production capacities and skills fully and effectively. In the plant affected by the INF Treaty some civilian products were already being produced. Indeed, as Chapter 8 records, this is a very common feature of defence production in centrally planned economies. Where there is excess capacity in the equipment required to produce the civilian products, labour can be easily transferred. However, it does not follow that the machinery used for the two sets of output is interchangeable and it seems that frequently the high level of skills required in military production is simply not necessary in making the civilian product. There could well, therefore, be an element of waste in automatically stepping up the civilian lines of production when military output is cut, although such a strategy may imply less social disruption than would be involved in closing the military plant completely.

Another point of contrast between socialist and market-oriented systems, relevant to the issue of conversion, concerns the enterprises' approach to capital stock. In countries with a high rate of productive investment the market value of old capital stock soon falls, capitalist enterprises then write it off and raise the funds for new investment. To raise new funds they must demonstrate the likelihood of sustaining reasonably high future profit rates. To some extent they can do this by take-overs and applying their own managerial and other expertise to existing enterprises in other lines of business. From a balance sheet point of view they have then successfully converted. In socialist countries it should be observed that: first, because of ministerial tutelage, enterprises are far more limited in what they can do; second, the technical sophistication of capital equipment changes less over the years so that its value falls more slowly; and third, the average annual rate of scrapping engineering equipment is very low, only 3.1 per cent annually until recently in the USSR.[16] Thus the average piece of equipment is expected to last 33 years. To that extent the pressures to make use of machinery are far greater than in market economies and as a result conversion, rather than scrapping, will be the more common. This gives rise to the apparently inefficient phenomenon of using tanks as tractors.

Under the new system of enterprise management in the USSR, a fall in profits will have a number of serious consequences: investment and R & D activities, which are financed out of enterprise profits, are likely to be affected, unless financed by special government grants, which is not in line with the new system's basic intentions. Moreover, allocations to the enterprise social development fund and the material incentives fund might be cut. Since these funds have a direct impact on the workers' personal and social incomes, i.e. on their fringe benefits and premia, this would result in a drop of workers' total earnings.

Under the current circumstances, subsidies have been earmarked to preserve defence workers' income levels, at least for 1991 and 1992. Other solutions available to ease conversion are to organise co-operatives in the converted plants, or to lease them to the work collectives in the hope that productivity will rise with a change in the incentive system, or, finally, to establish joint ventures with foreign participation and manufacture high technology equipment. By and large, while economic reform may make enterprises more cautious in their employment policies, it should on balance be beneficial for conversion. As pointed out in Chapter 9, with a better system of evaluating performance, productive enterprises should expand, and allowing the possibility of inter-enterprise trade in equipment and machinery would certainly ease the adjustment problem.

In China economic development through a measure of decentralisation has been assigned high priority since 1978, and important defence cutbacks were made to liberate resources for civilian production. The sharp reduction in defence expenditure, the decision to demobilise one-quarter of China's armed forces, i.e. 1 million men, and the conversion of the large defence industry, which

---

[16] A. G. Aganbegyan, "The new economic strategy of the USSR and its social dimensions", in *International Labour Review*, (Geneva) 1987, Vol. 126, No. 1.

had been built in the remote south-west region during the 1960s and early 1970s, resulted at first in considerable unemployment. This unemployment was tackled by a series of policy measures, often swift and authoritarian, but largely effective. The peculiarities of China's economic and military system enabled the potential unemployment impact of defence cutbacks to be minimised, for example, through direct labour reallocation. The conversion of China's large defence-related industries (either directly or indirectly controlled by the People's Liberation Army) to civilian production has freed significant material and skilled labour resources for economic development which, for perhaps unrelated reasons, has been rapid. Conversely, the large build-up of defence industries in an earlier period was a substantial drain on investment resources. Thus, while the short-term financial and social costs of demobilisation were considerable, as have been the adverse impacts on the south-west region of the country where defence industries are concentrated, these have in general been outweighed by accelerated consumer goods output (providing the necessary workers' incentives), by enhanced productivity and also by greater employment generation in civilian industries over both the short and long term.

III. Reactions and attitudes of the main decision-makers to defence conversion problems

1. Trade unions

Given constantly rising social needs, trade unions have been favourable to arms reduction and to the rechannelling of resources to civilian use, on condition that all efforts should be made to find alternative employment for defence industry workers. Workers in defence industries have on occasions joined the lobby for government subsidies to arms factories in periods of reduced arms procurement, in order to safeguard their jobs and earnings, but this has not been endorsed as policy at higher levels. On the contrary, many unions have adopted well-defined stands on conversion, often as part of general, peace-oriented, disarmament policies. As a result intra-union conflicts have arisen, the more so when the union includes workers from many branches of industry. While such conflicts are unwelcome in that they reduce the effectiveness of union action at the national level, they reflect an understandable view that the "peace dividend" need not be pure gain.

Particularly within the trade union movement in Western Europe numerous initiatives have been taken to address the conversion problem at the local level. These actions have been largely motivated by the need either to sustain employment in existing facilities by widening the product range or to search for alternative employment within the community. An important conversion initiative, which has continued to influence the debate, was taken in the United Kingdom in 1975-76, when the Lucas Aerospace Corporate Plan was worked out by the Shop Stewards Committee. Although the plan was never implemented because it required government purchase of certain products and because the management was never convinced of its profitability, it inspired other plant-based initiatives geared towards finding alternative and socially useful goods to produce, and provided blueprints for action of a much wider, national and international scope. The 1985 UK Trades Union Congress reaffirmed the TUC's commitment to arms conversion. How successful such attempts may be depends in part on how much co-determination and sharing of information has taken place in the plant or enterprise in question. It may also depend on the extent to which the industrial relations framework is plant rather than industrial-sector based.

In the Federal Republic of Germany trade unions have adopted anti-militaristic attitudes throughout the post-war period. At present, their demands include a decrease in the large engineering companies' dependence on defence contracting, a diversification of their production and a cut in investment in armaments producing plant. This is true particularly of IG Metall, the powerful union of metal-workers, largely represented in defence industry enterprises.

In Italy defence conversion has become particularly topical since the decline in arms exports in the early 1980s and the resulting threats to jobs in the defence industry. The unions, and especially the CGIL, have adopted a firm policy commitment to defence conversion. One of the union's concrete demands is that the process of conversion be supported by public funding based on detailed plans worked out by the defence industry companies. Since much of the Italian defence industry is state-owned, and since much state-owned industry in Italy has received capital investment on easy terms, this may be a reasonable demand. However, trading partners would not view the situation so simply and would see such support as unfair competition.

The list of these examples could be extended. The conversion issue has been taken up by trade unions at the European level. The attention of the European Commission has been drawn to defence conversion as an important economic issue, with implications for employment, technological change and economic growth within the Community. The easing of international tensions in Europe, combined with the need to bring solutions to urgent social problems at the European level, have made the issue highly relevant for future trade union policies.

However, while trade unions may, on the one hand, see a benefit in politicising the issue, more solid work is constantly being done through the collective bargaining process. It is essential for the workforce to be informed of the state of the enterprises' order books and to be given advance warning of closures. It is essential to reach agreement on criteria used in lay-offs and re-hires (and even conversion of existing plant would require a period of closure for retooling) and on severance pay or wage protection. It is essential to bring out in the open a range of issues relating to retraining. Management may well want to retrain younger workers, unions may want to stick to a seniority criterion. Most countries have systems for subsidising retraining, but there are still problems in deciding what occupation to train for, and in settling how such decisions are to be made. Some of these issues relate as much to redeployment within an enterprise in socialist countries as to the closure of a plant. Healthy industrial relations based on mutual respect are likely to make any conversion debate more fruitful, whether in terms of re-hiring elsewhere in a conglomerate enterprise, or in terms of finding successor enterprises to take over unwanted facilities.

However, many unions will inevitably find it difficult to meet the job challenge posed by disarmament. A union can scarcely sketch out a constructive role for itself in the conversion of defence facilities and retraining of the defence workforce unless it has a historical record of co-operation to raise productivity while preserving employment. Otherwise it would probably be marginalised in government-industry negotiations. Furthermore, plant closures and enterprise mergers are likely to set groups of workers against each other, even in the same union. A concerted programme of all unions to press for improved labour market measures at the national level, as well as for employment-preserving measures at the plant level, may be the most desirable strategy.

2. Enterprise managers

Reactions of top-level defence company managers and their bankers to defence cuts affecting them depend to a large extent on the economic environment, and growth trends in their countries and regions and, above all, on their expectations of the prospects for future demand for armaments. The immediate reaction of management to cuts in arms procurement is usually to reduce costs, stretch out existing production and possibly reduce sub-contracting. Employment is likely to decline and plant closure may result. Enterprises may merge to ensure that whatever production capacity remains is jointly owned and, hopefully, incorporates the best technologies available. Hostile take-overs may result in unwanted divisions being scrapped.

However, first of all management strategies would be likely to depend on their assessment of the nature and duration of the phenomenon. They might react differently if they perceived that the cuts were caused by a loss of competitiveness in comparison to other countries rather than by one-time events, such as the termination of a regional armed conflict leaving a core government procurement untouched. A sustained reduction in government procurement, caused either by budgetary pressures or by a long-term policy to reduce defence expenditure and channel national resources to civilian programmes, would be different again. If the defence cuts were considered temporary or if the problem was considered to be one of competitiveness, management might try to survive the difficult times while minimising losses through selective employment cuts and forward-looking reorganisation and investment. Certainly in the past labour has been hoarded during the down periods and alternative markets sought at reduced prices on favourable credit terms.

If the decline in demand was considered of a long-term nature, past reactions of defence companies have been to try to strengthen their market position through mergers and takeovers at the national and international level. These moves, sometimes checked and sometimes encouraged by governments, have occasionally led to considerable loss of employment at the regional and local level, particularly when production sites were sold off or closed. Sizeable, and profitable, diversification into other products seems to have been rare.

If defence production cuts and conversion to civilian production became an official policy which governments were be ready to support through alternative expenditures and guarantees, companies' reactions would again be different. They might adopt a wide range of solutions, from complete closure of "non-convertible" plants to a fairly rapid switch to civilian output. This would depend on the amount and type of assistance expected from the government and on its duration, particularly on the possibilities of government contracts for civilian goods, on their existing production capacities and the ease with which they could be adapted to civilian production, and last but not least on the market situation and on the demand for their prospective products. An eight-to-ten-year planning cycle might well be necessary, with a need for considerable managerial retraining. The outcome of negotiations with trade unions on training, retraining, transfer and remuneration of defence industry workers would also play an important role in influencing enterprises' decisions. As illustrated in some of the chapters, some managements might refuse to operate in civilian markets altogether. To what extent they could retrench themselves in the shrinking defence market, with a minimum of personnel as a strategy for survivial, is an open question. Other managements might welcome the opportunity of diversification into the civilian market, particularly if government aid was forthcoming on what they considered a satisfactory level.

3. Government policies concerning defence cuts and conversion

In all countries the government expenditure and taxation policies that would accompany a major defence cut would be crucial in determining the severity and cost of short-term economic adjustments. The form of such policy might be also critical in designing regional, local and even plant level conversion strategies. If defence cuts lead to reductions in government borrowing, creating a surplus of private sector savings, under certain conditions this could create problems of effective demand which would make the conversion process more difficult. The most promising form of compensation of a defence cut in order to promote conversion would be measures to rechannel the savings into investment. This would probably increase short-term growth in output and employment and provide opportunities for defence firms in civilian goods markets. Of course, in countries which already have a surplus of domestic savings, other measures would be needed.

A large number of scenarios can naturally be foreseen. Governments have intervened in the past to prevent major industries, or at least certain conspicuous segments, from going under. Often they have done this by subsidising retooling and reinvestment or by preventing foreign competition. But in the event of major arms reductions, the option of sustaining domestic demand at earlier levels is *ipso facto* ruled out. With that option removed, Western governments have certainly stated that they would prefer to rely on the market to reallocate the physical and human resources released by disarmament, i.e. that they would not provide a guaranteed market for "conversion" products. However, the formation of coalitions to exert pressure on governments to use public procurement programmes in this way must be expected. The use that governments make of the financial resources made available can vary from reducing tax levels (and it would make a difference which taxes were reduced) to increasing other expenditure programmes. It is highly unlikely that expenditure programmes would be selected on the basis of their employment-generating capacity; no doubt more common social and political criteria would be used. However, there is little value in speculating about the subsequent likely form of public sector fiscal policy except that the amount of resources probably committed to compensatory and training programmes could be expected to be a minor part of the resources freed.

In Central Europe it is premature to speak of the market's ability to reallocate industry for all that governments wish to introduce market principles. Intervention in some form seems inevitable. But a hands-off approach by central government would nowhere prevent local and regional governments from doing all they could to attract compensating new investment to absorb the labour displaced and make use of empty facilities. Indeed it is at that level that conversion planning can most fruitfully take place. However, the capacity of local governments is likely to have been shaped by the overall industrial policy framework as it has operated over the past decade, including its degree of decentralisation and use of regional investment promotion measures. In general, the role of local government would appear to have been most effective in the United States, although there are many instances of Swedish counties and the smaller West German provinces playing an active part in industrial conversion. So far as the displaced workforce would be concerned, countries have different experience of retraining and locational assistance policies, different social security and health insurance policies and different traditions of geographical mobility and wage flexibility, let alone perceived willingness to enter self-employment. Acceptance of lower wage levels and of a job requiring a different skill mix are likely to be essential components of conversion for a sizeable part of the released labour force, whether or not a spell of unemployment is experienced. However, these are not desirable outcomes on either social or economic grounds and they should be minimised either through legislation or collective barganining. A desirable central government role might be one of taking existing labour market policies one stage further, and ensuring full social security coverage, portable pension rights and early retirement, promoting efficient systems of employment information and encouraging flexible training systems possibly within the enterprise offering new employment, possibly on the demand of the workers in the enterprise which is shedding employment.

It might, however, be argued that the social benefits of moves towards disarmament are so widespread that a special effort should be made to fully compensate anyone (including shareholders?) who might be faced with even a short-term loss as a result. Such arguments were advanced in the United States in the context of the acceptability of trade adjustment assistance. Conversely, of course, recognition of the social benefits might be so widespread that the kind of coalitions which have emerged to prevent adjustment in certain industries threatened by foreign competition could not be formed, or at least, not publicly. It is very doubtful whether governments would accept any arguments as a reason for initiating new programmes specially targeted to defence industry workers (would employees of subcontractors be included?), although perhaps tax advantages could be envisaged for new investment in an old defence-related plant. But any scheme of specially targeted assistance can bear an element of moral hazard and could conceivably delay full adjustment, as has been argued in relation to income support under Trade Adjustment Assistance. Furthermore, in conditions of continued unemployment and of an abundance of already depressed areas, it is not obvious that it would be legitimate for governments to direct many resources to income support of workers from the defence industry.

None of this nullifies the value of conversion planning at the plant and local level, way in advance of serious demand cuts. Indeed, the nature of defence cuts ought to be such that they can be easily foreseen. Management should then take the workers' representatives fully into its confidence and, if corporate planning suggests closing a particular plant (without reabsorbing its labour force elsewhere), a buyer could be sought. In any event, conversion planning should encompass all aspects of the production of alternative products, with a review of markets and of the necessary extra investment, of existing schemes for encouraging investment and for retraining. But conversion planning should not in any way prevent personally chosen geographical and occupational mobility nor sidetrack governments from addressing general issues of disseminating employment information, encouraging retraining, addressing the causes of unwillingness to migrate, etc.

In planned economy countries conversion would depend practically entirely on enterprise management supported by government measures and funds. The likelihood of the work collective forming a profitable co-operative to run ex-defence plants is remote. Judging by the experience of the post-INF Treaty conversion process in the Soviet Union, and later efforts to raise the share of civil output in defence plants, the run-down of military production would pose the need for the retraining of personnel and would require state budget compensation for reduced projects and earnings. There might also be short-term problems in reconciling an at least partially centrally directed and planned conversion process with an economic reform designed to promote greater enterprise autonomy and financial self-reliance. In principle, the conditions for conversion are favourable. Most Soviet defence enterprises have prior (or actual) experience of civilian production, there is substantial unsatisfied demand for better quality manufactured goods, and the labour market position in most regions with concentrations of military productions is such that significant unemployment is unlikely to emerge. In fact there are problems in deciding which goods to produce and in using acquired skills productively. As a result the "peace dividend" in terms of higher living standards may be delayed.

IV. Conclusions

The main findings of this study might be summarised as follows:

1. The conflict between disarmament and employment is of a short-term nature. While in the short term, defence expenditure cuts could be expected to have negative impacts, particularly on employment, in the long term some studies discussed in Chapter 2 show that defence expenditure cuts and the rechannelling of resources to civilian use would have an employment-creating effect. In the United Kingdom merely redistributing military expenditure among other branches of government would lead to higher employment levels. In Norway a study showed that while this alone might not be enough, a bias towards spending on social services would create more jobs overall. The difference between the long-term employment effects of military and of alternative civilian expenditure is the implicit cost of national security.

2. Defence conversion can be considered as a particular case of industrial restructuring. In many countries there has been experience of restructuring at the macro- and micro-economic level in recent years. Also defence production cuts as such have been relatively frequent, caused by various internal or external, economic and political factors. Job security has, of course, not been an element in this restructuring and the emphasis has been on preparation for job flexibility. In the socialist countries there has been employment security but a demand for occupational flexibility. However, there is a wide range of experience from which useful lessons could be drawn, in order to minimise any unnecessarily negative impacts of the conversion process, if it were decided to undertake compensating targeted programmes of intervention.

3. The defence industry is concentrated in certain regions which tend to be dependent on it, to different degrees. In case of cuts in military expenditure, the defence-related employment in these regions would be particularly affected. The larger the proportion of defence employment in the regional labour force, the greater the problem would be.

4. In the regions of defence industry concentration, and particularly in the localities with important armaments-producing establishments, planning for conversion would be desirable, based on a review of existing measures of government assistance to new investment, a detailed analysis of the region's manufacturing profile, of the trends in service sector employment, of the local labour market, labour force structure, as well as of labour mobility, training and retraining possibilities, and other issues.

5. Useful lessons for conversion could be drawn from recent production cuts in the sunset industries in certain regions, such as steel or shipbuilding, even

if the analogies are only partial, due to the specific characteristics of the defence industry. Governments would in this way have good grounds for anticipating the response of the workforce to plant closures and the realism of programmes for the development of alternative projects.

6. The social partners have a very important role to play in the conversion process. An effective contribution by the trade unions, with the co-operation of the managements of defence-related companies, could ease the conversion process and considerably minimise negative impacts on employment and output. It could also prepare the ground for further sustained growth. Collective bargaining agreements need to cover a wide range of issues involved in redeployment and retraining.

7. Governments should see the possibility of significant arms reductions as an opportunity to review and improve their forms of labour market intervention. Different traditions will determine the trade-off between income security and wage flexibility. However, there is common consensus on the desirability of encouraging management-labour collaboration and co-operation in matters relating to the workforce and on providing a framework to assist retraining and informed job choice and adequate levels of social security.

8. A final point of general concern is data collection. This can be viewed both from a static angle, i.e. what is the weight of defence employment in different regions, economic branches, occupation, etc., and a dynamic one, i.e. what is the likelihood of a worker with certain characteristics finding an alternative job at a certain wage level? The latter requires longitudinal studies of recent labour market experience. Both types of data are needed and accelerating defence cuts would require policy-makers to have the capability to assess both how many workers will be in the labour market and what advice to give them.